THE BEST OF

CRAFTSMAN FURNITURE
Projects

THE BEST OF **W**OODWORKER'S **J**OURNAL

CRAFTSMAN FURNITURE
Projects

from the editors of *Woodworker's Journal*

Fox Chapel Publishing

1970 Broad Street • East Petersburg, PA 17520
www.FoxChapelPublishing.com

Our friends at Rockler Woodworking and Hardware supplied us with most of the hardware used in this book. Visit rockler.com.

Fox Chapel Publishing Company, Inc.
Publisher: Alan Giagnocavo
Acquisition Editor: Peg Couch
Editor: Gretchen Bacon
Series Editor: John Kelsey
Creative Direction: Troy Thorne
Cover Design: Lindsay Hess

Woodworker's Journal
Publisher: Ann Rockler Jackson
Editor-in-Chief: Larry N. Stoiaken
Editor: Rob Johnstone
Art Director: Jeff Jacobson
Senior Editor: Joanna Werch Takes
Field Editor: Chris Marshall
Illustrators: Jeff Jacobson, John Kelliher
Contributing Writers: John English, Mike McGlynn, Chris Marshall, Darrell Peart, Sandra Newman and Joseph Ebler, Rick White, Brad Becker, and Chris Inman

ISBN 978-1-56523-324-9

Publisher's Cataloging-in-Publication Data

Craftsman furniture projects. -- East Petersburg, PA :
Fox Chapel Publishing, c2007.

p. ; cm.

(The best of Woodworker's journal)
ISBN 978-1-56523-324-9

1. Furniture, Mission, 2. Furniture, Mission--Design and construction. 3. Furniture making. 4. Furniture making--Technique. I. Series. II. Woodworker's journal.

TT195 .C73 2007
684.1/04--dc22   0704

To learn more about the other great books from Fox Chapel Publishing, or to find a retailer near you, call toll-free 1-800-457-9112 or visit us at www.FoxChapelPublishing.com. For subscription information to *Woodworker's Journal* magazine, call toll-free 1-800-765-4119 or visit them at www.woodworkersjournal.com.

Printed in China
10 9 8 7 6 5 4 3 2 1

Note to Authors: We are always looking for talented authors to write new books in our area of woodworking, design, and related crafts. Please send a brief letter describing your idea to Peg Couch, Acquisition Editor, 1970 Broad Street, East Petersburg, PA 17520.

INTRODUCTION

We didn't exactly know what to expect the first time Woodworker's Journal magazine presented a project in the Arts & Crafts style some years back. After all, some would contend that the style's popularity "peaked" at the turn of the last century. But the designs of the Stickleys, the Greene Brothers, Frank Lloyd Wright and others never quite went out of fashion. Our first Stickley-inspired pieces, by then Journal editor Chris Inman and long-time contributing editor Rick White were very well received by subscribers. Some years later, when our good friend and contributing editor Mike McGlynn suggested we present a full-blown piece in the Greene Brothers' style, I thought he was crazy. But once again, readers voted by mail after Mike's first Greene and Greene project was published. They fell in love with both the style and Mike's well-conceived interpretations.

This compilation includes a number of Mike's pieces in the Greene Brothers' style, as well as a classic design based on the work of Frank Lloyd Wright. Other Woodworker's Journal regulars, including Brad Becker, Chris Marshall and John English also offered up their interpretations, from the most complicated pieces to Chris Marshall's end table, which we asked him to simplify so that even beginning woodworkers would be comfortable giving the style a try.

People like Craftsman furniture in their homes because it is unpretentious, functional, and comfortable. But woodworkers like to make it because it's composed mostly of solid wood, straight lines, and flat panels. We can build projects in this style using ordinary woodworking tools and machines, and sound but not overblown techniques.

It's accessible to us as makers for much the same reason that it is accessible to our families: we can understand it, we can enjoy both making it as well as using it, we can succeed with it.

Whether you call it, Mission, Stickley, Prairie-style or Craftsman, there's one thing most woodworkers agree on: Arts & Craft-style furniture is truly American furniture, expressing honesty and integrity through straightforward construction and the use of solid oak and other real materials.

Now, lets get to the shop and start making some quartersawn white oak sawdust.

Larry N. Stoiaken, Editor-in-Chief

ACKNOWLEDGMENTS

Woodworker's Journal recently celebrated its 30th anniversary—a benchmark few magazines ever reach. I would like to acknowledge both the 300,000 woodworkers who make up our readership and Rockler Woodworking & Hardware (rockler.com), which provided most of the hardware, wood and other products used to build the projects in this book. Our publishing partner, Fox Chapel, did a terrific job re-presenting our material, and I am especially grateful to Alan Giagnocavo, Gretchen Bacon, John Kelsey, and Troy Thorne for their commitment to our content.

Larry N. Stoiaken, Editor-in-Chief

CONTENTS

by John English

SLATTED BOOKCASE

Simplicity meets beauty, function and sturdy construction in this versatile Gustav Stickley Craftsman style storage project, featuring mortise and tenon joints.

Stickley emphasized the relationship between beauty, simplicity and function in all his designs. In my approach to this classic project, I used tenon joinery, matching wood plugs, triple slats and gentle curved lower rails to lend an understated elegance. The bookshelf isn't hard to build, although you may learn that cutting a perfect through tenon joint isn't as easy as it looks. (You'll probably end up with a few practice joints in your scrap bin, but it won't take long to get the technique down cold.) As far as function goes, the center shelves are adjustable and should suit anyone's library or assortment of collectibles. If you like what you see, round up some white oak and get started.

Mortise and Tenon Joinery

The key to building this bookcase is mortise and tenon joinery. All the cuts are square, so great results are just a matter of taking your time and laying out the joints with care.

Start by preparing stock for the stiles (pieces 1), according to the dimensions in the Material List, next page. Use the Elevation Drawings to lay out pairs of upper and lower through

Cutting Mortise and Tenon Joints

The usual convention for cutting mortise and tenon joinery, like the through mortise and tenon joints in this project, is to mill the mortises first, then cut the tenons to fit. The reasoning here is simple: your drill bit or mortising chisel automatically establishes the width of the mortise. It's easier to trim the tenons to fit the mortises than it is to tweak the width of the mortises.

If you bore your mortises as shown here with a drill press and Forstner bit, drill the ends of the mortise first, then make a series of side-by-side holes along the length of the mortise. Once these are cut, go back along the mortise and drill out the crescent-shaped waste areas that remain. Then shave the walls and ends of the mortise smooth and flat with sharp chisels. When the mortise extends all the way through the joint, as it does for the bookcase stiles, use a backup board beneath to keep the drill bit from tearing out the bottom surface as it exits the wood.

Table saws make quick work of cutting tenons. If you cut the wide tenon cheeks with the workpiece on end, as shown here, secure the wood in a tenoning jig or support it against a tall auxiliary fence mounted to the rip fence. It shouldn't rock or tip away from the fence as it passes through the blade, or a kickback could occur. Cut the short tenon cheeks with the workpiece held on edge against the saw table and backed up by the miter gauge.

Scribe a line around the mortise with *a sharp chisel or knife before you drill out the mortise waste. Scoring the wood fibers first will help minimize splintering. Once the primary waste is drilled out, smooth and square up the mortise with sharp chisels.*

You can cut the tenon cheeks *in the rails with a standard saw blade by standing the rails on end and against a tall auxiliary fence mounted to the rip fence. Or mount the rails in a tenoning jig for even more stability.*

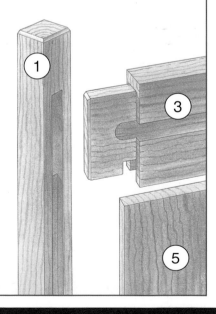

1
3
8
9
1
6
5
1
10
7
5
4
7
2
6

Chamfer Detail

Technical Drawings

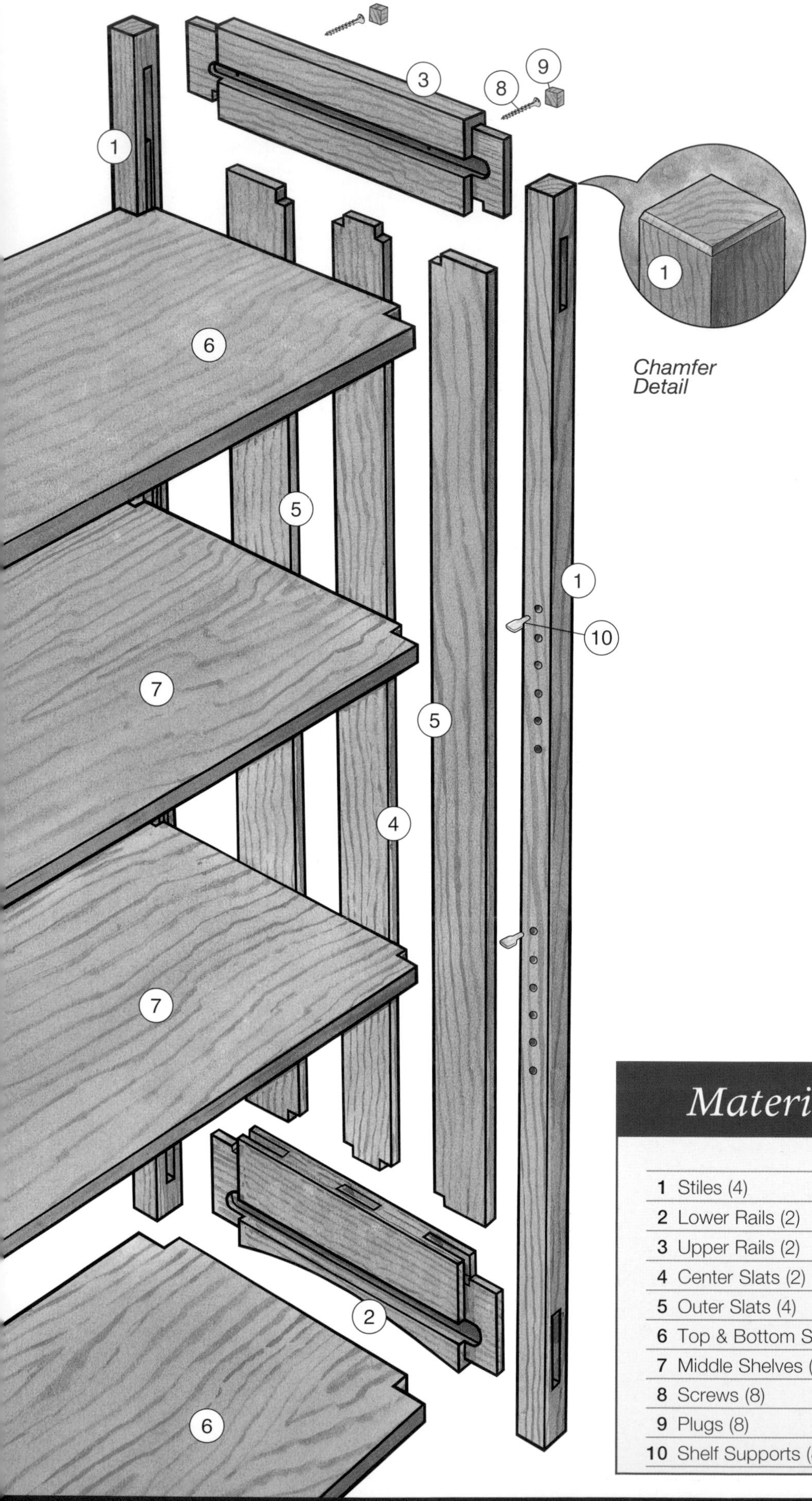

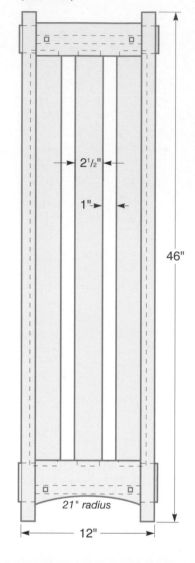

Side Assembly Elevation
(Side View)
2½"
1"
46"
21" radius
12"

Material List - Bookcase

	T x W x L
1 Stiles (4)	1¼" x 1¼" x 46"
2 Lower Rails (2)	¾" x 4" x 12½"
3 Upper Rails (2)	¾" x 3" x 12½"
4 Center Slats (2)	½" x 2½" x 37½"
5 Outer Slats (4)	½" x 2¾" x 37½"
6 Top & Bottom Shelves (2)	¾" x 11½" x 29"
7 Middle Shelves (2)	¾" x 11½" x 28½"
8 Screws (8)	#6 x 1¼"
9 Plugs (8)	⅜" x ⅜" x ¼"
10 Shelf Supports (8)	5mm Brass

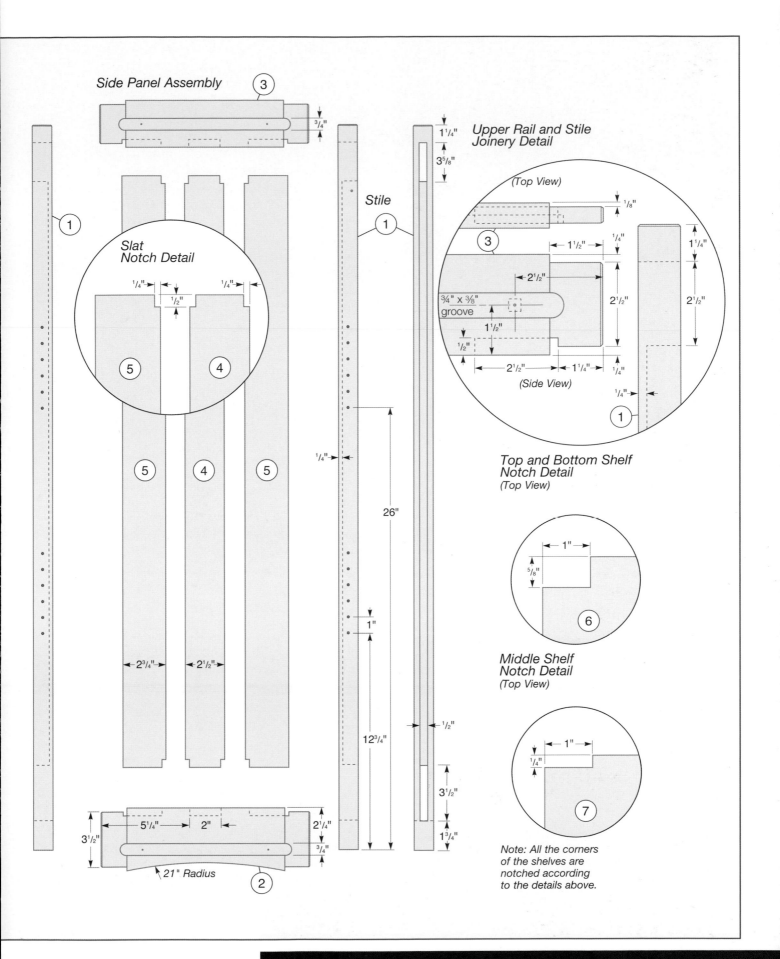

Side Panel Assembly

③

¾"

Slat
Notch Detail

¼" ¼"

½"

⑤ ④

⑤ ④ ⑤

2¾" 2½"

①

3½"

5¼" 2"

21" Radius

②

2¼"

¾"

Stile

①

¼"

26"

1"

12¾"

½"

3½"

1¾"

Upper Rail and Stile
Joinery Detail

1¼"

3⅝"

(Top View)

⅛"

③

1½"

¼"

1¼"

2½"

¾" x ⅜"
groove

2½"

2½"

1½"

½"

2½" 1¼" ¼"

(Side View)

①

¼"

Top and Bottom Shelf
Notch Detail
(Top View)

1"

⅝"

⑥

Middle Shelf
Notch Detail
(Top View)

1"

¼"

⑦

Note: All the corners
of the shelves are
notched according
to the details above.

Figure 1: *Plow grooves into the rails on your router table with a ¾" straight bit. Clamp stops to the fence to control the length of the groove.*

Figure 2: *Drill pilot holes to hold the screws that will secure the fixed shelves. Reshape the tops of the holes with a ⅜" chisel to accept square plugs.*

Figure 3: *Use a depth gauge on your drill bit and a template to place the holes for your shelf supports. A piece of pegboard works great for drilling these rows of holes.*

mortises in the stiles. These mortises will house tenons cut on the ends of the rails (pieces 2 and 3). If you're using quartersawn stock for the stiles, notice that the flake pattern only appears on two faces of the stile blanks. The other two faces are plain sawn. Keep the sides with the attractive flake patterns facing forward so they'll show prominently.

If you have access to a mortising attachment for your drill press, cutting true, square mortises is easy work. However, most of us drill out the waste on a drill press, then clean up with a sharp chisel (as shown in the sidebar on page 9). Whichever method you use, make a few test mortises first. Grain direction is a significant issue with wide grained species such as white oak: a sharp cut along the grain can cause splitting, so work across the grain whenever possible. One last tip on this procedure: be sure the surface you are drilling into is without voids to steer clear of unsightly tearout.

Once the eight through mortises are cut and cleaned up, mill a groove along the inside edge of each stile. Notice in the Side Panel Assembly Elevation that these grooves run from through mortise to through mortise and serve to capture the outer slats. The easiest way to mill the grooves is on the router table with a ½" straight bit raised to ¼". Test your setup on scrap stock, then use pencil marks on the router table fence and stock to start and stop the cuts at the mortises.

With the grooves completed, mill a chamfer around the top edges of the stiles using a router and ¼" chamfering bit or a block plane.

Riding the Rails

The upper and lower rails (pieces 2 and 3) join all the fixed structural elements of the bookcase. Rip and crosscut the rail stock to size, then cut three mortises into the edges of the rails to house the outer and center slats (pieces 4 and 5). Use the Side Panel Assembly Elevation to find the mortise locations.

Next, form tenons at the ends of the rails. See the Upper Rail and Stile Joinery Detail on the previous page to lay out the tenons. Use your table saw and a tenoning jig to make the tenon cheeks by slicing off each side of the rails. This will reveal a notch in the tenons because of the mortises you cut earlier. Now lower your saw blade to ¼" and switch to the miter gauge to nibble away the edges of the rails and form the tenon shoulders. Chamfer the ends of the tenons as you did on the stiles.

Install a ¾" straight bit into the router. Use this setup to plow grooves on the inside of each rail (see Figure 1 and the Upper Rail and Stile Joinery Detail). These grooves will accept the ends of the top and bottom shelves, so make them ⅜" deep and 10½" long. It's OK to leave the ends of the grooves rounded, as they will be hidden by the notched corners of the top and bottom shelves. On the bottom rails, lay out the 21" radius as shown in the Elevation Drawings. Use the bandsaw to cut these curved arches. Sand the edges to remove the saw marks while keeping the gentle curves identical.

Cut the slats to size (pieces 4 and 5) and notch the ends, following the Slat Notch Detail Drawing. The ends of the slats remain at full thickness and will fit into the stopped mortises you cut earlier in the edges of the rails.

Test-fit the side assemblies by placing the notched ends of the slats into the rail mortises, then drive the stiles onto the slat and rail subassembly. When everything fits correctly, disassemble, apply glue and clamp the parts together. Keep the side assemblies perfectly square and flat until the glue cures and scrape off any excess glue after it has set.

The Shelves and Their Supports

There are four shelves in this bookcase: two fixed shelves and two adjustable middle shelves (pieces 6 and 7). Cut them to size, now. Note that the middle shelves are shorter than the fixed ones: this is because the latter fit into the mortises you made in the rails. The top and bottom shelves are glued in place and then secured with screws (pieces 8) whose heads will be hidden by square wooden plugs (pieces 9), as shown in Figure 2. Make the plugs by ripping strips from your ⅜" plug stock and crosscutting the strips into plugs. Pre-drill pilot holes through the rails and then, with a chisel, cut ⅜" square mortises over the holes to receive the square plugs. (Note: Make these plug holes ¼" deep.)

Notch the ends of all the shelves by gang cutting them in pairs using the table saw and your miter gauge. See the Elevation Drawings to lay out the differing dimensions and shapes of the notches — those on the top and bottom shelves are deeper than the middle shelves. After checking the fit of the top and bottom shelves in the rails, apply glue in the rail mortises and insert the shelf tenons. Secure them with the screws, then glue the plugs in place.

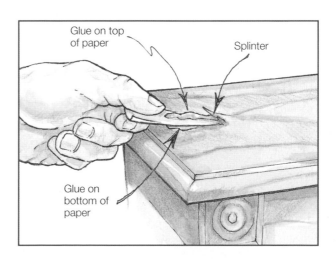

QuickTip

Get Slivers Under Control

Sometimes a sliver of wood may show up on your project, usually during the sanding process. Generally it's due to a grain anomaly in the wood, and oversanding just makes it worse.

Correcting this problem used to be rather difficult, but here's a quick way to deal with it. Simply place a drop of wood glue on both sides of a small piece of paper and slip the paper under the sliver. Clamp or weight the sliver in place until the glue dries, then sand the repaired area. The paper under the sliver will disappear, and you can proceed with finishing.

Glue on top of paper

Splinter

Glue on bottom of paper

While clear glass jars are handy for storing finishes, all it takes is a bit of residual finish on the rim to seal the lid and make it difficult to remove. Here's a simple solution: Teflon tape sold for sealing pipe threads. First, wipe the top of the jar clean, then wrap a couple layers of tape over the threads, winding it on clockwise. Let some tape lap over on the top lip of the container as well. Most finishes and paints won't stick to the tape, so the jar will open easily and safely the next time you need it.

Teflon tape

All that stands between you and the finishing room is to make four rows of shelf pin holes in the stiles of each side assembly for the two adjustable shelves. Refer to the Elevation Drawings again to determine the starting and stopping points of these rows. Drill the holes using a piece of pegboard as a template and with a sharp brad point bit fitted with a depth collar. Clamp the template evenly in place on each stile before boring the shelf pin holes.

Give all the project surfaces a thorough sanding up to 220 grit before proceeding with finish.

A Safer Stickley Finish

Stickley developed a unique method of fuming white oak with ammonia to create a glowing aged and mellow color. Mimicking the unique look of the Stickley finish was a challenge I took seriously. I used Bartley's honey gel stain to approximate the same fumed effect with much less fuss and danger. It's also convenient for staining vertical surfaces without the drippy mess. Just be sure to wipe all the excess gel out of nooks and crannies. Protect the wood with a few coats of satin varnish—the gel variety goes on smoothly and won't sag if you accidentally apply too much. It produces a rich luster that is much in keeping with the Arts & Crafts tradition.

There are other good, safe finish options for Arts & Crafts furniture that you may want to try instead of gel stain. For more more options, see Michael Dresdner's suggestions on the next page.

The shelf supports (pieces 10) are the brass plug-in type; install them after the finish dries thoroughly.

This is such a classic bookshelf that I'll wager you're making a second or third as soon as this one finds a prominent spot in the living room or den.

Woodworker's Glossary

Mortise and Tenon:
A type of joint used to attach two perpendicular pieces of wood where a protruding tenon on one workpiece fits into a matching mortise hole in the other.

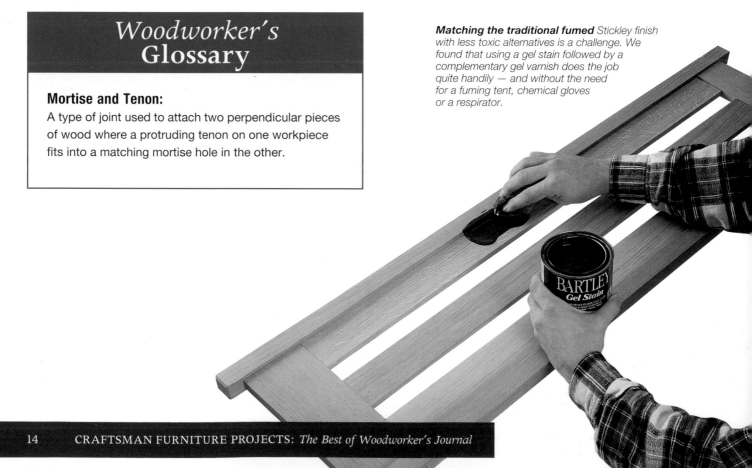

Matching the traditional fumed Stickley finish with less toxic alternatives is a challenge. We found that using a gel stain followed by a complementary gel varnish does the job quite handily — and without the need for a fuming tent, chemical gloves or a respirator.

A traditional-looking Arts & Crafts finish is easily attained through a variety of modern products, including asphaltum, Minwax Jacobean stain or a two-part finish called Old Growth.

One of finishing expert Michael Dresdner's favorite oak stains is a mixture called "asphaltum." It is a thickish tar made from a natural mineral, called gilsonite, ground into a drying oil, such as linseed oil or modified soya oil. In addition to being used in many dark stain formulas, asphaltum also shows up in roofing tar and tree pruning paint.

Finishers prize this dark brownish black paste for the richness of color it offers. Like an oil slick on water, it shows highlights of both green and red. It makes an excellent glaze between coats of finish as well as a deep rich stain for raw wood. If you are a purist, as he is, you can buy asphaltum in one-gallon containers from Sherwin Williams' commercial stores (Sherwood Wiping Stain Concentrate, stock #S64N44). Cut it 50/50 with mineral spirits and you have a wonderful stain for Arts & Crafts furniture.

For those who prefer their stains ready to use, Minwax offers a very close alternative. Minwax Wood Finish #2750 Jacobean, used right out of the familiar bright yellow can, will give you a color almost identical to the straight asphaltum stain mixture. Whether you choose asphaltum or stain, the application process is the same.

Fuming Without the Fumes

Recently, a new product arrived on the market that seeks to offer the look of fuming without the danger. "Old Growth" is a line of safe, water-based compounds that attempt to mimic many different chemical stains, including fuming. The fumed oak treatment consists of two clear liquids that are applied separately.

Old Growth is a water-based system designed to mimic different chemical stains. It's safe and effective. Apply it in a two-step procedure.

Using a clean brush for each solution, you first apply the #1 portion evenly. After it dries, follow with the #2 solution. As the second solution goes on, the wood immediately changes color, and it continues to get darker until the wood dries.

Because it is water-based, the treatment seriously raises the grain of the oak. You can make it less problematic by raising the grain first with water, letting the wood dry, and cutting it back with 320-grit sandpaper before you apply the chemical stain. Old Growth certainly has an interesting look and comes close to the real thing. However, placed side by side with fumed oak, you can still see the differences.

Once you've colored the wood with any of these products, topcoat with shellac or another protective finish of your choice.

Mix asphaltum in a fifty percent mixture with mineral spirits to create a beautiful Arts & Crafts style stain.

Flood the surface of your properly sanded project with the mixture. Then wipe the stain off quickly before it dries.

by John English

VINTNER'S VALET

This Gustav Stickley-inspired accent piece holds a full complement of wine glasses and champagne flutes, and it keeps a case of your favorite wine close at hand. Build it from quartersawn white oak to add some authenticity and durability to this project.

Figure 1: *A marking gauge (set to the right thickness with one of the side aprons, as shown in the inset) is used to lay out stopped rabbets in the legs.*

Gustav Stickley (1857-1942) began his working life as a mason in his native Wisconsin. In his late teens he moved to Philadelphia, where he found a position at an uncle's furniture business. Given his early experience working with stone, it's not surprising that he later professed a "love for working in wood and (an) appreciation of the beauty and interest to be found in its natural color, texture and grain."

My wine table follows Stickley's design tradition. However, remembering that the master had at his disposal a full complement of fine craftsmen, I've taken the liberty of simplifying some of the more complicated aspects. For example, the two bottle racks are set in stopped rabbets in the legs, rather than in the more daunting through mortises for which Stickley was famous. And the distinctively Arts & Crafts inspired slender slats in either end of the table are secured with spacers in a dado,

rather than being mortised directly into the stretchers.

So roll up your sleeves and head for the shop. But keep the wine for later, when the work is all done.

Choosing Quartersawn Stock

Quartersawn white oak was Stickley's wood of choice for the vast majority of his furniture pieces. Why quartersawn? According to Stickley, "the quarter-sawing method of cutting oak—that is, the making of the cut parallel with the medullary rays and thus largely

preserving them, instead of cutting across them and thus destroying their binding properties, renders quartersawn oak structurally stronger, also finer in grain, and...less liable to check and warp than when sawn in any other way."

Trouble is, 1¾"-square white oak is not always readily available as quartersawn stock. That's not necessarily a bad thing: If you look at a wide plain-sawn board, the stock near the edges—where the annual rings are tightly packed together—is, in effect,

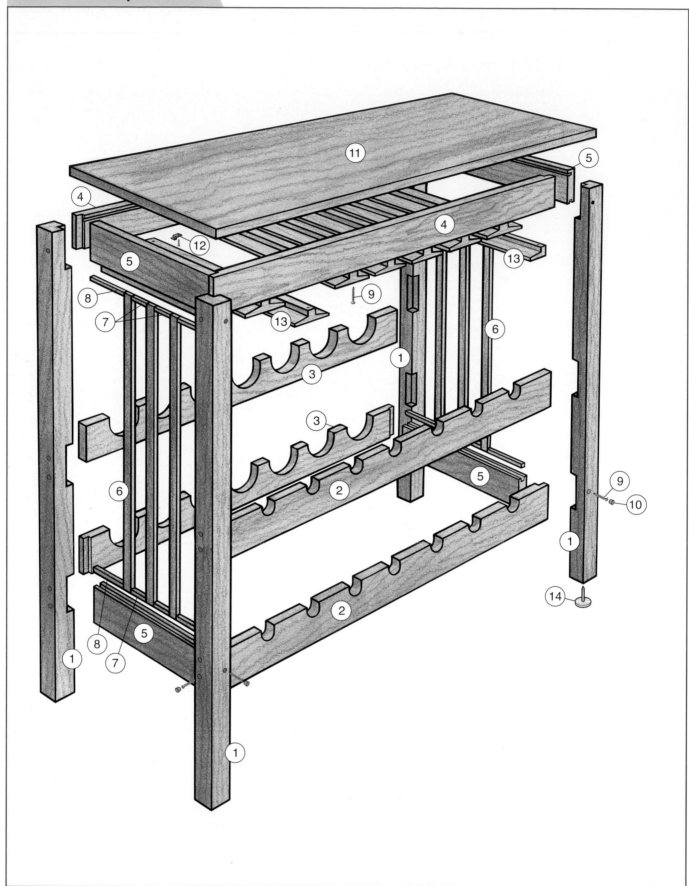

Material List - Vintner's Valet

		T x W x L				T x W x L
1	Legs (4)	1¾" x 1¾" x 35¼"		8	Large Spacers (8)	⁷⁄₁₆" x ⅜" x 2"
2	Front Racks (2)	¾" x 3" x 28¼"		9	Screws (46)	#8 x 2½" Flathead
3	Back Racks (2)	¾" x 3" x 28¼"		10	Plugs (28)	⅜" Oak Face Grain
4	Front & Back Aprons (2)	¾" x 3" x 28¼"		11	Tabletop (1)	¾" x 14¾" x 32¾"
5	Side Aprons, Stretchers (4)	¾" x 3" x 9"		12	Tabletop Fasteners (10)	³⁄₃₂" Steel
6	Slats (6)	⁷⁄₁₆" x 1" x 22¾"		13	Wine Glass Molding (7 or 8)*	¾" x 2¾" x 10¼"
7	Small Spacers (8)	⁷⁄₁₆" x ⅜" x 1"		14	Glides (4)	⅞" Nylon Glides

* Depending on your stemware (see Technical Drawings).

quartersawn. When you choose the lumber for your legs (pieces 1), just make sure you keep one of these quartersawn faces to the front.

Rip the four legs to size about ⅛" larger in each direction than the dimensions that are given in the Material List, above. (While you're at the saw, this is a good time to cut all the wine rack's parts to size.) Joint or plane the legs to final dimensions, then cut them to length.

The two racks that hold the wine bottles and the apron that supports the tabletop are all set in stopped rabbets cut into the legs (see the Exploded View on the facing page). For the locations and dimensions of these rabbets, consult the Technical Drawings. Mark these locations on the legs using a pencil and marking gauge (see Figure 1), then score the ends of each rabbet location with a sharp knife, as shown in Figure 2. Use a Forstner bit in your drill press to remove most of the waste, then clean out each rabbet with a sharp chisel (see Figure 3).

Figure 2: *To stop chipping and tearout, use a sharp utility knife to score across the grain at each end of the stopped rabbets.*

If You Don't Like Chisels…

An alternative to the traditional drill-and-chisel method for making stopped rabbets is to split each leg, cut dadoes in one half, then glue the leg back together. The only disadvantage to this method is that a joint line is created, but it could be located in the side, rather than the front of each leg. You'd also have to oversize your stock in one direction by ⅛" to compensate for the blade kerf.

Cutting Out the Bottle Racks

Your favorite beverage bottles will rest on two pairs of racks, each of which is scalloped out to hold seven bottles. The cuts in the two front racks (pieces 2) are 1⅛" diameter, while those in the back (pieces 3) are 3¼". You can create both the front racks at the same time by clamping them edge-to-edge, then drilling seven holes along the joined edges (see the Technical Drawings for locations) with a spade bit chucked in a drill press, as shown in Figure 4. The rough walls left by the spade bit can be cleaned up with a drum sander mounted in the drill press, as shown in the inset photo on the next page.

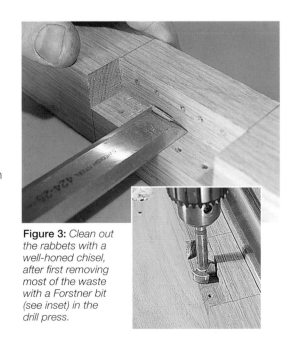

Figure 3: *Clean out the rabbets with a well-honed chisel, after first removing most of the waste with a Forstner bit (see inset) in the drill press.*

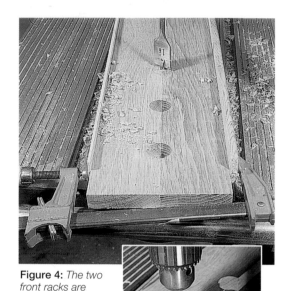

Figure 4: *The two front racks are clamped together when drilling the half circles along their top edges. A drum sander cleans up these borings (see inset photo).*

The larger semicircles in the back racks are best cut on a bandsaw (see Figure 5), because a 3¼" hole saw can really chew up a nice piece of stock. You might like to try a sharp circle cutter, since it's capable of making an acceptable cut. Either way, clean up these cuts with the drum sander, too.

Building Two Frames

The frame under the tabletop is made up of the front and back aprons (pieces 4) and two side aprons (pieces 5). Before that assembly can be completed, however, you need to do a little milling.

Start by creating a single saw kerf in the inside face of each top apron piece (see Technical Drawings) for the fasteners that will later hold the tabletop in place. Then cut a ⁷⁄₁₆"-wide dado into the bottom edge of each short apron and the top edge of each stretcher (pieces 5) as shown in the Technical Drawings). These dadoes will house the slats (pieces 6) that adorn the sides of the table and the spacers (pieces 7 and 8) that separate these slats.

Cut a rabbet on each end of the two longer aprons. This rabbet not only makes for stronger joinery, but it will keep the joints invisible by hiding them inside the legs. Cut these rabbets on your table saw with a dado head, then predrill for the screws (pieces 9), and assemble the apron frame with glue.

A second frame is created when the side stretchers are joined

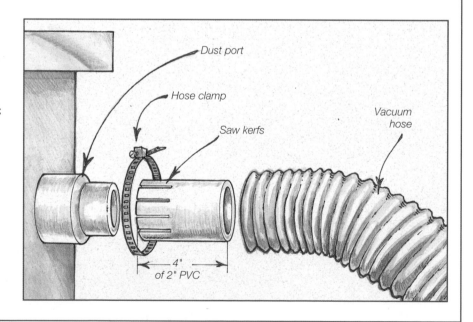

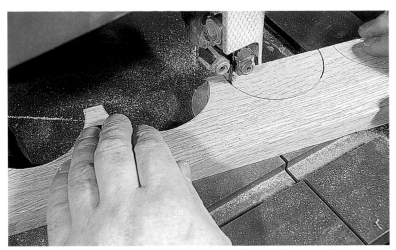

Figure 5: *Slice the large semicircles in the back racks on a bandsaw, then remove the kerf marks with a drum sander.*

to one front and one back rack in the same manner as the tabletop apron. Rabbet the racks just like you did with the long aprons (see Figure 6), then assemble this frame too.

Assembling the Frames and Legs

Dry-fit your two frames—and the six slats—to the stopped rabbets you cut in the legs (the apron frame goes in the top rabbets, and the bottle rack in the bottom one). Test the fit of the remaining rack elements in the middle rabbets, then use glue and screws to complete this assembly, setting the slats loosely in place without their spacers now, as you won't be able to install them until after the frame is glued up. To do so, drill large pilot holes through the legs (so the screws can move freely), and drill

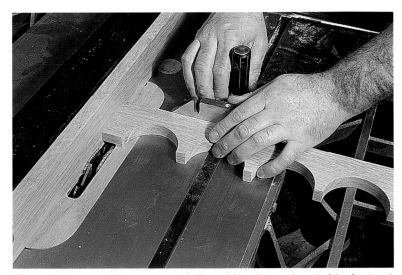

Figure 6: *Use your table saw to cut shallow rabbets into each end of the front and back aprons and the lower racks for attaching these parts to the legs.*

Many wines age well when cellared in a controlled environment. According to Bill Abrahamson of Sutler's Wines & Spirits in Stillwater, Minnesota, the temperature in a wine cellar should be between 55° and 58° F, while the ideal humidity range is a little more forgiving—40% to 60% works well. The most important aspect of both temperature and humidity is that, once set, they remain constant. Large variations in either can cause irreparable damage. Wine must also be protected from direct sunlight, which will break it down and cause an "early death."

Cellared wine should never be stored in a vertical (upright) position, where there is no contact between the wine and the cork. If the cork dries out, oxygen can come in contact with the wine, causing rapid aging. Wine laid on its side lets the entire bottom surface of the cork contact the liquid: This is ideal. However, some vintners prefer to store wine at an angle, an arrangement that allows a better view of the label. This is fine as long as at least some of the cork is immersed.

Abrahamson also points out that not all wines are intended for prolonged cellaring: Some wines are best when used closer to their bottling date. A good wine merchant can help you choose.

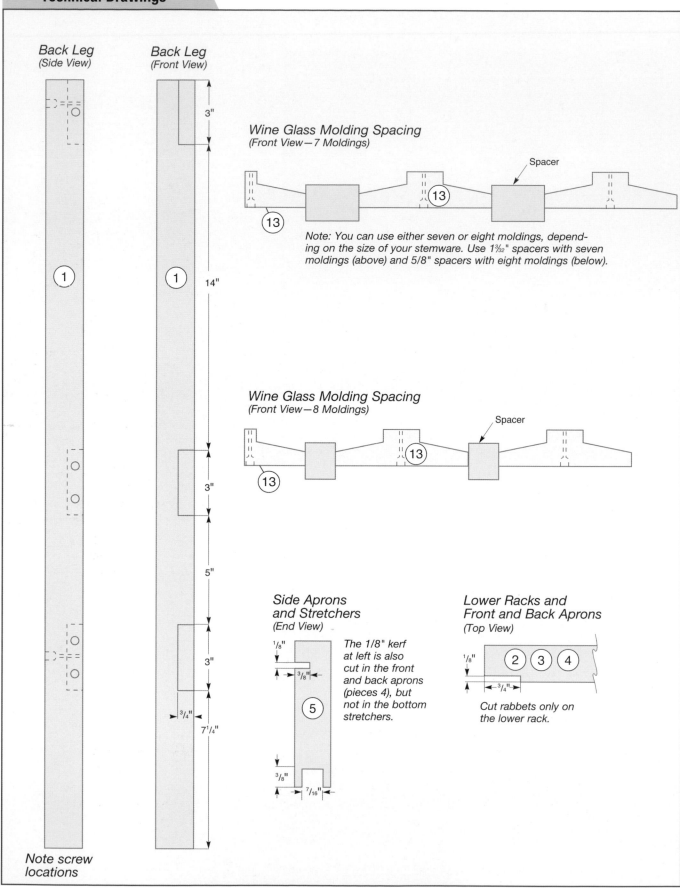

Back Leg
(Side View)

Back Leg
(Front View)

3"

14"

3"

5"

3"

³/₄"

7¹/₄"

Note screw
locations

Wine Glass Molding Spacing
(Front View—7 Moldings)

Spacer

Note: You can use either seven or eight moldings, depending on the size of your stemware. Use 1³/₃₂" spacers with seven
moldings (above) and 5/8" spacers with eight moldings (below).

Wine Glass Molding Spacing
(Front View—8 Moldings)

Spacer

Side Aprons
and Stretchers
(End View)

1/8"

³/₈"

The 1/8" kerf
at left is also
cut in the front
and back aprons
(pieces 4), but
not in the bottom
stretchers.

³/₈"

⁷/₁₆"

Lower Racks and
Front and Back Aprons
(Top View)

1/8"

³/₄"

Cut rabbets only on
the lower rack.

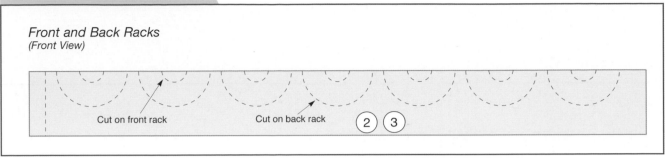

Front and Back Racks
(Front View)

Cut on front rack   Cut on back rack   ② ③

small pilot holes in the frames where the screws need to grip. Counterbore for the screw heads with a ⅜" Forstner bit, placing screws at the locations shown on the Technical Drawings, then cover their heads with oak face grain plugs (pieces 10).

Making the Tabletop

Three boards work well for the tabletop (piece 11), edge-joined and glued together. When the glue is dry, cut the top to size and sand it before installing it with tabletop fasteners (pieces 12). These lock into the saw kerf you cut earlier, and they are screwed to the underside of the top. Place three fasteners on each side and two at the ends.

Your wine glasses will be held in place by moldings (pieces 13) which are cut to length and screwed to the bottom edges of the long aprons. Note that the two outside moldings are made from

Figure 7:
Use scraps of wood between the clamps and workpiece when installing the slat spacers in their dadoes.

a single piece that's ripped in half. You can use either seven or eight moldings, depending on the size of your stemware (if in doubt, go with the wider spacing), and dimensions are given in the Technical Drawings on the facing page for scrap spacers for this installation.

Glue and clamp the slat spacers into their dadoes, as shown in Figure 7, then sand the project up through

the grits to 180 and apply your favorite finish: I chose a darker walnut stain to match Stickley's original furniture. Finally, tap a nylon glide (pieces 14) into the bottom of each leg, and call your best friends over to admire your new Stickley-style wine table.

QuickTip

Resawing on the Bandsaw with a Point Fence

Resawing makes two thin boards (say, ⁵⁄₁₆") out of one thick one (¾"). It's usually done on the bandsaw with a stiff ½"- or ⅝"-wide blade. The best way to guide the board is to clamp a point fence to the saw. That's just a V-shaped fence, where the point is positioned the thickness of the resawn board (⁵⁄₁₆") away from the blade. The idea is to keep the board vertical and pivot the board against the point the fence as needed to follow your layout line and keep an even width of cut.

by Mike McGlynn

TABORET PLANT STAND

Fine woodworking doesn't have to take forever. This project will help sharpen your stock preparation and joinery skills without keeping you in the shop for a month of Sundays. In the end, you get a classic Arts & Crafts reproduction for your efforts.

This little Arts & Crafts taboret is an adaptation of an original Stickley piece. It's a great introduction to building Arts & Crafts furniture and is easily completed in just a couple of weekends.

I made this table from quartersawn red oak, but a more traditional choice would be quartersawn white oak. It requires small amounts of ⁴⁄₄, ⁶⁄₄, and ⁸⁄₄ material. Select stock with a nice, but not too wide, decorative flake pattern. You could also make the table from mahogany or even cherry, but the flake pattern of quartersawn oak shows off particularly well on this simple design.

Beginning the Milling Routine

The first step in any construction process is to lay out and rough-cut your pieces. First, crosscut the parts in the Material List (see page 26) about 1" long, then joint, rip, and plane everything ¼" oversized in width and height and 1" in length. Finally (and this can actually be the hardest part if you're itching to do some woodworking!), leave the milled pieces in the shop for a week before

Three Steps to Achieving Stable Stock:
1. Crosscut all the pieces 1" oversized.
2. Joint, rip and plane them ½" oversized.
3. Store the prepared pieces for one week in your shop before continuing.

continuing. Then you can mill the workpieces to final dimension. This routine will save you the headache of watching pieces change shape when they are milled to final dimensions immediately. It's important to give the wood a chance to do what it's ultimately going to do anyway.

Making the Top

The top (piece 1) is made of two or three pieces of ¾" stock. Try to pick pieces that have very complementary grain—possibly out of the same board. Trim these pieces so you only have about ¼" to remove after glue-up. No need to worry about clamp dents this way. Reinforce and align these joints with three biscuits each, and glue up with Titebond® II or epoxy. (Regular Titebond will end up looking like a dark line after you apply the water-based aniline dye finish—if that's the route you decide to take for finishing.)

After the glue-up, trim the top to final size, sand, rout the edges with a ¼" roundover and set it aside.

Proceeding with the Feet

The crossed feet (pieces 2) come next. See the Elevation Drawings on page 26.

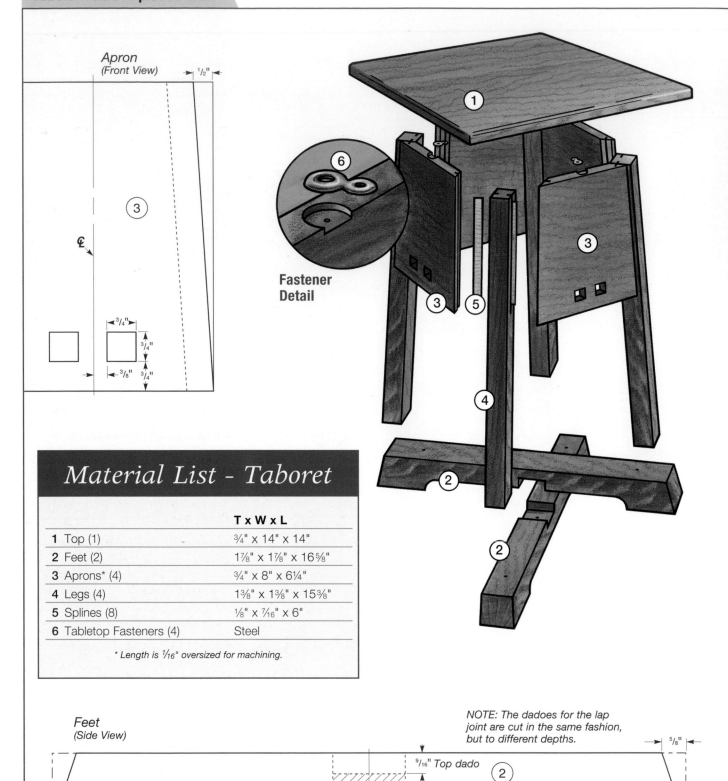

Apron
(Front View)

½"

③

₵

¾"

¾"

³/₈" ¾"

Fastener Detail

⑥

①

③

③ ⑤

④

②

②

②

Material List - Taboret

	T x W x L
1 Top (1)	¾" x 14" x 14"
2 Feet (2)	1⅞" x 1⅞" x 16⅝"
3 Aprons* (4)	¾" x 8" x 6¼"
4 Legs (4)	1⅜" x 1⅜" x 15⅜"
5 Splines (8)	⅛" x ⁷/₁₆" x 6"
6 Tabletop Fasteners (4)	Steel

* Length is ¹/₁₆" oversized for machining.

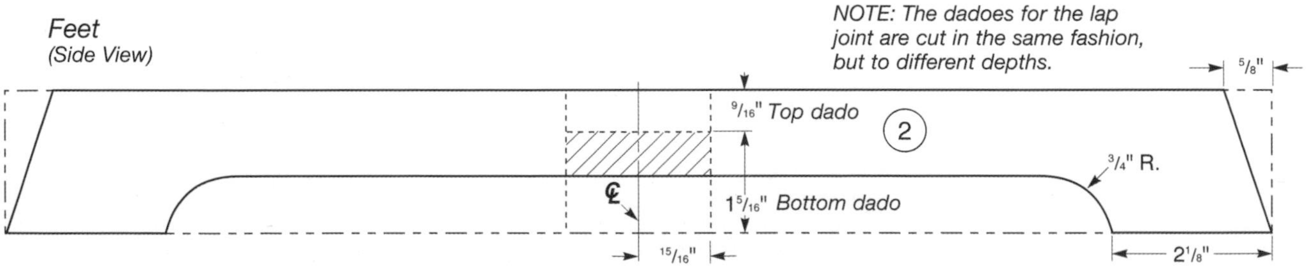

Feet
(Side View)

NOTE: The dadoes for the lap joint are cut in the same fashion, but to different depths.

⁵/₈"

⁹/₁₆" Top dado

②

³/₄" R.

₵

1⁵/₁₆" Bottom dado

¹⁵/₁₆"

2¹/₈"

Jig #1

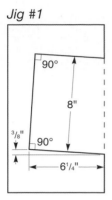

90°

8"

³/₈"

90°

6¹/₄"

Jig #2

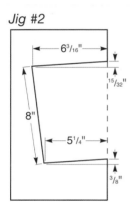

6³/₁₆"

15/32"

8"

5¹/₄"

³/₈"

Leg, Aprons and Splines
(Top View)

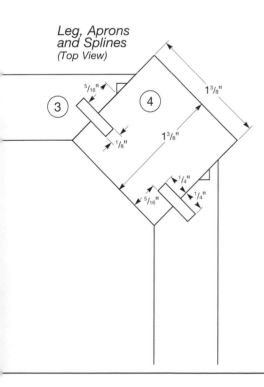

5/16"

③

④

1³/₈"

1³/₈"

1/8"

1/4"

1/4"

5/16"

Because of their trapezoidal shape and mitered edges, the aprons are the hardest pieces to mill on this table. A couple of easy-to-use jigs help simplify the process. Make them out of ¾" plywood (see *drawings*, below). Be sure to mark the inside and outside of the aprons before cutting their edges.

Tilt your blade *45° away from the rip fence and use Jig #1 to cut the right side of each apron first.*

Keep your blade and rip fence in position *and switch to Jig #2 to cut the left side of each apron. The scab piece on top keeps the newly mitered edge from riding up during the cut.*

Cleat must overhang opening by at least ¹/₁₆".

First make a ¼"-thick arch template from hardboard that you can use to both mark and template-rout the arch's shape. Trace the arch on your feet workpieces, but before cutting them out, make the crossed lap joint while the parts are still flat-edged. The lap joint is deceptively simple looking. The keys to this joint are accurate layout and to creep up slowly on the final fit. As can be seen in the drawings, each foot is dadoed halfway through. Do this milling work in a series of passes on the table saw, with the very tip of the teeth reaching the halfway layout mark (see top photo, page 29). This will leave you with a corrugated dado bottom that is easy to pare to a final, flush fit with a chisel.

Now it's time to form the arched underside, and it is best done with a combination of band-sawing and template routing. Saw the arch about ¹/₁₆" outside the layout line (see center photo, page 29), then use double-stick tape to mount the template you made previously to the foot workpiece, and

template-rout it to its final shape with a piloted flush-trimming bit. When you are done, form the angles on the ends of the feet at your miter saw.

Next comes the hardest part—the aprons (pieces 3). They're hard because they not only tilt inward, but also are tapered vertically and meet the legs in a miter. Because of their inward lean, the mitered edges are not 45° but instead are just strong. Start machining these pieces by cutting the top and bottom edges square and to size. Next, lay out and cut the square decorative mortises. It's much easier to lay these out and cut them now than after the panels are tapered. You can drill out most of the mortise waste with a Forstner bit and then clean it up with a sharp chisel, as shown in the photo on page 24, or use a mortising machine and make them in four overlapping passes instead.

Tapering the aprons requires the use of two fairly simple jigs (see the sidebar, above), one for each edge. The only trick to remember here is that the

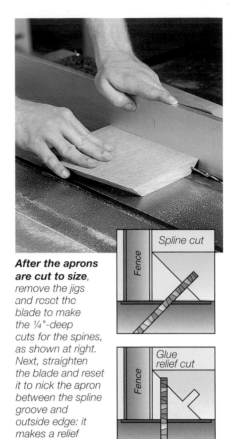

After the aprons are cut to size, *remove the jigs and reset the blade to make the ¼"-deep cuts for the spines, as shown at right. Next, straighten the blade and reset it to nick the apron between the spline groove and outside edge: it makes a relief groove to catch glue squeeze-out.*

jigs must be perfectly complementary or the aprons will end up asymmetrical.

The last step on the aprons is to cut the spline and glue relief grooves (see photo and illustrations at left). Tip your table saw blade to 45° for the spline cuts, then reset it to square for the glue relief cuts.

The final parts to make are the legs (pieces 4), which have a slight 5° miter cut on each end and stopped spline grooves to accommodate the aprons. Clamp a stop block to your table saw's rip fence to prevent cutting the spline grooves overly long (see bottom photo, page 29).

Prior to dry-assembling the table, cut some oak splines (pieces 5) to fit snugly into the apron and leg grooves.

Time for Dry Assembly

As with proper milling techniques, dry assembly is a critical step that you shouldn't skip. For this project, it involves assembling the legs and aprons with the splines and a couple of band clamps, assembling the feet and screwing them together from the bottom side of the lap joint, marking the landing points of the legs onto the feet, drilling holes and pilot holes and screwing them together from underneath.

At this point, take a small Forstner bit and drill a pocket on top of each apron for the tabletop fasteners (pieces 6). Screw the fasteners in place and attach the top with them. If everything fits well, disassemble all the pieces to prepare for finishing.

QuickTip

Gold Ball Outfeed Rollers

Outfeed rollers are essential for supporting long stock or wide panels as they leave a table saw. You can make an adjustable outfeed roller easily with a piece of ¼" steel rod, a length of bar stock, five golf balls and and some odds and ends from the scrap bin. Assemble the outfeed roller as shown here. Make the wooden T long enough so you can clamp it to a Workmate®. That way, you can adjust the roller to the height of your saw.

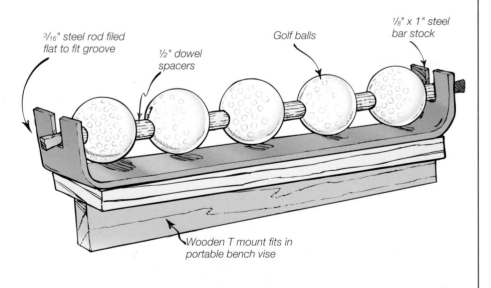

³⁄₁₆" steel rod filed flat to fit groove

½" dowel spacers

Golf balls

⅛" x 1" steel bar stock

Wooden T mount fits in portable bench vise

The lap joint is deceptively simple looking. The keys to forming this joint are accurate layout and creeping up slowly on the final fit.

Adding Dye Stain and Topcoat

Water-based aniline dye makes an attractive finish for Arts & Crafts projects because it colors the wood evenly without darkening the large open pores of the oak. The first step is to raise all the grain with a damp rag, wait for it to dry and sand everything smooth with 120-grit paper. Take care not to sand so much that the lap joint gets loose. With everything sanded and the edges broken, wipe stain on all the parts. If it's warm in your shop, remember to keep your head out of the line of fire. You don't want a big bead of sweat landing on your just dyed piece, or it will leave a stain.

When the parts dry thoroughly, burnish them lightly with a fine Scotchbrite™ pad to take off any minute fuzz. Assemble the pieces while wearing rubber gloves to prevent any sweat on your hands from marking the stained surfaces. The assembly follows exactly the same process as the dry assembly except now you should glue the aprons and splines and use soft rags to pad the band clamps so they don't scar the finish. Leave the top off for the time being.

I sprayed three coats of catalyzed lacquer as my topcoat, but most any finish will do as long as it isn't water-based, which would cause the stain to smear. Varnish or a wipe-on oil finish would be other good choices here.

The final step is to attach the top with four screws through the tabletop fasteners. The table is now complete.

This is a great project for someone looking to advance their skills without spending weeks in the shop to complete it. Set this taboret in a prominent spot, find a healthy plant to top it off and step back to admire your handiwork.

The lap joint dadoes on the feet are cut first. Clearly mark your stock, and remember to reset the blade height for the second foot.

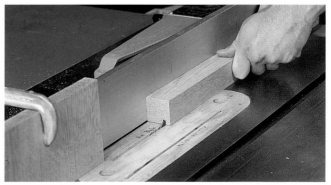

Once the dadoes are cut, move to the band saw to remove the waste at the bottom of each foot. Then template-rout the final shape.

With a stop block in place to create a 7" spline groove, cut the right side of each leg, then reset the fence to cut the opposite sides.

by Chris Marshall

MISSION-STYLE END TABLE

There are many signature features of Mission-style furniture, but one of the more prominent details are mortise and tenon joints where the tenons show. You might think they're difficult to make, but a simple drill press technique and a few chisels are all it really takes. This end table gives you ample opportunity to try these joints on for size.

Through mortise and tenon joints are attractive hallmarks of Mission and Arts & Crafts furniture. They also form rock-solid connections for table legs and other high stress parts. If you've been avoiding them because you don't own a mortising machine, there's a simple solution: all you need is a drill press with a sharp Forstner bit. The technique is accurate, quick and wonderfully low tech. If you can drill a series of holes, deep through mortises are a cinch to make.

Start with the Legs
Begin by planing 8/4 stock down to 1½" for the legs (pieces 1). Cut them to size and joint the faces smooth. As you can see from the Exploded Drawing on the next page, each leg has a number of mortises, and their arrangement can get a little confusing. Take time now to lay out all the mortises before you begin milling. Choose the best face of each leg (with nice quartersawn rays) to face forward.

Conventional wisdom for making mortise and tenon joinery is to cut the mortises first, then trim the tenons to fit. The logic is that you can always trim a

thick tenon thinner but you can't make a too-wide mortise narrower. On through mortises, this reasoning is especially sage. Since the mortises show, you'll want to make them as neatly and accurately as possible, then fiddle with the tenons to fit the joints together.

The sidebar on page 34 will guide you through the process of making the leg mortises, but here are some important tips. Whether you are cutting through or stopped mortises on the legs, start at one end of the mortise and bore a series of holes along its length. Space the holes so they touch but do not overlap, to keep the bit from wandering into the previous hole. Drill all the way through the legs for the through mortises, boring down into the show faces, hiding any tearout on the back beneath the tenon shoulders. When you are about two bit widths from the end of the mortise, skip to the end and drill it out, then back up and drill out the remaining waste. Slide the leg along the jig's fence to drill each hole. Once the first round of drilling is complete, repeat to remove the crest-shaped waste areas that remain.

One jig setup on the drill press allows you to tackle all of this table's mortises except those for the drawer supports, which run perpendicular to the rest. You can align the bit by eye for hogging these out. Note that the mortises for the upper drawer support are open at the tops of the legs to house the bare-faced upper support tenons.

Turn to the Tenoned Parts
Start the tenoning process by cutting the aprons, drawer supports, side rails and shelf supports (pieces 2, 3, 4, 7, 8 and 11) to size. These pieces all have ⅜"-thick tenons. A wide dado blade in the table saw will make quick work of trimming the tenons to the correct thickness and length. Use the rip fence to index the first long shoulder cuts with parts held face-down against the miter gauge. Make additional passes over the blade to rough out the broad tenon cheeks, and then trim the tenons to width on the band saw. Refine the tenons with a shoulder plane or sandpaper until they slide into their mortises with just a bit of resistance.

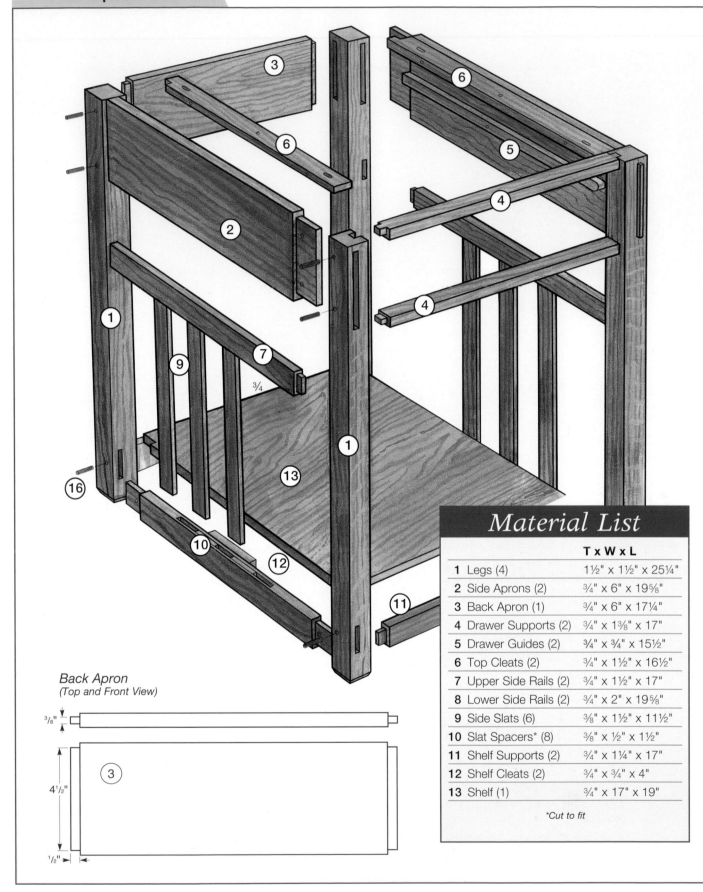

Back Apron
(Top and Front View)

	Material List		
		T x W x L	
1	Legs (4)	1½" x 1½" x 25¼"	
2	Side Aprons (2)	¾" x 6" x 19⅝"	
3	Back Apron (1)	¾" x 6" x 17¼"	
4	Drawer Supports (2)	¾" x 1⅜" x 17"	
5	Drawer Guides (2)	¾" x ¾" x 15½"	
6	Top Cleats (2)	¾" x 1½" x 16½"	
7	Upper Side Rails (2)	¾" x 1½" x 17"	
8	Lower Side Rails (2)	¾" x 2" x 19⅝"	
9	Side Slats (6)	⅜" x 1½" x 11½"	
10	Slat Spacers* (8)	⅜" x ½" x 1½"	
11	Shelf Supports (2)	¾" x 1¼" x 17"	
12	Shelf Cleats (2)	¾" x ¾" x 4"	
13	Shelf (1)	¾" x 17" x 19"	

*Cut to fit

Front and Back Table Legs
Mortise Location Details

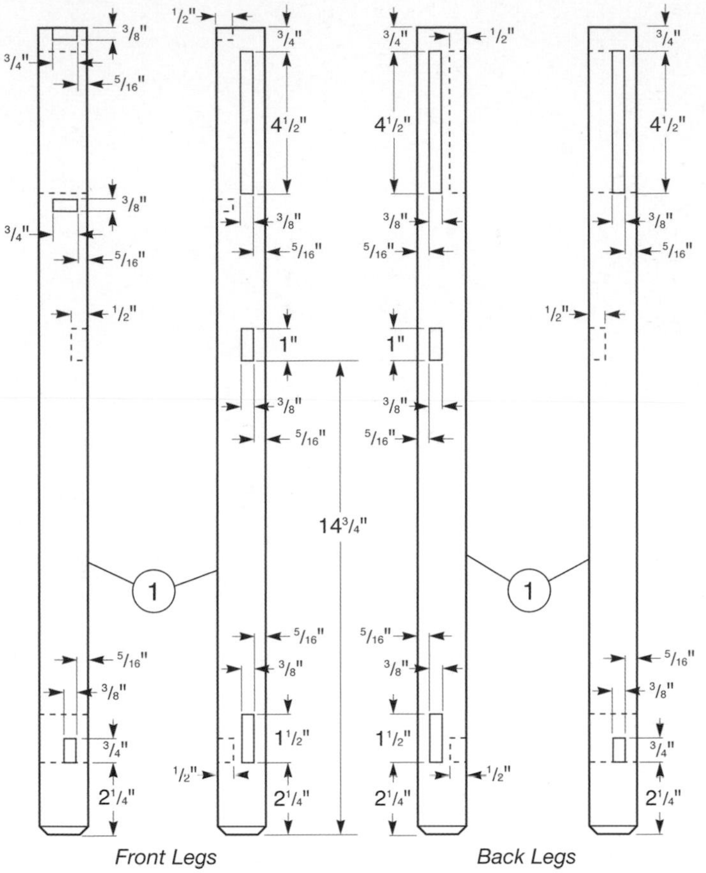

Front Legs

Back Legs

Side Apron
(Top and Front View)

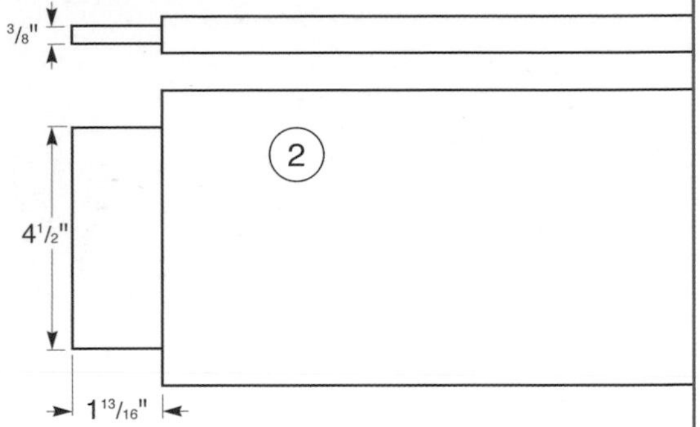

$3/8"$

$4^1/2"$

②

$1^{13}/_{16}"$

Shelf Support
(Top and Front View)

$3/8"$

$3/4"$

⑪

$1/2"$

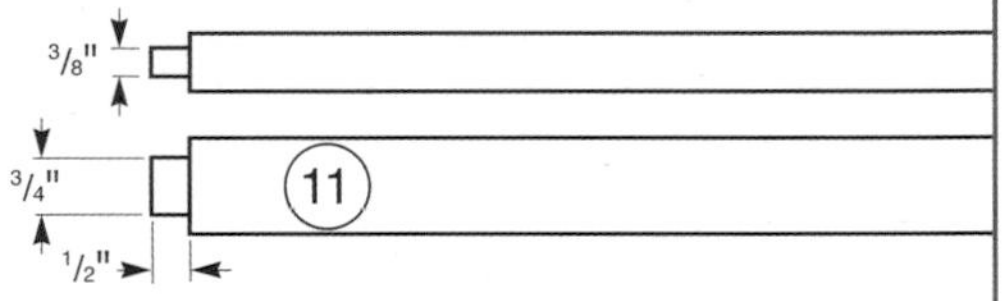

Upper Side Rail   *(Top and Front View)*

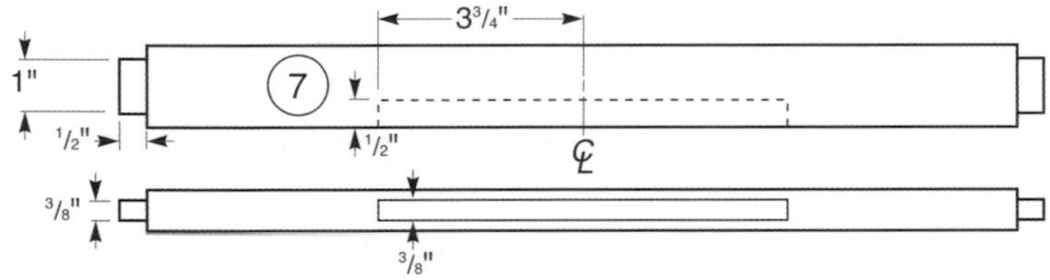

$3^3/4"$

$1"$

⑦

$1/2"$

$\cancel{C}$

$3/8"$

$3/8"$

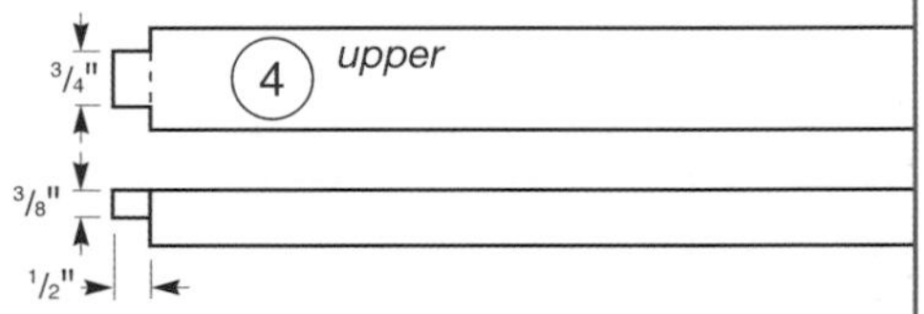

Lower Side Rail   *(Top and Front View)*

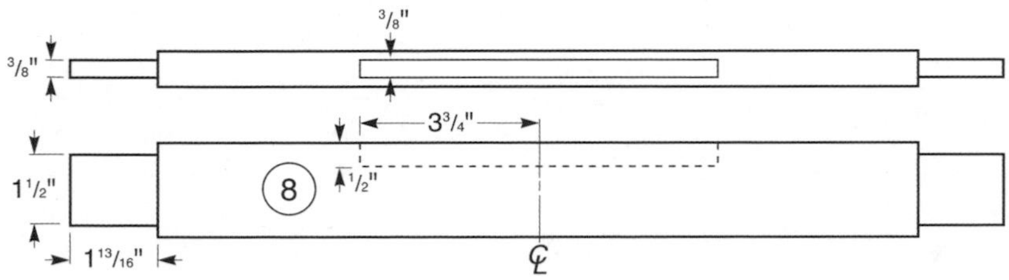

$3/8"$

$3/8"$

$3^3/4"$

$1^1/2"$

⑧

$1/2"$

$\cancel{C}$

$1^{13}/_{16}"$

Drawer Support
(Top and Front View)

$3/4"$ ④   upper

$3/8"$

$1/2"$

Drawer Support
(Top and Front View)

$3/4"$ ④   lower

$3/8"$

$1/2"$

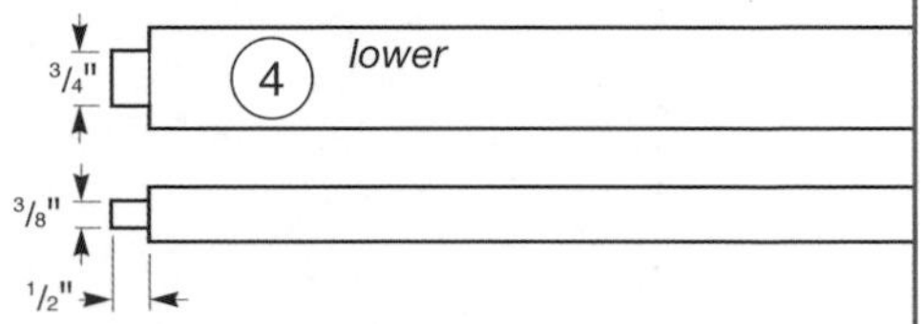

Drilling Through Mortise and Tenon Joints

Drill press mortising sure beats hand chiseling, and it works well for cutting deep through mortises that would otherwise require a long router bit or dedicated mortising machine. The technique doesn't demand a burly floor-model drill press or complicated tooling to complete. Armed with a only benchtop drill press and sharp Forstner bit, you'll have great success. It also helps to have a combination alignment fence and hold-down jig to assist the drilling operation. It's easy to make: just screw a straight piece of stock, 1/16" thicker than the legs, to a piece of scrap plywood. Then fasten a couple

Lay out all the leg mortises with a combination square before you begin milling them. This will help keep their order and orientation clear on each leg.

of hold-downs to the top of the jig fence (about 5" apart). The fence will align the multiple borings required to create the mortises, and the hold-downs will keep the bit from lifting the legs off the drill press table when clearing chips.

Clamp the hold-down jig to the drill press table so the drill bit spur is centered inside the mortise. Drill a series of adjacent holes along the mortise to remove the waste.

Square up the mortise ends with a chisel and mallet. For deep through mortises, a mortising chisel works best. Keep the chisel held square to the leg as you tap it home.

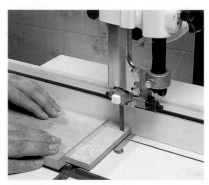

Cut the tenons to thickness and length with a dado blade on the table saw, then make the end cheek and shoulder cuts on the band saw. Guide your work against a fence.

Take shavings off the tenon until it fits its mortise, then chamfer the ends and edges. The chamfers help smooth the assembly and become distinctive visual details.

Preparing the Rails and Slats

Rather than drill separate mortises for each side slat, I'll mill a stopped groove into the side rails for all three slats, then fill the gaps with spacers. Cut these grooves on the router table, and square the ends. Now plane enough 3/8" stock to make the slats and spacers (pieces 9 and 10). Cut the slats to size, but wait on the spacers for now.

Assembling the Table Frame

After all this mortise and tenon work, it's time for some assembly. Start by preparing two side frames consisting of two legs, a side apron, the upper and lower side rails and three slats. Dry-fit the parts first, then disassemble and do your finish sanding. Glue and clamp the side frames, but fit the slats into their grooves dry. When gluing the through tenons, spread glue on the tenons only, not their mortises. Keep the first 1/2" or so of the tenons free of glue and you'll have no glue to clean off the exposed ends after sliding the parts together. With the side frames clamped, drill and insert six dowel pins to lock the joints. Now, cut the spacers to fit and glue them between the slats.

Join the two side frames together by gluing and installing the drawer supports, back apron and shelf supports in place. Spread clamps across the frame to close the joints.

Making and Hanging the Drawer

There are no surprises in the construction of the flush-fit drawer. Cut the face, sides and back (pieces 17 through 19) to size, then mill all the corner joinery. Use a dovetailing jig and router to form the half-blind dovetails and a dado blade to cut the back rabbet and dado joints. After milling the corner joints, rout grooves along the appropriate inside faces to accept the bottom panel. Be sure to stop this groove on the face or it will show after assembly. Sand the parts and glue up the drawer box. Cut the bottom panel

(18) $2\frac{3}{16}$" $\frac{7}{16}$" $\frac{7}{8}$"

$\frac{7}{8}$"

1" $\frac{7}{8}$"

$1\frac{7}{8}$" $\frac{7}{8}$"

Front Corner Dovetail Layout (Side View)

$\frac{1}{4}$" $\frac{1}{2}$" $\frac{3}{8}$" $\frac{7}{16}$"

$\frac{3}{8}$" $\frac{3}{8}$"

(19)

(20)

(18)

Back Corner Joinery Detail (Top View)

(19)

(18)

(20)

(18) (20)

(17)

(21)

(Section View)

Material List - Drawer

	T x W x L			T x W x L
17 Drawer Face (1)	$\frac{3}{4}$" x $4\frac{3}{8}$" x $15\frac{7}{8}$"		**20** Drawer Bottom (1)	$\frac{1}{2}$" x $14\frac{7}{8}$" x $16\frac{1}{2}$"
18 Drawer Sides (2)	$\frac{3}{4}$" x $4\frac{3}{8}$" x $16\frac{1}{2}$"		**21** Pull	Hammered copper
19 Drawer Back (1)	$\frac{3}{4}$" x $3\frac{5}{8}$" x $15\frac{1}{8}$"			

(piece 20) to size, slide it into place and pin it to the drawer back with brads.

The drawer hangs on a pair of guides (pieces 5) that fit into stopped dadoes in the sides and attach to the side aprons. Plow the guide grooves into the sides with a $\frac{3}{4}$" straight bit in the router table. Now rip and crosscut the drawer guides, round their front ends and sand them until they slide easily in the drawer grooves.

The trick to hanging the drawer is locating the precise positions of the drawer guides on the aprons. Here's how I did it: First, fit the entire drawer assembly into place with the guides in the drawer grooves. Hold it in place with a scrap block clamped to the back apron. Adjust the drawer face for

a flush fit. Mark the top and bottom edges of the guides on both aprons near the back. Pull the drawer out, position the guides on the aprons and fasten them through their rear pilot holes with screws. Replace the drawer and insert thin shims of cardboard around the face to center it evenly in its opening. Then, mark the drawer guide positions on the aprons near the front. Finally, adjust the guides to your front reference marks with the drawer removed, and drive in the remaining screws.

Adding the Tabletop and Shelf

Breadboard tops aren't typical features of Arts & Crafts tables, but I chose this style because the

breadboard ends help keep the top flat and hide its end grain. To make the top, glue up a wood panel for the center section (piece 14), and cut the breadboard ends (pieces 15) to size. Next, chuck a $\frac{1}{4}$" straight bit in the router table and plow a long stopped groove into one edge of each breadboard end. With the grooves cut, mill the center panel tongues just as you made the tenons (see Elevation Drawings). Notice that the tongues are $\frac{1}{4}$" narrower and $\frac{1}{8}$" shallower than the grooves to allow for wood movement.

Attach the breadboard ends to the panel with six dowels (pieces 16) driven through the tabletop. Be sure to first form slotted holes in the tongues

Rout evenly spaced pins *across the sides with a dovetailing jig and ½" dovetail bit. Test the setup on scrap before cutting the parts.*

Mill tails *into the drawer face to complete these half-blind joints. On this jig, a stopblock clamped to the fence limits the depth of the cuts.*

for the outermost dowels so the center panel can expand and contract. Spread glue along just the center 4" or so of the tongues when installing the ends. Use a light film of glue on the dowels to keep excess glue off the tongues.

The center panel will expand and contract across the grain far more than the breadboard ends will move along the grain, so the parts won't always line up. To help minimize this mismatch, be sure to use lumber kiln-dried to at least 8%. If there's room in your budget, choose quartersawn stock for the top—it will move significantly less than plainsawn lumber.

To install the tabletop, cut the top cleats (pieces 6) to size and shape, outfitting them with round and slotted screw holes.

Align the cleats flush with the tops of the aprons, then attach them with glue and screws. Position the tabletop and adjust it for an even overhang. Use a scratch awl to mark the screw locations, drill stopped pilot holes and drive the four screws into the slotted holes. Use washers under the screwheads to ensure that these joints will slip when necessary.

Now for the shelf (piece 13). Glue up a solid panel and cut it to size, notching the four corners so they fit around the legs with ⅛" of extra clearance for seasonal expansion. Cut and screw two shelf cleats (pieces 12) to the lower side rails, and attach the shelf to the cleats with screws.

*Quick*Tip

Strengthening Spline Joints for the Long Haul

Spline joints are a great way to join two long edges. But while most woodworkers have no problem routing the grooves for the spline, they often let the ball drop when it comes to making the actual spline. A ripped piece of hardwood won't work, as it will tend to split along the grain—right where you need the most strength. Plywood is the perfect answer: its alternating grain prevents splitting, and it comes in thicknesses that are perfectly suited to the router bits you use to make the grooves. The only time plywood won't be desirable is if your splines show, but a little re-designing may easily solve this problem.

Since the tabletop's ends and panel form crossgrain joints, they need to be able to to move independently of one another. This is accomplished by hidden tongue-and-groove joints. Slotted holes on the tongues allow a slip fit around the outer dowels.

Breadboard End *(Top View)*

Material List - Top				
	T x W x L			**T x W x L**
14 Tabletop Center Panel (1)	¾" x 21" x 24"		**16** Dowel Pins (18)	¼" Dia. x 1¼"
15 Breadboard Ends (2)	¾" x 2½" x 24"			

Finishing Up

Give the tabletop and shelf a final sanding. Tint the end table with a medium-dark stain, followed by a topcoat of varnish and paste wax. While you're at it, wax the drawer guides and their grooves for slippery smooth drawer action. Attach a reproduction Stickley drawer pull (piece 21) to complete the table.

I hope this drill press mortising technique draws you into building more Mission-style furniture. Now that through mortise and tenons are within your reach, you'll probably get hooked!

Half-blind dovetails are a nice touch when assembling the flush fitting drawers.

by Darrell Peart

The author's admiration for Arts & Crafts designers inspired a series of furniture pieces, including this end table made of cherry and ebonized walnut.

GREENE & GREENE END TABLE

Regardless of your design tastes, every woodworker wants to build furniture that will stand the test of time. One sure bet for durability is Craftsman-style engineering. Our end table features wedged and pinned through tenons at all critical joints and finger joints in the drawer. Will it stand up to an atomic blast? Maybe not, but it will surely bear the brunt of ordinary wear and tear without complaint.

Irony is the word I use to describe my introduction to the Arts & Crafts Movement. A cabinet shop I worked for secured a contract to build several Stickley-style tables and display cases. What I thought would be a chance to make some fine furniture turned out to be an exercise in fraud. The pieces were made with pasted-on joinery and an abundance of particleboard—exactly the kind of poor craftsmanship and low-grade materials that gave rise to the movement in the first place.

Despite the shoddy construction of these pieces, I was drawn to the designs and philosophy of the movement. At the library I learned about Gustav Stickley and the brothers Charles and Henry Greene. The end table featured here is my latest effort in a series inspired by their original pieces. A friend and fellow woodworker dubbed an earlier, stouter version of this table "atomic furniture" (see page 45). In the event of a nuclear attack, he explained, this table would be the only object left standing! I couldn't tell if this was a compliment or a criticism, but I still reveled in the notion that something

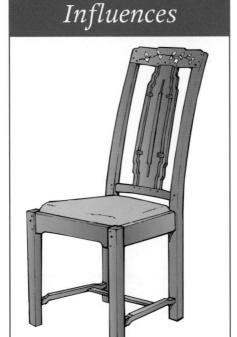

Greene Influences

The abundant use of exposed ebony pegs and projecting tenons was a hallmark of the furniture designed by Charles and Henry Greene. Compared with other Arts & Crafts builders, the Greene brothers incorporated more Oriental styling and flowing, organic carvings in their unique designs.

I built could withstand a nuclear blast. In any event, this comment made me reconsider the table design, and the result is what I now call "atomic lite."

Setting First Things First

This table is made of cherry, which breaks a little with the Arts & Crafts tradition. Historically, quartersawn white oak was the wood of choice, although mahogany was preferred by the Greenes. Any hardwoods will work just fine for this project.

To get your project going, mill stock for the legs, aprons, rail and stretchers (pieces 1 through 6), making sure the lumber is flat and free of any twist or warp, with edges that are perfectly square to the surfaces. Beginning with material that meets these criteria will ensure a smooth work progression throughout the project.

Now set aside the major parts of the table so you can cut the tenon wedges, crosspins and drawer pull (pieces 7, 8, 9 and 17). Getting these pieces going early gives them plenty of time to soak in the black aniline dye (see page 50 for more on using aniline

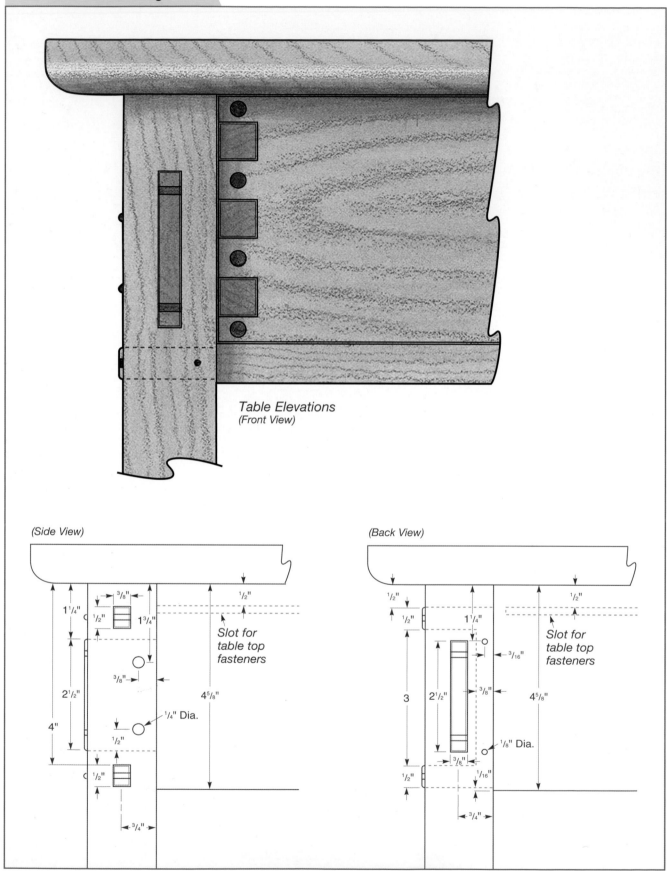

Table Elevations
(Front View)

(Side View)

3/8"   1/2"

1 1/4"   1/2"   1 3/4"

Slot for table top fasteners

2 1/2"   3/8"   4 5/8"

1/4" Dia.

4"   1/2"

3/4"

(Back View)

1/2"   1/2"   1 1/4"   1/2"

3/16"

Slot for table top fasteners

3   2 1/2"   3/8"   4 5/8"

1/8" Dia.

1/2"   3/8"   1/16"

3/4"

dye). Cut the wedges (see Figure 1) and drawer pull (see the Drawer Pull Elevation on page 42) from scrap walnut, and cut the pins from walnut dowels. Roundover one end of each pin using a drill press and file (see Figure 2), and file a chamfer on the top edges of the pull. Now soak all the pieces in water-soluble aniline dye for at least one week. Be sure to use a glass container—metal could adversely affect the dye and the wood.

Cutting Mortise and Tenon Joinery

The aprons, stretchers and legs are held together with mortise and tenon joints. The only difference from what you might be used to is that with this project many of the tenons stick out about ⅛". This detail draws attention to the joinery, making it an important part of the table's decoration.

Start by laying out all the mortises on the legs and stretchers, as shown in the Table Elevations at left. Use a plunge router with a straightedge fence and a spiral cutter to hollow out the longer mortises (see Figure 3), and switch to a drill press with a ¼" bit for all the smaller mortises. After completing the machining, square the corners of the longer mortises and chop the smaller mortises to full size with a chisel. Be sure to work from both outside surfaces to avoid tearing out the rims of the mortises.

Now take a look at the tenon elevations on this page and cut them with a table saw, making repeated passes over a ½" dado blade (see Figure 4).

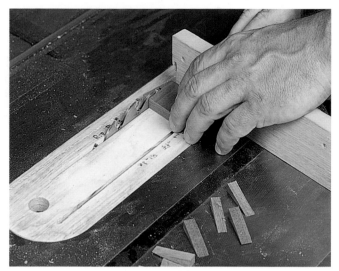

Figure 1: *To slice off your wedges, turn your miter gauge 5° and use a tight-fitting throat plate to keep the wedges from falling alongside the blade.*

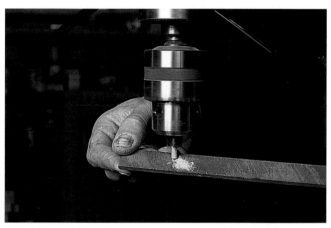

Figure 2: *Rounding over one end of each cross pin is easily accomplished by chucking the dowels in a drill press and holding a file to the spinning wood.*

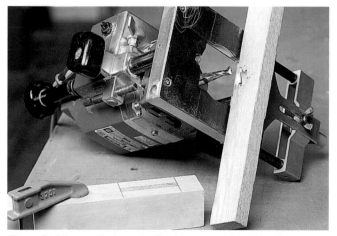

Figure 3: *A fence attachment will guide your router during the mortise cuts, and a spiral bit clears out the chips as the bit moves through the wood.*

QuickTip

Twine Around Your Laminate

The next time you're laying up laminate on a substrate, try using heavy twine instead of sticks or dowels to float the laminate above the cemented surface. Start at one end of the substrate and, leaving about six inches hanging over the edge, cover the glued area in loops about three inches apart across the entire width and length of the workpiece. When satisfied with the position of the laminate, press down at one end, making contact with the glue below. This will prevent the piece from shifting as you pull the twine from the leading six inch "starter." As the twine pulls out, the laminate drops down into place right where you want it…it's foolproof.

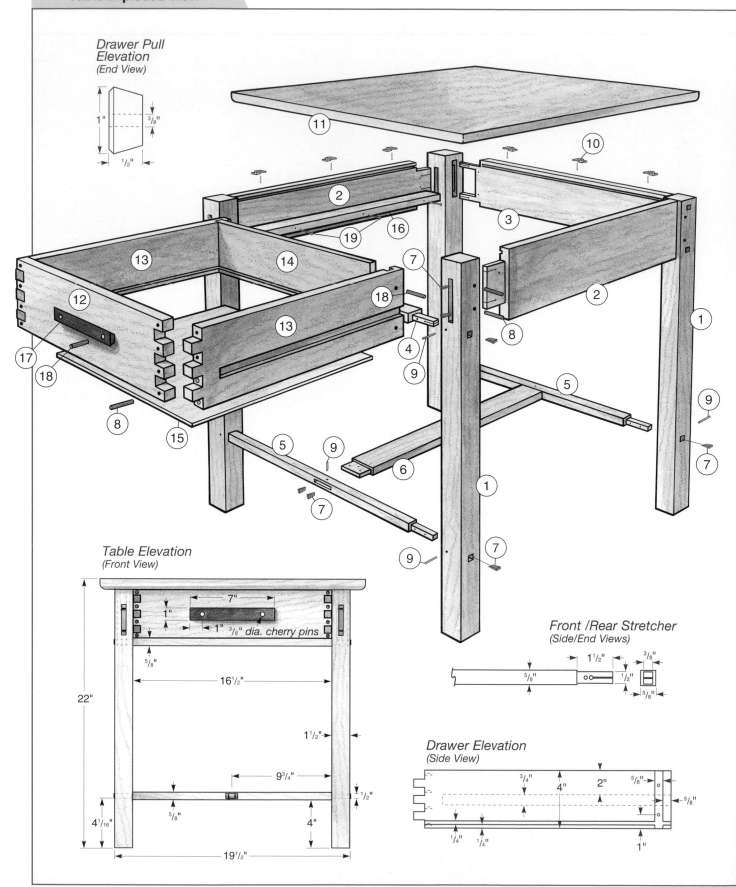

Drawer Pull
Elevation
(End View)

1"   3/8"

1/2"

Table Elevation
(Front View)

7"

1"

1" 3/8" dia. cherry pins

5/8"

16 1/2"

22"

1 1/2"

9 3/4"

1/2"

4 1/16"

5/8"

4"

19 1/2"

Front /Rear Stretcher
(Side/End Views)

1 1/2"   3/8"

5/8"   1/2"

5/8"

Drawer Elevation
(Side View)

3/4"   4"   2"   5/8"

5/8"

1/4"   1/4"   1"

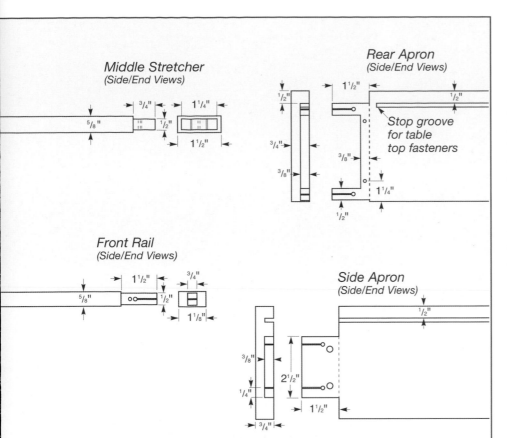

Middle Stretcher
(Side/End Views)

Rear Apron
(Side/End Views)

Stop groove for table top fasteners

Front Rail
(Side/End Views)

Side Apron
(Side/End Views)

Material List - End Table

		T x W x L
1	Legs (4)	1½" x 1½" x 21¼"
2	Side Aprons (2)	¾" x 4⅝" x 19¾"
3	Rear Apron (1)	¾" x 4⅝" x 19¾"
4	Front Rail (1)	⅝" x 1⅛" x 19¾"
5	Front, Rear Stretchers (2)	⅝" x ⅝" x 19¾"
6	Middle Stretcher (1)	⅝" x 1½" x 18⅞"
7	Wedges (22)	¼" x ⅜" x 1½"
8	Pins (20)	¼" Dia. x 2"
9	Pins (12)	⅛" Dia. x 2"
10	Table Top Fasteners (9)	Steel with screws
11	Top (1)	¾" x 22" x 22"
12	Drawer Front (1)	⅝" x 4" x 16¾"
13	Drawer Sides (2)	⅝" x 4" x 17¾"
14	Drawer Back (1)	⅝" x 17¼" x 15¾"
15	Drawer Bottom (1)	¼" x 17¼" x 16"
16	Drawer Runners (2)	¾" x ⅞" x 16½"
17	Drawer Pull (1)	½" x 1" x 7"
18	Drawer Pull Pins (2)	⅜" Dia. x 1⅛" (Cherry)
19	Screws (6)	#8 x 1½"

I recommend machining the tenons a little fat and then shaving them to fit with a shoulder plane and chisel. To remove the additional waste on the back apron tenons, raise the dado blade 1¼", stand the pieces on end and push the stock over the blade with your miter gauge (see Figure 5). Cut the edge shoulders a little fat following the same method, then pare them to size with a chisel. Next, lay out the slots for the wedges and use a band saw for the cuts. Follow up by drilling a ⅛" hole at the end of each slot to reduce the chance of splitting when driving in the wedges.

To make the tenons easier to insert in the mortises and more pleasing to look at, file the ends to a slight roundover. As a final step before assembly, cut a saw kerf in each apron for housing the table top fasteners (pieces 10), as shown in the Table Elevations.

Assembling the Table Base

After sanding all the legs, aprons, rail and stretchers to 220 grit, and completing a successful dry fit, break the table base down into subassemblies for the final glue up. Prior to gluing up, however, wipe the ends of all the exposed tenons with a coat of oil/varnish finish. This will prevent any glue from sticking to the exposed tenon areas during the table assembly. After the oil dries, glue the front legs to the front rail and stretcher. Square the clamped subassembly, then shoot some glue into the wedge slots with a syringe and tap in the wedges. Later, when you've removed the clamps, cut and file the wedges flush with the tenons and touch them up with black aniline dye using a fine brush.

Now glue the two rear legs to the rear apron and stretcher, and drive in the wedges. Complete the base by joining the front and rear subassemblies

Figure 4: *Form tenons using a ½" dado blade, a set-up block and a miter gauge, adjusting the blade height for the various tenon layouts.*

Figure 5: *To remove the extra waste for the back apron tenons, screw a tall fence to your miter gauge and clamp the stock for each pass.*

with the side aprons and middle stretcher. Drive in the remaining wedges and lay out the holes on the legs for the crosspins (see the Table Elevations). Bore the holes using a ¼" bit, making sure they pass through the tenons plus ¼". Next, cut the dyed pins to length, allowing for the ⅛" projection of the rounded ends. Squirt glue into the holes and drive in the pins with a hammer and a simple jig (see Figure 6).

Before moving on to the drawers, glue up the top (pieces 11). Later, cut the top to size, rout the edges and sand to 220.

Building the Drawer

The drawer is held together in the front with finger joints and in the back with dado joints. (Note: Any conventional table saw finger joint jig will work fine.) After constructing the jig and milling the drawer stock to size (pieces 12, 13 and 14), cut the finger joints, as shown in the Table Elevations. I recommend cutting a sample joint first to make sure the finger size and spacing work out with your jig and blade. Be sure the bottom edges of the drawer align.

QuickTip

One Clamp is All You Need

Short on clamps and don't want to use biscuits or dowels? Duplicate a spring joint and with only one clamp in the center…bring your boards together. First, plane the very center of each board's edge with one stroke of your #6 or #7 plane. Next, increase your planing area about one third; finally, plane the complete board. More smaller strokes will give you a greater bow.

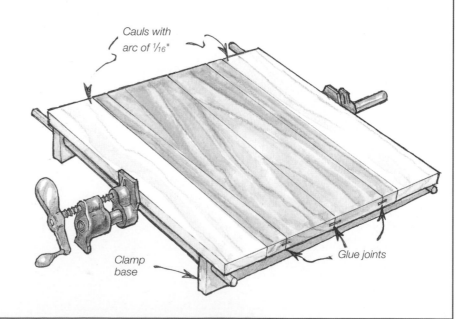

Cauls with arc of 1/16"

Clamp base

Glue joints

Once you've perfected the finger joints you can complete the machining on the drawer parts. Cut dadoes in the drawer sides for the back, as shown in the Drawer Elevation on page 42, then use your router table and a ³⁄₁₆" bit to rout grooves in the drawer walls for housing the bottom. Make two sets of passes with this undersized bit to get a tight fit with the plywood bottom (piece 15). Be sure to stop the groove in the drawer front to keep it from showing. Complete the drawer bottom grooves, then switch to a ¾" bit and plow ⁵⁄₁₆"-deep stopped grooves in the drawer sides for the drawer runners (pieces 16), as shown in the Drawer Elevation. Square the ends of all the stopped grooves with a chisel.

Now position the drawer pull (pieces 17) on the drawer front and use your drill press to bore two ³⁄₈"-diameter x 1"-deep holes for the cherry pull pins (pieces 18). Dry-assemble the drawer and drill ¼" holes for pinning the sides to the back, as shown in the Drawer Elevation, then take the drawer apart and round over the corners of the fingers with a file.

Glue and clamp the drawer parts together, then squirt glue into the holes for the back pins (pieces 8) and drive them into place. After removing the clamps, shave the back pins and front fingers flush with the drawer sides, and re-file the sharpened finger edges. Lay out and drill the cross pin holes in the drawer front joints, as shown in the Table Elevations, and drive in the ebonized cross pins.

Now round over one end of each pull pin using the drill press and file technique shown in Figure 2. Squirt glue in the drawer pull and drawer front holes and drive the pins home. Finally, cut the drawer runners to length, round the front end a bit and mount them in the table base with screws (pieces 19), as shown in the Table Elevations.

Finishing Up

Finish your project with three coats of the same oil/varnish product you used earlier on the tenon ends, but avoid getting too much in the drawer runner grooves and on the runners—the drawer will stick. When the last coat of finish is dry, secure the top to the base with the table top fasteners.

Hopefully you'll agree that I've captured the spirit of the original Arts & Crafts designs. Even though my new "atomic lite" table may fail in a nuclear blast, I am confident it will last more than a few generations in your family.

Figure 6: *Make a pad for driving in your pins by boring a shallow dimple in one end of a piece of scrap wood.*

¼"-dia. dimple

Our author's first version *of this design was called the "atomic table" for its apparent ability to survive even the most severe conditions.*

GREENE & GREENE WALL MIRROR

Take your shop skills to the next level with this Arts & Crafts style mirror. It's made of Honduras mahogany with ebony plugs decorating the joints.

by Mike McGlynn

This large mahogany mirror is an adaptation of a design by Charles and Henry Greene. The original piece is now part of a collection at the David B. Gamble House, a home in Pasadena, California, which was designed by the Greene brothers in 1908. Apart from their woodworking talents, the Greenes were registered architects. Perhaps that explains why their work incorporates both solid aesthetic values and superb structural integrity.

The original mirror is vertical and embellished with wavy, secondary stiles that would be rather difficult to reproduce. I kept that in mind when building this reproduction, opting for a horizontal version with simple, straight stiles. The reproduction does, however, remain true to the original in most other aspects. For example, this mirror's design features identical mahogany stiles and rails, the Greenes' signature ebony plugs and aniline dye stain. (If you've never worked with aniline dye, see page 50 for some helpful tips.)

Honduras mahogany isn't difficult to find and is only slightly more expensive than red oak. If you don't want to pay for ebony, substitute maple for your plugs and stain them with black aniline dye.

Milling the Mahogany

I built this entire project from one $^5/_4$ plank of rough-cut Honduras mahogany. To some degree, the three true mahoganies (African, Cuban and Honduras) are interchangeable, but each has some defining color characteristics. African and Cuban are a bit darker than Honduras; both are difficult to find, and what does come on the market is about twice as expensive as Honduras.

Honduras mahogany boards are generally quite flat, and it's not unusual to find them 24" wide and 15' long. It's a very clear wood with almost no knots, and it rarely warps. Most of the time the

Historical Fact

Charles and Henry Greene's furniture is distinguished by rounded edges and corners. This effect contrasts with the strong lines found in the work of their contemporaries, Gustav Stickley and Frank Lloyd Wright.

Charles & Henry Greene

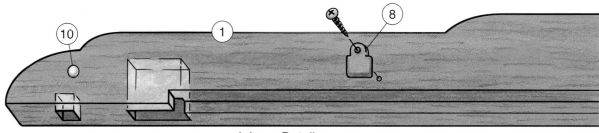

Joinery Details
(Back view)

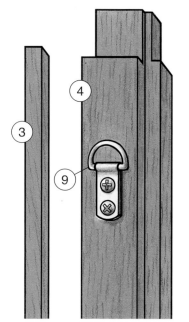

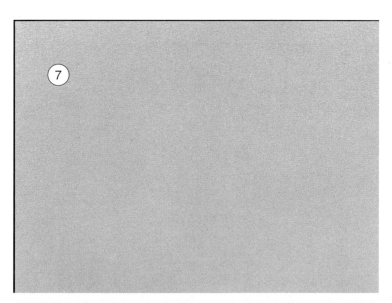

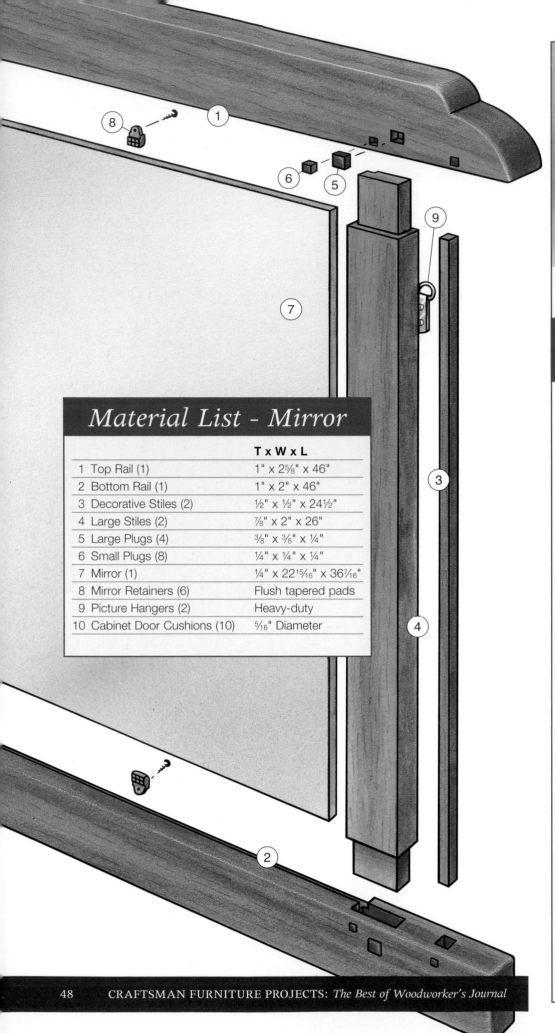

Material List - Mirror

		T x W x L
1	Top Rail (1)	1" x 2⅝" x 46"
2	Bottom Rail (1)	1" x 2" x 46"
3	Decorative Stiles (2)	½" x ½" x 24½"
4	Large Stiles (2)	⅞" x 2" x 26"
5	Large Plugs (4)	⅜" x ⅜" x ¼"
6	Small Plugs (8)	¼" x ¼" x ¼"
7	Mirror (1)	¼" x 22¹⁵⁄₁₆" x 36⁷⁄₁₆"
8	Mirror Retainers (6)	Flush tapered pads
9	Picture Hangers (2)	Heavy-duty
10	Cabinet Door Cushions (10)	⁵⁄₁₆" Diameter

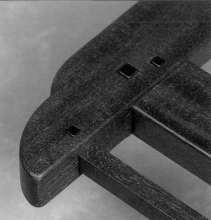

The ¼" and ⅜" square ebony plugs add a decorative touch to the mahogany.

Making Ebony Plugs

Creating the decorative plugs for this mirror requires that you first make two sticks, each at least 12" long, to safely run through your planer. Ebony was the Greene brothers' choice for decorative plugs. Or use black-dyed maple as a more economical substitute.

We made the large ⅜" square plugs first, aiming for a perfect friction fit (no glue) in the mortises. We also made sticks from both ebony and maple, using the maple sticks to get an exact setting before running the expensive ebony through the planer. Once the ⅜" plugs fit perfectly, follow the same procedure to cut the ¼" square plugs.

An alternative to the friction fit (also known as a press or a tap fit) would be to make the plugs a hair smaller than the mortise and secure them with a drop of poly glue.

Once you've achieved perfect fits, cut each end of your sticks square. Using 220-grit paper, sand a very slight dome on each end. Then put a buffing wheel on your bench grinder and, using some buffing rouge, polish both ends to a nice glossy finish. Slice off a ¼" thick piece from each end at the band saw. Break the bottom corners of each plug with sandpaper and tap the plug in place with a rubber mallet or a hammer wrapped in cloth. Repeat the whole process until you've filled all 12 mortises.

figure and grain are easy to see, even when the boards haven't been planed. That's because Honduras mahogany is usually cut on a bandsaw mill as opposed to a circular mill. For this project, you'll need a board that's 8" wide and at least 54" long.

Generally, it's a good practice to let lumber sit around in your shop for a week or so in its rough state, especially in the winter. This allows it to acclimate to its new environment. Then, to be absolutely sure that there are no surprises, cut the pieces oversized from that rough stock and let them sit for a few more days. Be especially patient in the winter if the temperature in your shop is radically different from that in the lumberyard. By the way, mahogany moves both widthwise and through its thickness, but not as much as some other woods do.

Once you've cut the pieces to rough size, dimension them to final size as shown in the Material List, on page 48. First, face joint all the pieces so one side is flat, then plane them to finished thicknesses. Joint one edge straight and rip the piece oversized by ⅟₃₂". When you take that last ⅟₃₂" off on the jointer, all evidence of saw marks goes, too.

Cutting the Mortises and Tenons

Layout and cut the mortises on the top and bottom rails (pieces 1 and 2). It's a lot easier to form these mortises now, while the profile of the top rail is still square.

The narrow stiles (pieces 3) are purely decorative and are centered front to back on the top and bottom rails. Their tenons don't have shoulders, so their mortises are a full ½" x ½". I used a mortising attachment on a drill press for making these square holes, but a ⁷⁄₁₆" drill bit and sharp chisel work equally well.

The mortises for the large stiles (pieces 4) are milled to hold a ½"-thick tenon and are cut 1¼" deep. These mortises are positioned so the backs of the stiles are flush with the backs of the rails, while the fronts are a little shy — a common feature in the Greene brothers' designs.

Cut the tenons for the large stiles on the table saw. I used a shop-made tenoning jig to make these cuts, as shown in Figure 1. Or you could cut them face-down on the table saw with a dado blade instead.

Use the sketch on page 51 to make a full-size drawing and a template from ¼" hardboard for scribing the top rail shape. Use the same template for both ends of the rail, so the cloud-lift shapes match. There are several sound reasons for making a template here. First of all, it's easier to get lines straight on ¼" thick material with no grain than it is on a 1"-thick piece with grain. It's also cheaper to fix mistakes on hardboard or plywood than it is on expensive mahogany. Best of all, if you want to make another mirror, you'll have a template for the most complex part of the project.

To make the template, tape a copy of the pattern to your hardboard blank and cut it out on the bandsaw. Stay just outside the line, then refine the template with files and sandpaper.

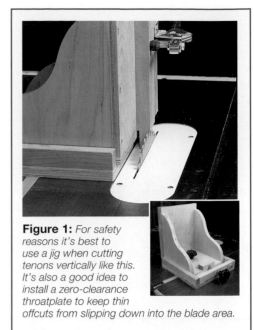

Figure 1: *For safety reasons it's best to use a jig when cutting tenons vertically like this. It's also a good idea to install a zero-clearance throatplate to keep thin offcuts from slipping down into the blade area.*

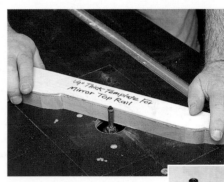

Figure 2: *Final shaping of the rail is completed with a flush-trim bit. The bearing rides the template to provide a clean surface. Be careful with the end grain on the curves. Several passes will help eliminate tearout.*

Figure 3: *To hold the mirror, both rails have stopped rabbets on their back sides. Alignment marks on you fence and rails define the starting and stopping points for these cuts.*

Aniline Dye Tips

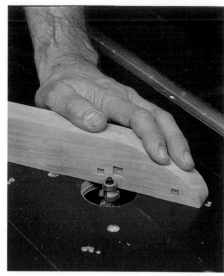

Figure 4: *When rounding over the outside edges of the rails, make sure the bearing on the bit is positioned to avoid the decorative plug mortises.*

We mixed brown and red aniline dyes for the Greene and Greene mirror, testing different mixtures until the color was right. An alternative would be a pre-mixed medium reddish brown color.

Here are 10 tips to keep in mind from contributing editor Mike McGlynn when using aniline dyes:

1. Using a sponge and some warm water, lightly wet all the surfaces just enough to raise the grain before applying the dye. Then sand lightly with 220-grit paper, just enough to take off all the fuzz.

2. Keep aniline dye away from mortises and tenons. Because aniline dye is waterbased, the dye won't affect the polyurethane glue that holds these joints together, but it can build up in the joints and could bleed out into the wood later, altering the color.

3. Mix the powdered dye in warm water according to the manufacturer's instructions. Let the mixture set for an hour so the dye totally dissolves before you apply it.

4. Aniline dyes have an almost indefinite shelf life, if you store them in airtight containers.

5. Add a little liquid dish soap — about one teaspoon for each quart of water — to your dye mixture. The soap helps break the surface tension of the water, allowing the dye to fill in all

the grain. This is especially helpful when dyeing oak.

6. Mix and store your dye in plastic or glass containers. Don't use steel containers because they'll rust, changing the color of the dye.

7. Use a foam brush to apply aniline dye. Wear rubber gloves; aniline dyes will stain your hands.

8. Before you stain your project, figure out how you're going to set the pieces down after wiping off the surfaces. (For this project, rest the tenons of the mirror stiles on some scrap pieces of wood. Rest the back sides of the rails on the points of nails pounded through scrap, as shown below.)

Drive several nails up through a piece of scrap to support your workpiece while it dries.

9. After you've applied the dye with a foam brush, use a soft, clean, lint-free cotton cloth to wipe the dye off. Wipe off any fingerprints so that moisture from your skin doesn't cause blotching.

10. If you apply the aniline dye before you assemble your project, wear thin rubber gloves during the assembly process. Any water, including sweat, that touches the dyed but unfinished surfaces will leave a spot on the wood.

When you're satisfied, use two-sided tape to attach it to the top rail. Make this cut with a ¼" blade in the bandsaw, staying ¹⁄₁₆" away from the template. Then, with the template still taped to the workpiece, switch to your router and let the bearing on a flush-trim bit ride the template to trim the piece to size. Take light cuts to avoid tearout on the end grain, as shown in Figure 2.

The Decorative Plugs

The next step is to cut holes for the decorative plugs (pieces 5 and 6) on the fronts of the rails. The Greene brothers frequently used such plugs to hide screws that held the mortise and tenon joints together. I decided against the screws because they're not needed with today's superior glues. To make the ⅛" deep plug holes, we used a drill press mortising attachment with ¼" and ⅜" chisels. Locate the plugs by eye, following the elevation drawing on page 51. Make the matching ebony plugs using the technique described in the sidebar on page 48.

Cut the stopped and through rabbets for the mirror (piece 7) next. Size the rabbets to the mirror's thickness (ours was ¼" thick, so we cut ¼" x ¼" rabbets). Mill the backs of both large stiles first, then dry-assemble these pieces to the rails. Use the rabbets on the stiles to mark the locations for the corresponding stopped rabbets on the backs of the rails. Make these cuts on the router table (see Figure 3) and square their corners with a sharp chisel.

Sanding and Finishing

To stay true to the Greene and Greene look, soften all the edges on this piece. Start with 120-grit sandpaper on the decorative stiles — there's no need to use coarser grits first. Then use a ⅛" roundover bit in your router table to soften the front edges of the rails and large stiles, making sure the bit's bearing is positioned so it won't run into the plug mortises (see Figure 4). Use 120-grit paper to break the outside edges of the back (avoiding the joints) and the top rail's profile where the router couldn't reach. Wrap up this step by finish-sanding all the parts to 280 grit.

Now you are ready to apply a medium reddish brown aniline dye. (For some tips on using aniline dye, see the sidebar on page 50.) Applying the dye now, before assembly, is preferable because it's difficult to get inside those narrow corners after everything is assembled.

Aniline dye will bleed into some finishes, especially waterbased polyurethane varnish. I used Bartley's Satin Topcoat (after assembly), but you can apply any finish over the dye, as long as you start with two coats of the appropriate sanding sealer.

Gluing Everything Together

After the aniline dye dries (at least two hours), glue the parts together. You can't use yellow woodworkers glue with aniline dye because both products are waterbased and they will react with each other, creating a dark line. I've had good success using polyurethane

glue. Because it's not waterbased, it won't react with the dye. It's also ideal for gluing dense imported woods, where surface penetration is restricted. Another advantage is its long open time.

After the glue is dry, you're ready to install the mirror. Check your yellow pages for glass suppliers who specialize in mirror glass, and have one of them cut your mirror ⅛" smaller than the opening in the frame. Remember that wood will expand and contract with the seasons, but glass won't.

Install the mirror using at least six tapered retainer pads (pieces 8). You'll also need to use strong picture hangers (pieces 9), as this is a heavy mirror. Finally, attach some cabinet door cushions (pieces 10) to the back to keep the mirror from scratching your walls.

Technical Drawings

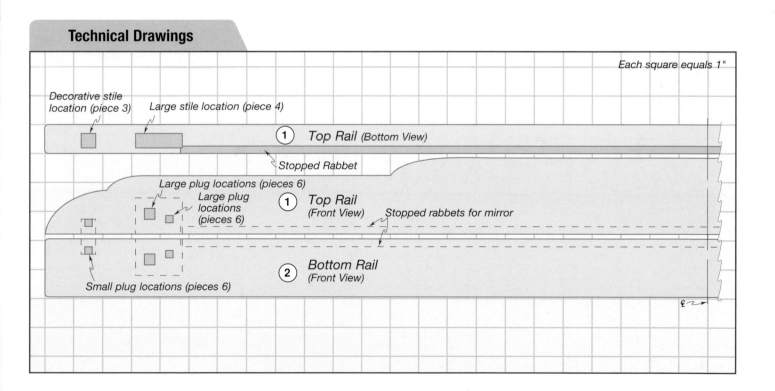

Each square equals 1"

Decorative stile location (piece 3)

Large stile location (piece 4)

(1) Top Rail (Bottom View)

Stopped Rabbet

Large plug locations (pieces 6)

Large plug locations (pieces 6)

(1) Top Rail (Front View)

Stopped rabbets for mirror

(2) Bottom Rail (Front View)

Small plug locations (pieces 6)

by Sandra Newman and Joseph Ebler

ARTS & CRAFTS PICTURE FRAME

Sure, the focal point of most artwork is generally the art and not the frame that contains it. But that's no reason to ignore the need for a proper and visually pleasing frame. Our double-frame design features pinned mortise and tenon joints for durability. Its proportion, wood grain and warm finish contribute to a harmonious whole.

The craft of framemaking has a long and rich history comparable to that of furnituremaking. In recent times, however, the use of pre-cut and pre-finished moldings has reduced most picture framing to little more than gluing and underpinning ready-made molding lengths to size. We believe the joy of framemaking comes from designing and carrying through your own individual creation.

Striking a Balance in Frame Design

Ideally, a frame design should complement both the art's subject matter and style, with the relationship between the framing components—artwork, mat and frame—established through rules of proportion. It is also important to relate the width of the frame to the overall size of the print, making sure that the frame appears sturdy enough to support the perceived visual weight of the artwork. Keep in mind that a print containing large shapes often calls for a wider frame than a print of the same size containing very small details.

Regarding Grain Selection

Arts & Crafts period furniture was left unpainted both to display the methods of construction and to reveal the beauty of the wood. The wood of choice was quartersawn white oak. Although the designation of quartersawn is usually thought of as specific, the variations within that classification actually are quite wide. When considering a frame design, you'll be confronted with the enjoyable decision as to which one of the grain patterns to use. They range from rift (straight grain with a combed effect), through small flakes and tiger stripes, to patterns that look like lightning strikes.

Considering both subject and style of the artwork helps when choosing your material. In this frame, the moderately heavy

Chop mortises *into the appropriate frame members first and then make tenons to match. Later they will be pinned to create simple and long-lasting joints. Mortise and tenon joints must fit perfectly to be attractive.*

When building your own frames, *select wood with an annual grain pattern that enhances the art being displayed.*

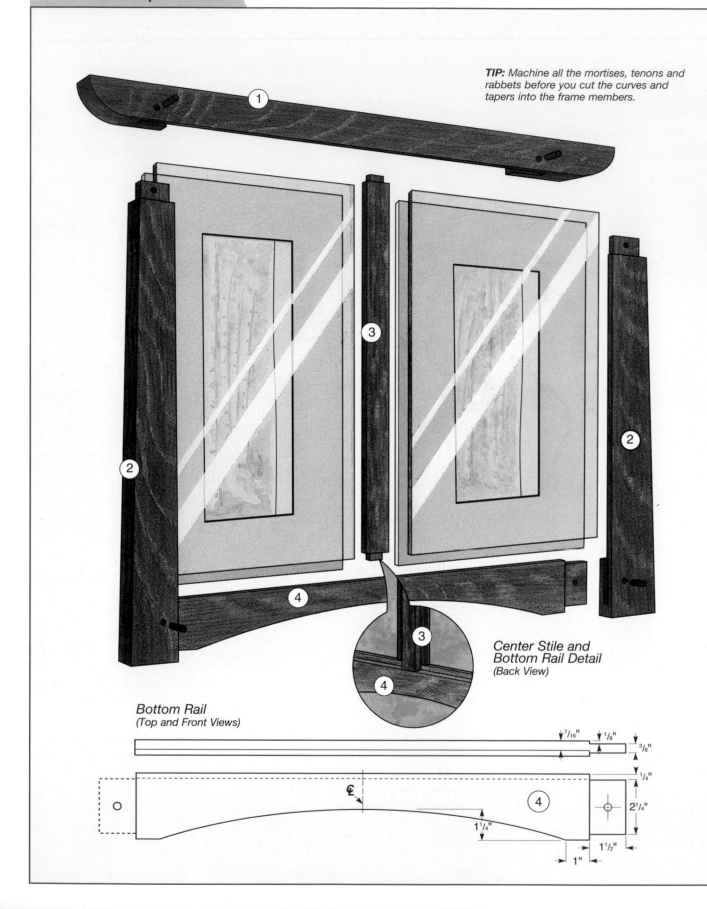

TIP: *Machine all the mortises, tenons and rabbets before you cut the curves and tapers into the frame members.*

Center Stile and
Bottom Rail Detail
(Back View)

Bottom Rail
(Top and Front Views)

Material List - Picture Frame

		T x W x L
1	Top Rail (1)	⅞" x 1½" x 26⅛"
2	Side Stiles (2)	¾" x 2½" x 21⅞"
3	Center Stile (1)	⅝" x 1" x 18¼"
4	Bottom Rail (1)	⅝" x 2¾" x 21¾"
5	Pins (4)	⅜" Dia. x ¾"

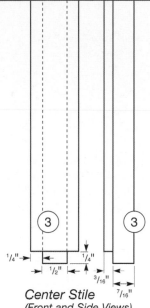

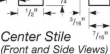

Center Stile
(Front and Side Views)

Side Stile
(Side and Front Views)

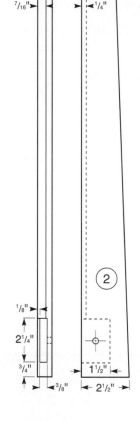

Hanging Hardware:
1- or 2-hole D hangers are preferable to screw eyes, because they allow the frame to hang straight on the wall. Install the hangers a third of the way down from the top edge of frame. Use braided picture wire of sufficient strength to support the frame, glass and art.

Top Rail
(Front and Bottom Views)

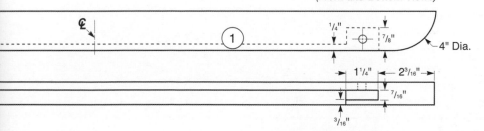

grain selected enhances the "woodsy" feel of the images without competing with them. Always strive for harmony.

Once you've selected an appropriate grain, you must balance the wood grain placement in the frame. This means the sides should somewhat mirror each other, and the top and bottom pieces should be of similar grain pattern.

While the finished frame is quite elegant, the joinery is very basic. The primary joint here is the pinned blind mortise and tenon, which adds to the project's simplicity. But in this simplicity still lies complexity—there's "no room to hide." Simple joints must still fit together well.

Making Tenons and Mortises

Machine all the tenons and mortises while the stock is sticked up, and take special note of the thickness dimensions. Cut the frame pieces to length and width as shown in the Material List. Next form the mortises in the top rail and sides (pieces 1 and 2). A mortising machine makes short work of this task, but any method, from traditional to modern, will work. Refer to the Elevation Drawings at left for all of the construction details. Now that you have the mortises prepared, move on to making the tenons. As shown on page 53, we used a radial arm saw outfitted with a dado head to reveal the tenons, including those on the center stile and bottom rail (pieces 3 and 4).

In our shop, we've found that it is more effective to match the tenons to the mortises rather than make the mortises match the tenons. Test-fit your joints as you go: they should be snug, but not too tight. Now step over to your router table and, with a straight bit chucked in your router, set up to shape the rabbets along the inside edges of the frame pieces. As you can see by the Elevation Drawings,

tenons you will be pinning. Cut your pins so they will be just a bit proud of the frame members and prepare for final assembly.

Putting It All Together

Glue, clamp and pin the frame together, making sure that the assembly is square and flat in your clamps. Secure the center stile with a bit of glue and one tiny brad at each end. Pre-drill for the brads…it would be a catastrophe to split your wood at this point. Once the glue cures, sand the pins flush and give the entire frame a final finish-sanding. Stain the frame to complement the art you are framing and complete the job with low-luster polyurethane.

Next, you need to mat and mount your art (see the sidebar, on page 57) and hang the frame on the wall. (There are several options for frame hangers available.) Once it's up, you will get to experience the bittersweet reality of a quality picture frame maker. Without a doubt, your guests will comment and compliment the art that you are displaying…but you'll know that they are also experiencing the pleasure of a well-made picture frame. Your work may not be the star of the show, but talk about an award-winning supporting cast!

A well-applied coat of Minwax® *dark walnut stain produces a reasonably close approximation to ammonia fuming. It's an appropriate tone for Arts & Crafts-styled pieces like this.*

these rabbets are stopped within the length of all the frame members except the center stile. With this step you create left and right versions of the side stiles, so take a moment to plan.

Adding Tapers, Curves and Rounded Corners

With those tasks completed, you are ready to cut the tapers, gentle curves and rounded corners that announce the Arts & Crafts influence of this picture frame. Grab your side stiles and mark out the taper cut on each piece. To achieve this cut, use a simple taper jig on the table saw. But again, method takes a second place to accuracy, and you could easily cut the tapers on the band saw or by hand if you choose to do so.

And speaking of the band saw, use it to shape the curve and corners on the bottom and top rails. Mark a 4" radius on each of the top rail's corners. Cut them on the band saw and sand the saw marks smooth later. The curve or arc that details the bottom edge of the bottom rail is also simple to mark. Measure up 1¼" from its bottom edge at the center point and then flex a thin strip of hardboard or a metal ruler from two corner marks (shown on the Elevation Drawings) to the indicated center point. Trace the curve onto the rail (ask a friend to help you), and you are ready to band saw. Sand the sawn edge smooth as well as the various pieces up to 180 grit. Now is also the proper time to test-fit all the pieces and be sure the whole assembly goes together without problems.

With the frame dry-assembled and clamped together, mark the locations of the joint pins (pieces 5). Step over to your drill press and bore holes deep enough to go all the way through the

For the authors, one of the most important aspects to proper framing is to protect the art in an archival frame package, as described at right. You can find archival material at a quality art supply store.

Protect Your Art...from the Frame

Proper framing preserves your artwork and prevents future problems. An archival frame package consists of a backboard or support for the art (which must be properly hinged or mounted), a window mat, glazing and a dust cover. As a wood frame ages it becomes acidic, which is damaging to artwork. Use aluminum-faced frame sealing tape to isolate the art from the frame's rabbet.

Glazing: Select glass or Plexiglas™ that has been coated to filter out the UV rays. Clean glazing with an anti-static brush prior to assembling the frame package. Hinging: Japanese rice paper attached with wheat or rice starch is our choice. Matting: Use only pH neutral mat board. Attach the window mat to the back support with archival linen tape along their longest side. Dust cover: Acid-free paper must cover the entire back of the frame, affixed to the outer edges with double-sided tape (ATG 924). Finally, keep the frame away from the wall with small bumpers (cork, plastic or felt buttons) placed in the bottom corners.

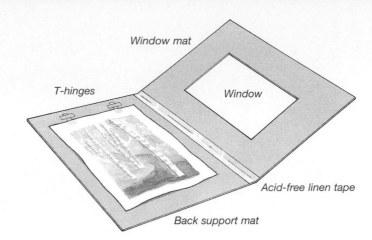

Window mat

T-hinges

Window

Acid-free linen tape

Back support mat

Alone or in concert with other Arts & Craft furniture, the authors' double picture frame adds elegance to the art, the room and the owner's life.

QuickTip

Tape Clamps
There's nothing quite as elegant as clear strapping tape when it comes to clamping unusual shapes. A good-quality tape can be stretched to its limits and, as its memory makes it try to shrink back to its original size, it draws parts together for a perfect bond. Mitered corners are especially suited to this technique. First, apply a short strip of tape to create a hinge, then spread the glue and close the miter. Finally, stretch the tape across it to draw it tight.

by Mike McGlynn

GREENE & GREENE SERVING TABLE

Moving from the verdant east to a dry, southern California landscape had a formative effect on the Greene brothers. Charles and Henry moved to Pasadena in 1893 and shortly thereafter created their own distinct architectural style.

Espousing a similar philosophy to the celebrated Frank Lloyd Wright, the Greenes believed an architect's duty lay beyond floor plans: They designed the furniture, lighting and accents in many homes they built. Charles, who had been affected by a Japanese furniture exhibit at the World's Columbian Exposition in 1893, was primarily responsible for creating those classic interiors. This reproduction serving table features many of the facets that set Charles' designs apart. Bold horizontal lines, wide aprons and a cantilevered top suggest strength, functionality and honest craftsmanship. A broad expanse of Honduras mahogany is deftly balanced by small, ebonized accents. Square plugs hide the screw heads, and splines hold the tabletop's breadboard endcaps in place.

Buying Materials

It's always a good idea to buy stock for a project several weeks in advance of when you plan to start building. That's what I did for the mahogany used on this table. Doing so allows the wood to acclimate to the temperature and humidity of your shop. This is especially true of the board used to make the top (piece 1) of this server: Because of the large cantilever on either end, the tabletop must be a stable, properly cured piece of stock. Another

important note before you start: If you will be using the water-based aniline dye I recommend for this project (see page 62), it is important to use a brown polyurethane glue. This will prevent dark lines from appearing, because the water-based glue will absorb the dye at a different rate than the mahogany.

After cutting the top to size (see the Material List on page 61), use a bearing-guided straight bit in your portable router to create the tenon on each end. (Refer to the Exploded View Drawing on page 60 and the project's Elevation Drawings shown on pages 64 and 65 for machining and assembly details.) It's a good idea to cut these tenons before jointing the long edges of the top, as any blowout will be cleaned up by the jointer. If the piece is too large to handle comfortably on your jointer, another option is to clamp a long straightedge to the workpiece and joint the edges with a straight bit chucked in your router.

Milling the Tabletop

The procedure for creating the breadboard endcaps (pieces 2) is described in detail in the sidebar on page 63. These caps serve two functions: they dress up the ends of the tabletop, and they also help prevent this wide piece from warping widthwise.

Refer to the sidebar on "Making the Ebonized Plugs and Splines," page 64, before chopping the square mortises in the endcaps for the ebonized plugs (pieces 3) that hide the screws (pieces 4). A good technique here is to drill out most of the mortise waste with a Forstner bit, then use a sharp knife to score the squared-up ends before trimming to their final dimensions with a sharp chisel. This will reduce tearout and create sharp, crisp corners on the mortises. Use the same technique to create the spline mortises on both the top and the endcaps. Note that these are matching mortises that accept a single piece between them. Use the Elevation Drawings to lay these out.

Screw (don't glue) the breadboard endcaps to the top through the equally spaced mortises and pre-drilled screw holes. These holes are drilled slightly oversized through the endcaps so the screw shanks have extra play all around. Space created by the enlarged holes allows the top to expand or contract across its grain and will help prevent cracking. Cover the holes with the ebonized plugs, secured with just a drop of glue. Gently break the long edges of the top with sandpaper, then sand the entire top and set it aside while you build the leg assembly.

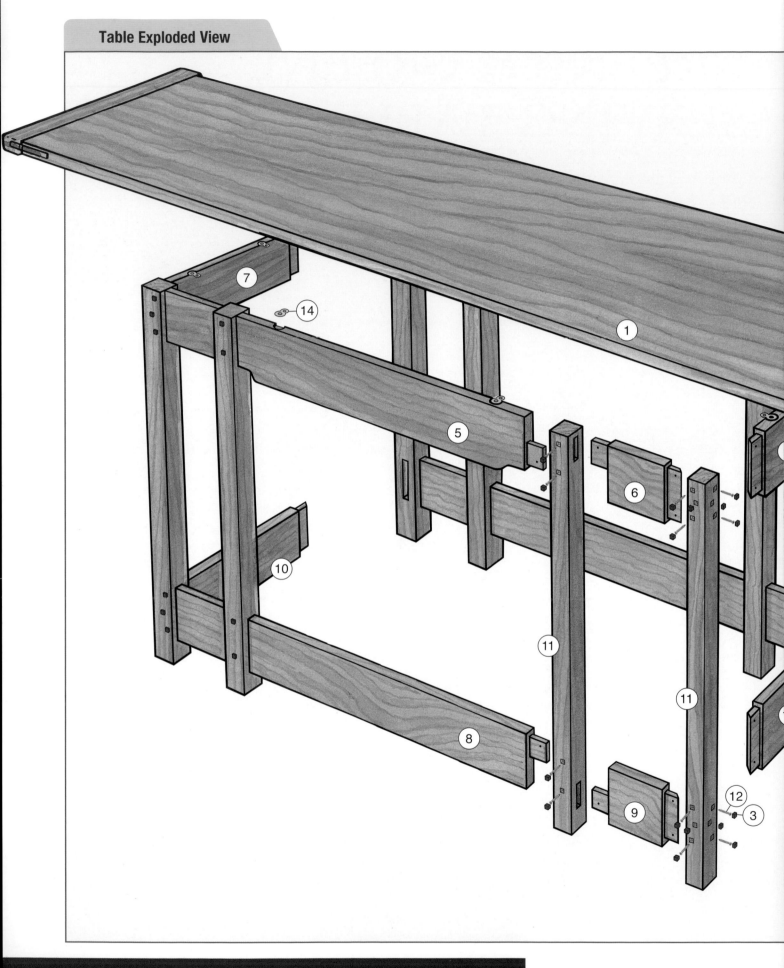

Material List - Server

		T x W x L
1 Top (1)		1" x 15⁷⁄₁₆" x 73"
2 Breadboard Endcaps (2)		1¼" x 1⅞" x 15¾"
3 Ebonized Plugs (70)		⅜" x ⅜" x ³⁄₁₆"
4 Endcap Screws (6)		#8 x 1¾"
5 Top Center Aprons (2)		¾" x 5" x 24⅝"
6 Top Side Aprons (4)		¾" x 4½" x 4¾"
7 Top End Aprons (2)		¾" x 4½" x 9¹¹⁄₁₆"
8 Bottom Center Aprons (2)		¾" x 4½" x 24⅝"
9 Bottom Side Aprons (4)		¾" x 4½" x 4¾"
10 Bottom End Aprons (2)		¾" x 4½" x 9¹¹⁄₁₆"
11 Legs (8)		1¹³⁄₁₆" x 1¹³⁄₁₆" x 26⅞"
12 Screws (48)		#6 x 1"
13 Ebonized Splines (4)		⅜" x 1½" x 4"
14 Tabletop Fasteners (10)		*Metal*

Making the Tenoned Aprons

Harmony and simplicity were guiding principles of the Arts & Crafts movement, so it's a good idea to keep both concepts in mind when selecting stock for the top and bottom aprons (pieces 5 through 10). Above all, the wood should be consistent in color. If its grain patterns also match, so much the better.

Cut all sixteen of the apron parts to size, according to the Material List on this page, then lay out the asymmetrical and mitered tenons on the ends of the aprons. Use the Elevation Drawings on pages 63 and 65 to create the proper offset for the aprons joining the central legs. You can cut all these tenons on the table saw using a dado head and the saw's miter gauge, as shown on the next page. Note that some of the tenons are notched and some are mitered. Cut the notches on the band saw and the miters on the full-width tenons with your table saw. After cutting the tenons, use the Top Center Apron elevation drawing on page 63 to lay out, then band saw the stepped profile on the bottom edge of both the top center aprons. Clean up the saw marks with a drum sander mounted in your drill press.

Mortising the Legs

If you own a mortising machine or an attachment for your drill press, chopping mortises in the legs (pieces 11) should be a quick and easy task, as all of them are the same width (see the Elevation Drawings on pages 63 and 65 for details). Even doing it the old-fashioned way (see the sidebar on the next page) is a relatively simple task. Carefully lay out the mortises for each individual leg. (The four inner legs are similar and the four corner legs match each other in the same fashion.) The apron tenons are asymmetrical and the mortises must match them exactly. Clamp a fence to your drill press and, as the Forstner bit removes most of the waste, slide each leg across the table against the fence. Clean up each pocket with a sharp chisel, then stay at the drill press to make all the small, square

Making the Mortise and Tenon Joints

Before cutting the shaped profile on the top center aprons, reveal the tenons on their ends using a dado head in your table saw.

A Forstner bit chucked in your drill press will remove most of the mortise waste, and the bit's design leaves a nice, flat-bottomed cavity.

After laying out the matching mortises in the legs, score them with a sharp utility knife to avoid tearout as you drill.

Clean up with a sharp chisel, cutting across the grain on the top and bottom first, then with the grain along the sides.

mortises in the legs for the plugs (these are similar to the plug mortises you already cut in the breadboard endcaps). When you're done, switch bits again and drill pilot holes for all the screws. Chisel the plug mortises square.

Using the Exploded View drawing on page 60 as a guide, dry-fit the aprons to the legs. Make any necessary adjustments, then use the screw holes in the legs as guides to extend pilot holes into the apron tenons. Disassemble the legset and give all the pieces their final 120-grit sanding before raising the grain with a water-dampened sponge. When this dries, sand with 220-grit paper before applying a stain or other colorant to bring out the richness of the wood. Before you go on, mask off the areas

where the aprons and the legs meet. This will keep those areas free of dye as you proceed with the finishing process.

Applying an Aniline Dye Finish

In keeping with the habits of the Greene brothers, I applied a water-based aniline dye to all the legset and tabletop mahogany parts. If you haven't used aniline dyes before, here are some tips to help you get top-notch results: Use a drop of dish soap in water-based dye to break the surface adhesion, and apply the product with a foam brush. Wipe it off immediately with paper towels, then let it dry. It is important to dye the wood before you assemble the piece. It is virtually impossible to achieve uniformity of color if you try to dye the assembled server.

From this stage on, you should wear utility gloves (latex medical versions or standard household rubber gloves will both work fine) whenever you handle any of the dyed parts: otherwise you may leave oil residue on the dye or dissolve the dye with ambient moisture from your hands. Both will show up as smudges on the finished piece. A little caution here will save you heartache later.

After the dye dries, remove the masking tape and use a utility knife to create small, V-shaped channels in the hidden surfaces, wherever glue might squeeze out of a joint. These little glue traps (see Figure 1, on page 64) will save you frustration — they're an excellent alternative to refinishing all the parts that might be affected by squeeze-out, since

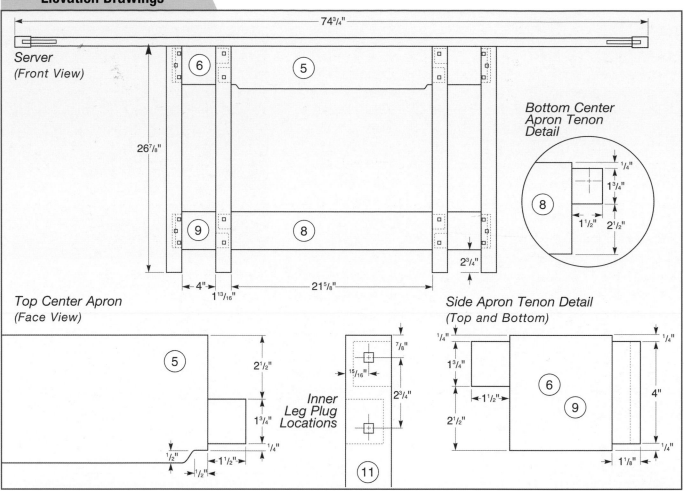

Server
(Front View)

74³/₄"

26⁷/₈"

4"
1¹³/₁₆"
21⁵/₈"
2³/₄"

Bottom Center
Apron Tenon
Detail

¼"
1³/₄"
1¹/₂" 2¹/₂"

Top Center Apron
(Face View)

2¹/₂"
1³/₄"
¹/₂"
1¹/₂"
¹/₄"
¹/₂"

Inner
Leg Plug
Locations

⁷/₈"
¹⁵/₁₆"
2³/₄"

Side Apron Tenon Detail
(Top and Bottom)

¼"
1³/₄"
1¹/₂"
2¹/₂"
4"
¼"
1¹/₈"

Making the Ebonized Plugs and Splines

Polish the Ebon-X plugs and splines to their final luster with a polishing wheel mounted in a bench top grinder.

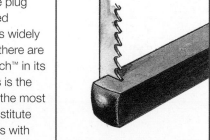

Early in the new century, Charles Greene had the luxury of being able to specify ebony for the plug and spline accents in his most accomplished furniture pieces. While ebony is no longer as widely available or as inexpensive as it once was, there are some viable modern alternatives. Exotic Birch™ in its Charcole Ruby shade is a sound choice, as is the idea of ebonizing your own stock. Perhaps the most appealing option is Ebon-X™, an ebony substitute made by impregnating domestic hardwoods with non-toxic chemicals. Making plugs (pieces 3) with this material is relatively simple.

Rip a length of material to 3⁄8" x 3⁄8", then create a gentle crown to both of its ends with a sander. Buff the ends of the stick on a grinder equipped with a polishing wheel to create an ultra smooth finish. Saw off ³⁄₁₆"-long plugs, then repeat the entire plug making process.

Cut the splines (pieces 13) to the shape shown in the Elevation Drawings on page 65. Again, use a sander to help create the gently rounded profiles. Move to the buffing wheel and repeat the buffing technique you used on the plugs. Polish the Ebon-X smooth as silk, bringing it to a high, rich luster.

wiping off the wet glue will also smudge the dyed surfaces.

You can now reassemble the legset using glue sparingly. Make sure everything is square and plumb as you tighten the clamps, then set this subassembly aside to dry. After the glue has cured, remove the clamps and drive home the screws (pieces 12) to complete the joint.

Final Thoughts

After all the plugs (pieces 3) and splines (pieces 13) are made, there are a couple of items that need your attention before these accents can be installed. First on the list is attaching the tabletop to the legset. Refer to the Exploded View or Elevation Drawings to locate and drill simple round mortises with a Forstner bit in the top of the legset for the tabletop fasteners (pieces 14), then screw the fasteners to the legset. Lay the top face-down on a soft surface (towels laid across cardboard works well), and drill pilot holes in its underside (be careful!) for the fastener screws. Then, screw the legset and top together.

Apply three coats of a satin or semi-gloss finish to all surfaces to achieve the soft yet durable finish the Greenes preferred. One of the best options out there is a gel varnish such as Bartley's — it's tough, easy to apply and has great visual depth. As mentioned earlier, a brown polyurethane glue is a good choice for securing the plugs and splines in their mortises. However, only glue the splines to the tabletop and not to the endcaps. This will allow your top to expand and contract with the seasons during a lifetime of useful service.

Charles and Henry Greene became known for their fine architecture and furniture design, developing a style of their own from a world of influences. Now you can serve your food from atop a stylish piece of true Americana that you've built yourself.

Figure 1: *Slice tiny v-channels around the perimeter of the joint areas with a sharp chisel or utility knife to help prevent glue squeeze out from smudging the dye.*

Making Breadboard Ends

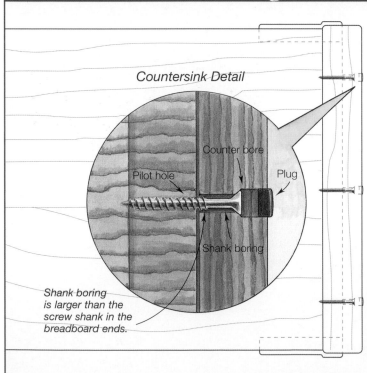

Countersink Detail

Counter bore

Pilot hole

Plug

Shank boring

Shank boring is larger than the screw shank in the breadboard ends.

Whether it's a glued-up lamination or a single wide board, wood likes to wiggle with the weather. Old-time cabinetmakers tried to eliminate this movement in breadboards by capping the ends with strips of solid hardwood. This treatment worked, but had its problems. You'll hear tales of folks awakened in the middle of the night by the loud report of maple and oak parting company under the tremendous pressures of moisture-related wood movement.

To prevent such a calamity from happening on this project, the tongue and groove joints on the breadboard ends allow the cross-grain joints to slip past one another as needed. The exclusion of glue here also helps. We used screws driven into counterbores with oversized shank holes to secure the ends. The space provided by these extra-large holes allows for the expansion and contraction of the top. Square up the counterbores to accept the ebony plugs that cap the screw heads and also add decorative detail.

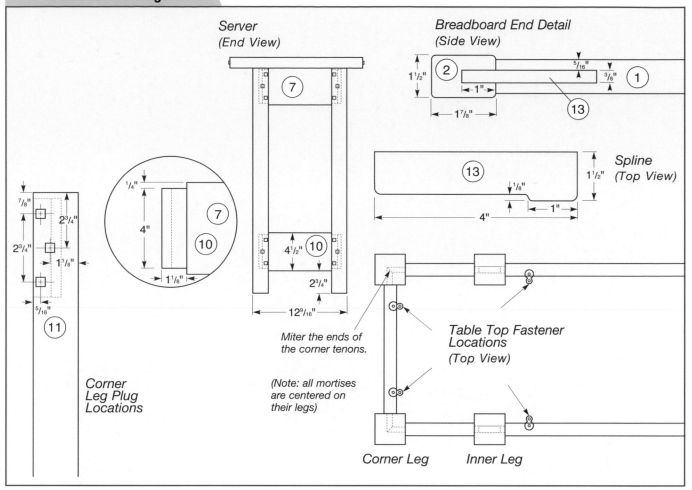

Server
(End View)

Breadboard End Detail
(Side View)

Spline
(Top View)

Corner
Leg Plug
Locations

Miter the ends of
the corner tenons.

(Note: all mortises
are centered on
their legs)

Table Top Fastener
Locations
(Top View)

Corner Leg   Inner Leg

---

*Quick*Tip

Go with the Grain

If you're getting a little tearout or feathering on boards as you run them across the jointer, flip the board end for end to reverse the direction of the feed. Tearout usually means you're planing against the grain. By switching the front of the board to the back, the blades will shear with the grain direction and produce a much cleaner cut. If the knives are nicked, just loosen one and move it left or right, as far as it will go. Leave the others as they are and you'll get clean, sharp cuts.

Snipe Remedies

Snipe is that annoying little concave area that a jointer or thickness planer can leave on the last couple of inches of a board. It is caused by an outfeed table that is set lower than the knives or on workpieces that are just too short. Dealing with it involves adjusting the outfeed table, planing longer boards, or buying one of a new breed of planers that are marketed as being snipe-free. Or you can cut your stock 6" or 8" too long, then trim off the snipe on the miter saw. It's not thrifty, but it works.

STICKLEY-INSPIRED DINING TABLE

Function and style, true tenets of the Arts & Crafts philosophy,
are combined here to create a project that will last for many generations.

by Rick White

This sturdy and attractive dining table came about after I designed and built the Arts & Crafts Dining Chairs featured on page 130. My wife wanted a table that would complement the details in the chairs, so necessity became the mother of invention here. True to its Mission influence, the table features pegged through mortise and tenon joinery and butterfly keys in the top.

Two Suggestions Before You Start

Throughout this project, you'll be chopping stopped and through mortises to fit the various tenons and plugs. If you don't already own a dedicated mortising machine, or if you plan to build both the table and a set of matching chairs, investing in a mortiser will be money well spent. A mortiser looks like a small drill press but drills square holes. Alternately, you could use a mortising attachment in your drill press. It uses the same hollow chisel bits as a dedicated mortiser to produce square-ended mortises more economically.

Gustav Stickley built most of his furniture from quartersawn oak for good reasons. It's attractive and one of the strongest species in North America. If your budget allows, it's good to use the same wood for your table. Quartersawn red or white oak yields straight boards with tight, parallel grain — ideal for tables.

Laminated, Quartersawn Legs

The legs of this table are built up in two major laminations (pieces 1), and the first step in construction is to cut these to the dimensions shown in the Material List on the next page. If the wide faces of these boards are quartersawn lumber, the thin edges will be plain sawn. The leg's most visible face after machining and glue-up would be the plain sawn view so, for appearance's sake, it must be hidden.

To accomplish this step glue quartersawn leg veneer (pieces 2) to each leg, after the first two have been milled and glued up.

Machining the Legs

Each leg is mortised twice for a couple of rails. The dadoes for the top and bottom rails (pieces 3 and 4) are easily created on the table saw, as shown in Figure 1. Both are machined into the leg laminations before they are assembled. Follow the locations and dimensions given in the Leg Subassembly and Half-mortise Detail Drawings on page 73 to lay out both mortises. After milling, glue and clamp each leg together. Once the glue dries, sand each leg thoroughly and chisel out any excess glue left in the mortises.

Although both of these openings are technically through mortises, you'll cover the top mortise with the leg veneer (pieces 2) to create, in effect, a stopped mortise. The bottom mortise is continued through the leg veneer to expose the chamfered end of the lower rail's tenon.

Making the Rails Next

After cutting all the rails to the dimensions given in the Material List, refer to the Top Rail and Bottom Rail Tenon Detail Drawings (also on page 73) to lay out and mill their tenons. This is a job for your dado head and miter gauge on the table saw. (Don't forget to chamfer the tenon ends on the bottom rails.)

If you decided to invest in a mortising machine, this next step will be your first chance to use it. Refer to the Face View Drawings for the top and bottom rails on page 73 to lay out and chop the five mortises in each rail (see Figure 2). In the bottom rails, these mortises are a strong $\frac{3}{8}$" deep, while those in the top rail are deeper. If you don't own a mortising machine, remove most of the waste on your drill press and square up the mortise walls and ends with chisels. This is also a good time to chop the small mortises in the legs for the plugs—the details are on the Leg Subassembly Elevation (page 73).

Apply the same technique for chopping the large through mortise for the beam (piece 10) in each bottom rail. Work from the outside so any minor tearout will occur on the inside, hidden face. Then use a strip of ¼" hardboard flexed in an arc to lay out and band saw the arches on the bottom edge of each top rail. The deepest point of this arch should be 1¼" from the bottom rail edges. Sand these curves smooth.

Completing the Leg Sets

There's just one more task to perform before you can assemble the leg sets: you must make the 10 slats (pieces 5 and 6). Cut all

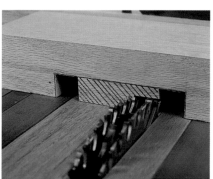

Figure 1: *The leg mortises are formed before the legs are glued up. Simply slice wide dadoes to form one half of each mortise.*

Figure 2: *A dedicated mortising machine will make short work of the many mortises featured in this project's Stickley-inspired joinery.*

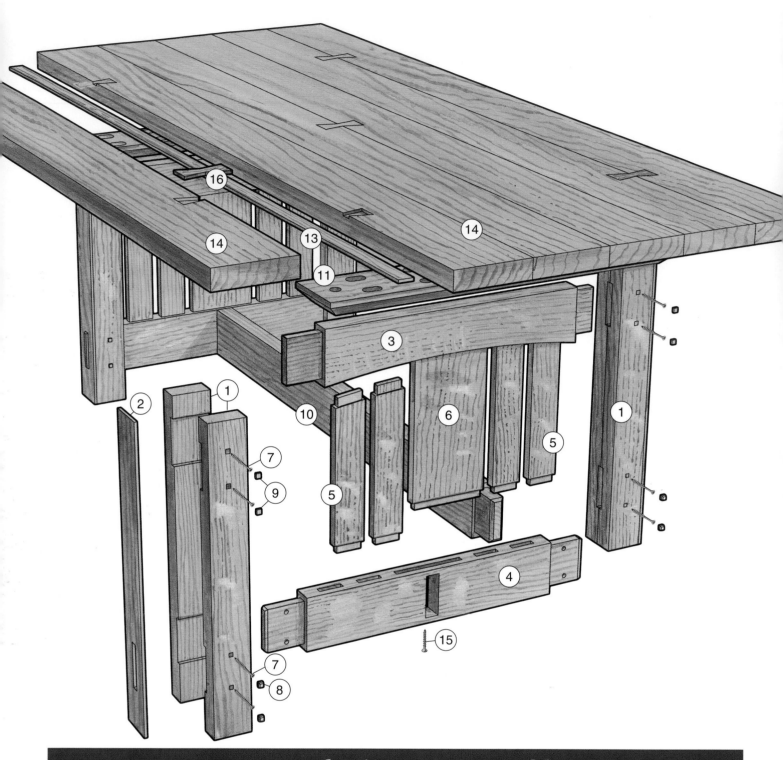

Material List - Dining Table

		T x W x L			T x W x L
1	Leg Laminations (8)	1¾" x 3¼" x 26¾"	**9**	Flush Plugs (16)	½" x ½" x ½"
2	Leg Veneer (4)	¼" x 3½" x 26¾"	**10**	Beam (1)	1¾" x 5" x 56¾"
3	Top Rails (2)	1¾" x 5" x 31"	**11**	Tabletop Supports (2)	1¾" x 6" x 35"
4	Bottom Rails (2)	1¾" x 5" x 32"	**12**	Support Leg Screws (4)	#12 x 3"
5	Edge Slats (8)	½" x 2¾" x 14"	**13**	Splines (5)	½" x 1" x 84"
6	Center Slats (2)	½" x 7" x 14"	**14**	Tabletop Segments (6)	1¾" x 7" x 88"
7	Rail Screws (16)	#8 x 2"	**15**	Support Top Screws (16)	#8 x 2"
8	Pyramid Plugs (16)	½" x ½" x ⅝"	**16**	Decorative Butterflies (5)	¼" x 2" x 4"

Table
(Side View)

1³/₄"

15"

18³/₄"

3"

Table
(End View)

3¹/₂"

1¹/₂"

28¹/₂"

12¹/₄"

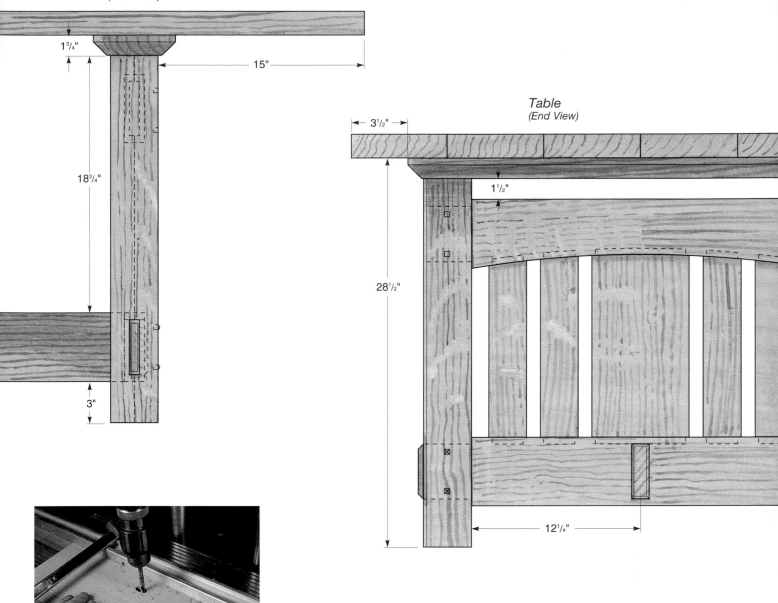

Figure 3: *The glued-up tabletop will expand and contract to a significant degree. Oblong slotted screw holes allow that movement to take place while firmly securing the top to the leg sets.*

³/₈"

³/₄"

¹/₄"

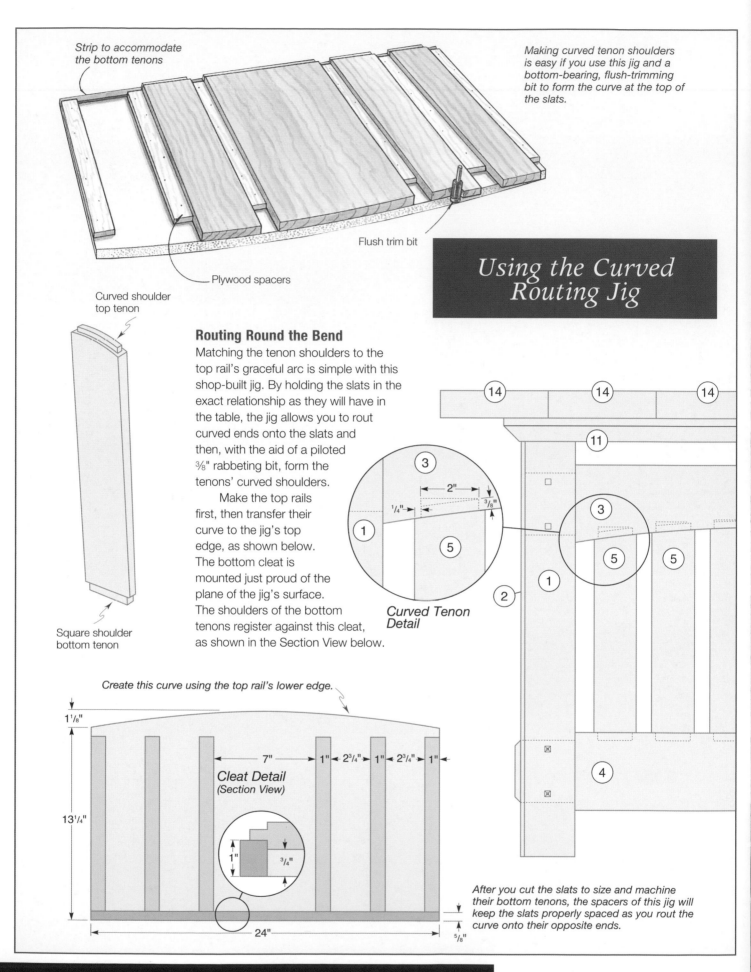

Strip to accommodate the bottom tenons

Making curved tenon shoulders is easy if you use this jig and a bottom-bearing, flush-trimming bit to form the curve at the top of the slats.

Flush trim bit

Plywood spacers

Curved shoulder top tenon

Square shoulder bottom tenon

Using the Curved Routing Jig

Routing Round the Bend

Matching the tenon shoulders to the top rail's graceful arc is simple with this shop-built jig. By holding the slats in the exact relationship as they will have in the table, the jig allows you to rout curved ends onto the slats and then, with the aid of a piloted ⅜" rabbeting bit, form the tenons' curved shoulders.

Make the top rails first, then transfer their curve to the jig's top edge, as shown below. The bottom cleat is mounted just proud of the plane of the jig's surface. The shoulders of the bottom tenons register against this cleat, as shown in the Section View below.

Curved Tenon Detail

2"
1/4"
3/8"

Create this curve using the top rail's lower edge.

1⅛"

7" — 1" — 2¾" — 1" — 2¾" — 1"

Cleat Detail (Section View)

1"
¾"

13¼"

24"

⅝"

After you cut the slats to size and machine their bottom tenons, the spacers of this jig will keep the slats properly spaced as you rout the curve onto their opposite ends.

Cutting Curved Tenons

Set the slats in place *between the jig cleats and clamp them all in position. Use a flush-trimming, bottom-bearing router bit to shape the gentle curve onto the top end of the leg set slats. Set the bit depth so the bearing rides along the jig's top curve.*

Move to your router table *and use a ⅜" piloted rabbeting bit to form the shoulders of the curved tenons. Cut the cheeks on a bandsaw.*

10 to the dimensions in the Material List, then lay out and mill ⅜" long tenons on their bottom ends. Use a dado set on the table saw or a router table and rabbeting bit for this work.

The tenons on the top ends are a little trickier. I used a jig similar to the one I designed for the dining room chairs. Details for how to make the jig in this project are shown on the previous page.

Dry-fit the leg sets together and, when everything is fitting well, start the assembly process by gluing and clamping the rails and slats together. Next apply glue and seat the rail tenons into their leg mortises. Predrill for the screws (pieces 7) and drive them home. Then cap the bottom ones with glued-in, pyramid plugs (pieces 8, see Pyramid Plug Detail, page 73) and the top ones with flush plugs (pieces 9). After the glue dries, sand the top plugs flush.

Building the Beam

The long, one-piece beam (piece 10) is tenoned on each end to fit the mortises you chopped earlier in the bottom rails. This would be an unwieldy job for the table saw, so use the Beam Tenon Detail to lay out the tenons and mill them with a handheld router. Chuck a straight bit in the router and clamp guide blocks to the beam to keep the cuts straight. When the tenons are completed, switch to a chamfering bit or use a block plane to create a traditional profile for the tenon ends.

Dry fit the beam in the leg sets, then temporarily clamp it in place. Cut the tabletop supports (pieces 11) to size next, and use your table saw to mill the large chamfer all around both of these pieces (see Tabletop Support Detail, page 73). Next, use your drill press to create oblong screw holes in the supports, as shown in Figure 3. These allow for wood movement in the tabletop.

Predrill for the large screws (pieces 12) used to attach the supports to the legs, then apply glue to the top of each leg, set the supports in place and drive the screws home.

Gluing Up the Top

The top of this table is the most critical element, simply because it's the most visible. Choose defect-free, straight, quartersawn boards and cut them a bit longer than their final 88". Equip your router table with a featherboard to machine the ½" wide by ½" deep grooves in these long, wide pieces, stopping the cuts 2" from each end of your boards. (Mill both edges of the internal pieces, and the inside edge

After forming the tenons, create the arc by flexing ¼" hardboard between two endpoints.

Top Rail *(Face View)*

③

1½"

3¾"

7½"

5¼"

Bottom Rail *(Face View)*

9"

④

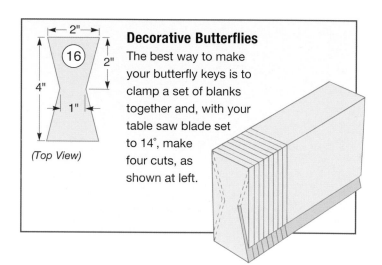

of the outside pieces.) Rip five splines (pieces 13) from oak lumber, and then test fit the top (pieces 14) together. The splines aid in registering these long pieces of lumber during glue-up and add considerably more glue area to the top joints. When everything fits, glue and clamp the top together.

The next step is to smooth the glue joints in the tabletop. You could sand them with a belt sander or take your top to a local cabinet shop and have them run it through their wide belt sander. (Make sure they can handle the 42" width before you haul the top to their shop, and scrape off any excess glue. You don't want to clog up their belts.)

After sanding, trim the ends with a clamped-on straight edge and a straight bit chucked in your router. Then gently break all the edges with sandpaper. Glue and fasten the beam to the leg sets with screws (pieces 15). Center the top on the supports and, after extending the pilot holes through the support pieces into the top, secure the top to the supports with the same screws (pieces 15). Don't glue the top to the supports. Restricting its movement widthwise could cause it to eventually split.

Making Decorative Butterflies

Aside from the exposed joinery and plugs, the only truly decorative elements in this project are the five butterflies (pieces 16) inlaid into the solid oak top. Before the advent of modern glues, these butterflies would have been cut deeper than the ¼" shown here, and they would also have served to hold the top together. Note the grain pattern of the butterflies

Use a template to rout the mortises for the decorative butterflies. A rub collar mounted in your router, coupled with a ¼" straight bit, will get you started right. Be sure to test your setup in scrap lumber before you move to the tabletop.

Decorative Butterflies

The best way to make your butterfly keys is to clamp a set of blanks together and, with your table saw blade set to 14°, make four cuts, as shown at left.

2"
16
2"
4"
1"
(Top View)

is at odds with that of the tabletop. These butterflies are easier to complete than you'd think. My usual approach is to create several at once on the table saw, cutting them to the shape shown in the Decorative Butterflies Drawing above. Then I clean up the edges with files, rasps and sandpaper.

Once the butterflies are made, make a melamine or hardboard template of the butterfly outlines to be used with a rub collar and a ¼" straight bit in your router. It's important to rout a couple of practice butterfly mortises in some scrap lumber to test the template before you move on to your actual tabletop. Locate the butterfly positions on the tabletop (see the Top View of the Table Elevation, next page), and mark each butterfly's outline

Woodworker's Glossary

Mission Style:
An American version of the Arts & Crafts movement in furniture design created by Gustav Stickley that features the simple and symmetrical designs found in Southwestern missions.

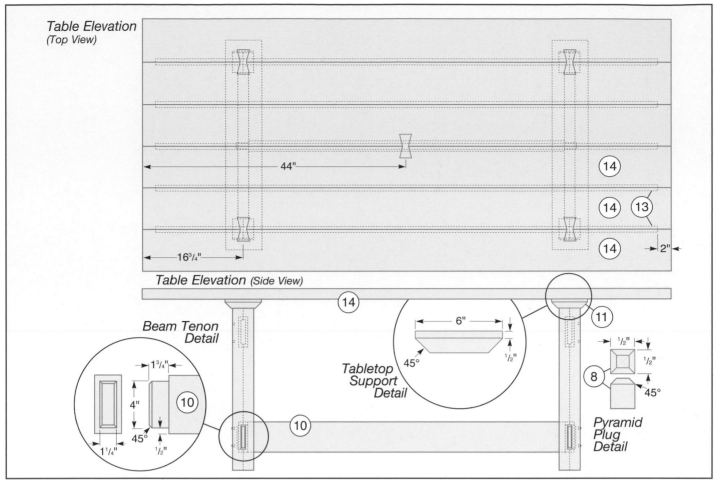

Table Elevation (Top View)

44"

16³/₄"

14

14   13

2"

Table Elevation (Side View)

14

11

Beam Tenon Detail

6"

45°   ¹/₂"

Tabletop Support Detail

10

1³/₄"

4"

45°   ¹/₂"

1¹/₄"

10

¹/₂"

8

45°

Pyramid Plug Detail

---

with a pencil. Use your template to safely remove most of the inlay mortise waste with the router. Make the mortise depth ¹/₁₆" shallower than the thickness of the butterflies. Clean up each outline with sharp chisels, then glue the butterflies in place. After the glue dries, simply sand them flush.

Finishing Up

After thoroughly sanding all surfaces of the entire project, apply the stain of your choice (I used Bartley's dark walnut gel stain), followed by several coats of clear satin varnish. Or try the aniline dye technique described on page 50. As far as durable topcoats go, polyurethane varnish or catalyzed lacquer are the best choices for a tabletop whose primary use is serving food and drink. Apply a couple of extra layers to the top. Remember, a thorough knockdown sanding between coats with 400-grit wet/dry paper is the key to building a great-looking, smooth finish.

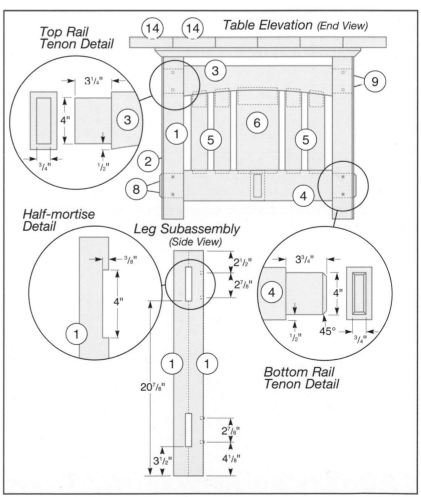

Top Rail Tenon Detail

14   14   **Table Elevation** (End View)

3¹/₄"

4"

3

¹/₂"

3

9

1

5   6   5

2

8

4

Half-mortise Detail

Leg Subassembly (Side View)

³/₈"

2¹/₂"

2⁷/₈"

Bottom Rail Tenon Detail

3³/₄"

4"

4

¹/₂"   45°   ³/₄"

4"

1

1   1

20⁷/₈"

2⁷/₈"

3¹/₂"   4¹/₈"

by Brad Becker

STICKLEY-INSPIRED LEATHER-TOP DESK

Without sacrificing any of the charm or structural integrity of our Stickley-inspired design, modern methods and materials bring this white oak desk within the reach of almost any woodworker's skills.

Sometimes, building a beautiful, practical piece of furniture can remind you of of all the reasons you started woodworking in the first place. Such was the case for me, when I originally built this Stickley-inspired oak desk. My sentiments rang true for other readers as well, making this project one of the more popular Arts & Crafts pieces we've published.

The desk is a series of simple frame and panel subassemblies joined with modern biscuits, hidden screws and glue. I designed the desk with basic joinery so that anyone with a little experience, a good router and a table saw will have no problem building it.

Starting with the Back

The back of the desk is made up of two rails, two stiles and three panels (pieces 1 through 4). Cut these and all the other parts to the dimensions shown in the Material List on page 77. With any project, measuring and test fitting each part as you make it is wise. The cabinet shop proverb—measure twice, cut once—holds true for all woodworking. Chuck a ¼" bit in your table-mounted router, set the fence, and mill ½" deep grooves

in both edges of both stiles, plus the appropriate edges of the top and bottom rails. (All dimensions are on the Elevations and Exploded Drawings on the next two pages.) The groove cuts should be made in several passes, raising the bit about ⅛" each time to avoid tearout and excessive wear on the router.

These stiles and rails have ¼" wide tenons centered on their ends. Form them using a fine crosscut blade in the table saw coupled with the saw's miter gauge and nibble away the waste in successive cuts.

The tenons at each end of the bottom rail are notched ¼" from the bottom. These cuts can be made on a bandsaw or with a sharp backsaw. With that done, you're ready to dry fit the frame together and check your joinery. When you're pleased with the fit, apply glue to the stile and rail joints (but not the plywood panels, as they need to float freely). Make sure the subassembly is flat and square as you clamp it up.

After the glue cures, use a router and straightedge to plow a vertical ¼" deep groove on the inside face of the stiles. These grooves are 1¼" wide and will be used to join the interior frames to the back.

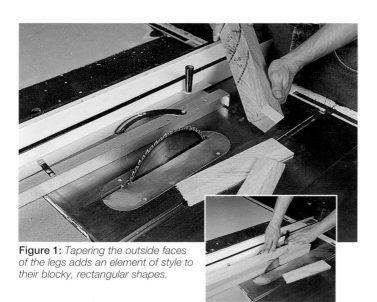

Figure 1: *Tapering the outside faces of the legs adds an element of style to their blocky, rectangular shapes.*

This project uses simple joinery and modern materials, like this white oak veneer plywood, to create an authentic Arts & Crafts appearance.

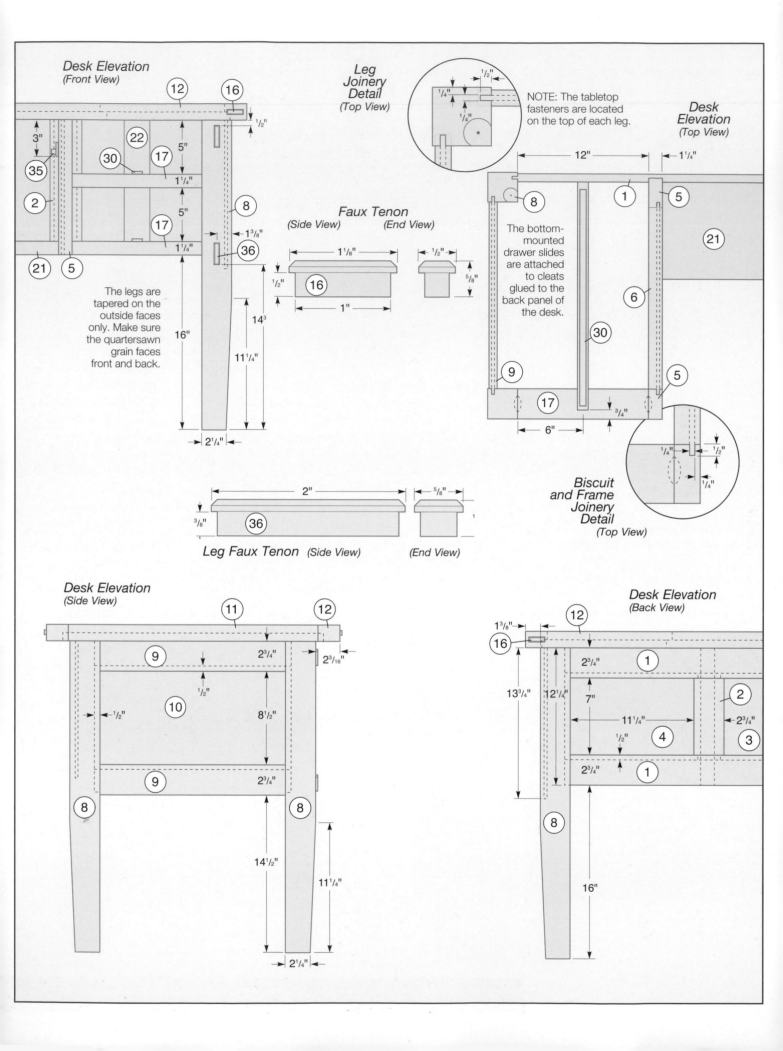

Desk Elevation *(Front View)*

⑫ ⑯
½"
3"
㉒
㉟ ㉚ ⑰
② 5"
1¼"
⑰ 5"
1¼"
⑧
21 ⑤ 1³⁄₈"
㊱

The legs are tapered on the outside faces only. Make sure the quartersawn grain faces front and back.

16"
14³
11¼"
2¼"

Leg Joinery Detail *(Top View)*
½"
¼"
¼"

NOTE: The tabletop fasteners are located on the top of each leg.

Desk Elevation *(Top View)*

12"
1¼"
⑧ ① ⑤
21
⑥

The bottom-mounted drawer slides are attached to cleats glued to the back panel of the desk.

⑨ ⑰ ⑤
㉚
¾"
6"

Faux Tenon *(Side View)* *(End View)*
1⅛" ½"
½" 5⁄₈"
⑯
1"

Biscuit and Frame Joinery Detail *(Top View)*
¼" ½"
¼"

Leg Faux Tenon *(Side View)*
2"
⅜"
㊱
5⁄₈"
1
(End View)

Desk Elevation *(Side View)*

⑪ ⑫
⑨ 2¾"
2³⁄₁₆"
½"
⑩
½" 8½"
⑨ 2¾"
⑧ ⑧
14½" 11¼"
2¼"

Desk Elevation *(Back View)*

1³⁄₈"
⑫
⑯
2¾" ①
13¾" 12¼" ②
7"
11¼" 2¾"
½" ④
③
2¾" ①
⑧
16"

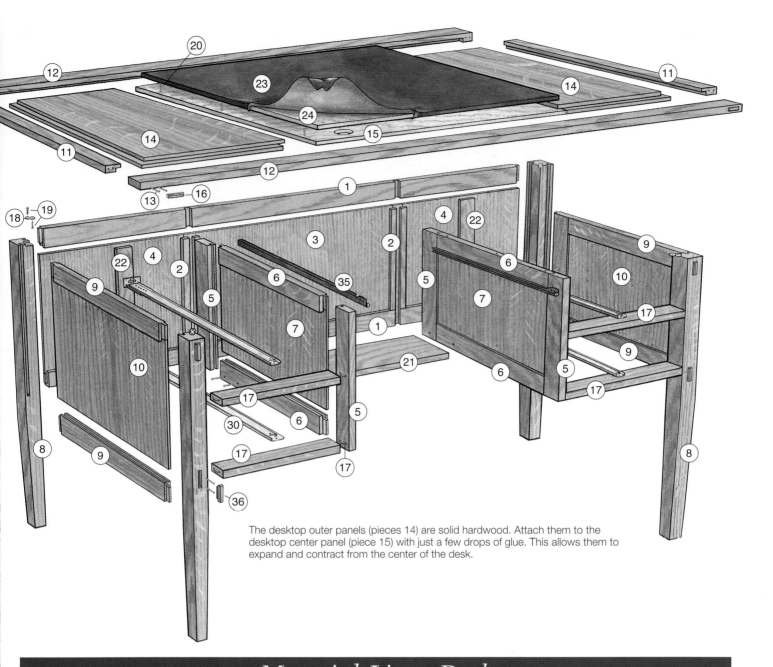

The desktop outer panels (pieces 14) are solid hardwood. Attach them to the desktop center panel (piece 15) with just a few drops of glue. This allows them to expand and contract from the center of the desk.

Material List - Desk

		T x W x L			T x W x L
1	Back Frame Rails (2)	¾" x 2¾" x 49¼"	**13**	Large Screws (12)	#10 x 3"
2	Back Frame Stiles (2)	¾" x 2¾" x 8"	**14**	Desktop Outer Panels (2)	1½" x 12" x 24"
3	Back Frame Center Panel (1)	¼" x 21" x 8"	**15**	Desktop Center Panel (1)	¾" x 24" x 30½"
4	Back Frame Side Panels (2)	¼" x 12⅜" x 8"	**16**	Top Faux Tenons (4)	½" x 1⅛" x ⅝"
5	Interior Frame Stiles (4)	1¼" x 2¾" x 12½"	**17**	Drawer Dividers (4)	1¼" x 2¾" x 12"
6	Interior Frame Rails (4)	1¼" x 2¾" x 17½"	**18**	Tabletop Fasteners (4)	Steel
7	Interior Frame Panels (2)	¼" x 17½" x 8"	**19**	Tabletop Fastener Screws (8)	Steel
8	Legs (4)	2¾" x 2¾" x 28½"	**20**	Tabletop Screws (12)	#8 x 2"
9	Exterior Frame Rails (4)	¾" x 2¾" x 18⅛"	**21**	Leg Space Shelf (1)	1¼" x 9" x 21¾"
10	Exterior Frame Panels (2)	¼" x 18⅛" x 9½"	**22**	Drawer Cleats (2)	¼" x 3" x 7"
11	Desktop Sides (2)	1½" x 2" x 23"	**23**	Leather (1)	25" x 31"
12	Desktop Front & Back (2)	1½" x 2" x 56½"	**24**	Leather Backer (1)	¾" x 29½" x 23"

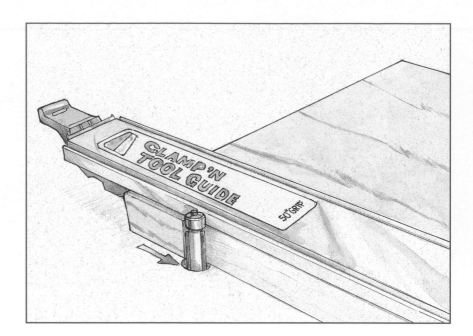

Building the Interior Frames

The interior frame subassemblies house the drawers and surround the desk owner's legs. Begin machining them at the router table by plowing a ½" deep groove in each stile (pieces 5) and rail (pieces 6) at the locations shown on the Elevation Drawings. Then move to the table saw to mill tenons on the ends of each rail. These are relatively simple cuts as no shoulder is required. Glue and clamp the two subassemblies together, again letting the panels (pieces 7) float freely in the frames.

Machining the Legs

Use either solid or glued-up stock to make blanks for the legs (pieces 8). Either way, have the quartersawn grain showing on the front and back faces of each. After cutting the legs to size, taper their two outside faces, as shown in Figure 1. Use a tapering jig and great care to slice the angles off the legs (see Desk Elevation Front and Side Views for taper dimensions).

Move back to the router table to mill the ½" deep stopped grooves in each leg to accommodate the sides and back. Stopping the grooves in the right spot is simply a matter of matching up pencil marks on the leg and the router table fence. Wrap up the legs by using a router equipped with a ¼" straight bit to create the small mortises for the legs' decorative faux tenons (see the sidebar on page 79).

Building the Exterior Frames

Cut and mill the four rails for the exterior frames (pieces 9), using the same techniques as you did for the interior frame rails; just notice that the lengths are different. Notch the tenons on the two bottom rails (see the Elevation Drawings) to create ¼" shoulders.

Test the tenons' fit in the legs, then cut the panels (pieces 10) to size. Glue and clamp the rails to the legs while slipping the panels in place without glue.

Woodworker's Glossary

Arts & Crafts:

A design style originated in the mid-1800s by William Morris to offset the elaborate detailing of the Victorian styles. Its purpose was to show a simple handcrafted artist's approach to furniture design. The popular Mission furniture is a variation of this style.

Figure 2:
Assemble the desktop frame and cut a rabbet in its bottom edge with a bearing-guided bit. Square the corners with a sharp chisel.

Figure 3: *Before final assembly, test fit the joints between pre-made subassemblies, such as the back sub-assembly and the legs.*

Building the Top

Begin making the top by creating a simple, butt-jointed frame with the front, back and sides (pieces 11 and 12). Start by cutting the parts to size, then chop the small, shallow mortises for the faux tenons and screws on the long frame pieces. Predrill each piece to properly accept the screws (pieces 13), then assemble the frame without glue. Turn the frame upside down and, using a bearing-guided bit, mill a rabbet around the inside edge (see Figure 2). Square the corners with a sharp chisel after you're done routing the rabbeted edge.

Select solid hardwood stock with beautiful grain and figure for the two outer desktop panels (pieces 14). Form rabbets on the edges of each panel. (Note that on three sides, this rabbet is milled on the top face while on the fourth side it is milled on the bottom face.) Cut the center panel (piece 15) from ¾" plywood and, after predrilling screw holes, attach it to the frame with screws only. Test fit the two outer panels to the center panel and frame. When all the parts fit together well, remove the screws and reassemble the top with glue and screws. Apply a couple drops of glue to the joint between the center panel and the inverted rabbet on the outer panels. This will ensure both panels will expand and contract out from the center of the desk. Finally, glue the top faux tenons (pieces 16) in place.

Assembling the Desk

Sand the subassemblies down through the grits to 220, and test fit all your joints (see Figure 3). Then lay out and mill the eight biscuit slots for the drawer dividers (pieces 17). Glue and clamp the two interior frames in their dadoes in the back, then glue the subassembly into the stopped grooves in the legs (don't glue the panels in place during this process). Before this glue begins to set, install the drawer dividers with glue and biscuits. Make sure everything is square as you tighten the clamps. Once the glue dries, use a Forstner bit to create round mortises in the tops of the legs (see Leg Joinery Detail, page 76), then screw the tabletop fasteners (pieces 18) to the legs (19).

To join the top and bottom subassemblies, start by placing the desktop on the lower desk assembly. From the underside, mark where the interior frames touch the desktop's center panel. Remove the top and drill pilot holes for screwing through the top into the interior fames, countersinking the holes from the upper face. Center the top on the desk body, then drive your screws (pieces 20) down through the center panel into your predrilled pilot holes in the interior frame's top rails (pieces 6). Finish securing the frame in place by driving screws (pieces 19) up through the tabletop fasteners into predrilled pilot holes in its bottom face, then attach the leg space shelf (piece 21) with screws (pieces 13). Take a moment to glue the drawer cleats (pieces 22) to the plywood panels inside the drawer cavity (refer to the Elevation Drawings on page 76).

Drill a finger hole in the top's center panel to help lift the removable leather covered panel, then cut the leather (piece 23) and its backer (piece 24) to shape and dry-fit them to the top of the desk. When the fit is right, glue the leather to the backer with 3M's 77 spray adhesive.

Faux Tenons

There are two different size faux tenons on this desk. The top frame set have larger tails and cover a set of screws. The leg set are machined with tiny tenoned tails to glue into ¼" mortises. They're easy to make and ensure a clean attractive look.

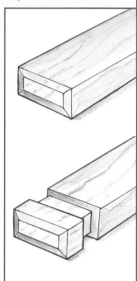

Machine the faux tenons in three steps: Chamfer the ends and edges of your stock on a sander, relieve the tenon tails on your table saw, and slice them free with a bandsaw and miter gauge.

Be sure to make *each size faux tenon in sets. Use a registration block clamped to your miter gauge to ensure uniformity.*

Finisher's Scorecard:

Choosing the best finish for your project doesn't have to be difficult if you know the basic characteristics of these eight common finishes. Incidentally, chatoyance refers to the ability of the finish to enhance depth and figure, popping the grain.

☐ **Wax** – thin; apply by rag; easy to repair; poor chatoyance; sheds water but takes water marks; poor solvent, scratch and heat resistance; fair stain resistance.

☐ **Oil and Danish oil** – thin; apply by rag; easy to repair; good chatoyance; good water, heat, and solvent resistance; poor scratch resistance; fair stain resistance.

☐ **Shellac** – apply thin or thick by rag, brush or spray; easy to repair; good chatoyance; poor heat and alkali resistance; good water and scratch resistance; fair solvent resistance; good stain and acid resistance.

☐ **Lacquer** – apply thin or thick by brush or spray; easy to repair; good chatoyance; poor to fair heat resistance; good water, scratch, stain and solvent resistance.

☐ **Oil varnish** – apply thin or thick by rag, brush or spray; not easy to repair; good chatoyance; good water, heat, solvent, scratch and stain resistance (if thick).

☐ **Polyurethane (oil base)** – apply thin or thick by rag, brush or spray; not easy to repair; good chatoyance; good water and stain resistance; excellent solvent, heat, and scratch resistance.

☐ **Waterborne acrylic-polyurethane** – apply thin or thick by pad, brush or spray; moderately easy to repair; poor chatoyance; good water, stain, solvent, heat, and scratch resistance.

☐ **Two part coatings (catalyzed lacquer, conversion varnish, automotive polyurethane)** – apply thick by spray; very difficult to repair; excellent water, stain, solvent, heat and scratch resistance; chatoyance varies.

Making the Drawers

Refer to the illustrations and photos on the facing page to mill the joinery on the sides, fronts and backs of the four deep drawers and the shallow pencil drawer (pieces 25 through 35). Assemble each box and sand smooth. Cut the drawer faces from attractive hardwood stock. Mount the drawer pulls with their bolt heads counterbored into the back of the drawer faces.

With the drawer boxes complete, install the drawer slides according to the manufacturer's instructions, then slide the drawers into their openings. Use double-sided tape to temporarily position and mark the locations of the drawer faces, then screw the faces in place. Install the remaining faux tenons. Remove the drawer faces and hardware for finishing.

Wrap up this project by applying a light walnut oil stain, topped by at least three coats of clear matte lacquer. Sand between these coats with 400-grit paper. Reinstall the drawer faces and drawer pulls after the finish dries.

QuickTip

Yet Another Way to Use Post-It Notes

Marking the spot to drill for hardware on a freshly finished piece can be trying. Next time you are confronted with this dilemma try placing a Post-It note in the approximate location of the intended hole and make your marks on it instead.

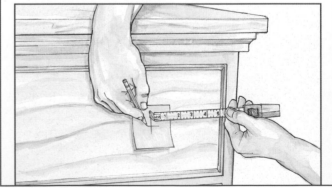

Corner Locking Drawer Joint

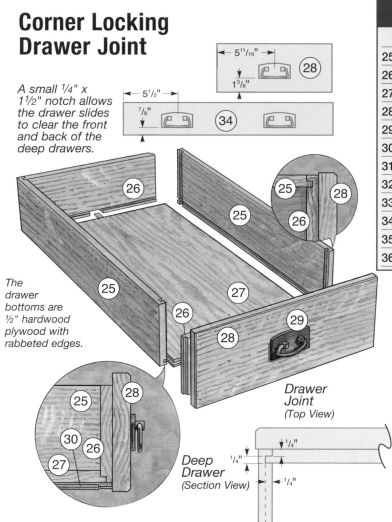

A small ¼" x 1½" notch allows the drawer slides to clear the front and back of the deep drawers.

The drawer bottoms are ½" hardwood plywood with rabbeted edges.

Drawer Joint (Top View)

Deep Drawer (Section View)

Material List - Drawers

		T x W x L
25	Deep Drawer Sides (8)	½" x 4¼" x 19¾"
26	Deep Drawer Fronts & Backs (8)	½" x 4¼" x 10¾"
27	Deep Drawer Bottoms (4)	½" x 10¾" x 19⅛"
28	Deep Drawer Faces (4)	¾" x 4⅞" x 11⅞"
29	Drawer Pulls (6)	Mission style
30	Deep Drawer Slides (4)	21"
31	Pencil Drawer Sides (2)	½" x 2½" x 18"
32	Pencil Drawer Front & Back (2)	½" x 2½" x 20¼"
33	Pencil Drawer Bottom (1)	½" x 20¼" x 17½"
34	Pencil Drawer Face (1)	¾" x 3¼" x 21⅝"
35	Pencil Drawer Slides (1 pair)	18"
36	Faux Tenons (4)	⅝" x 2" x ½"

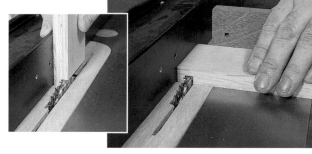

The drawer fronts and backs are rabbeted on their ends (left inset). Drawer sides (above right) have ¼" dadoes milled across their ends. Both steps can be done on the same setup, as shown above. The ¼" drawer bottom grooves are also formed on the same table saw setup.

QuickTip

Taper Jig Set-up

Setting a taper jig to the correct angle is a snap if you use your table saw miter gauge and a square. Slide the miter gauge into a table saw slot and set the gauge to the angle you want for the taper jig. Now slide the saw fence and taper jig over to the miter gauge and use the square to position the jig at the angle you need.

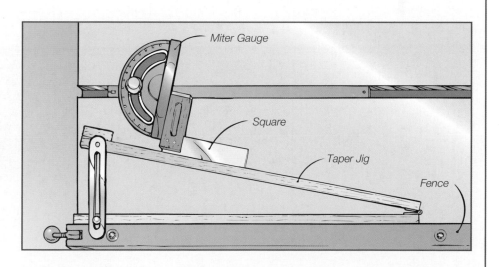

by Mike McGlynn

ROBINSON DINING TABLE

Graceful and lovely to look at, but demanding and rigorous to build, this multi-leaf Greene and Greene-inspired dining room table will test your skills. It's without a doubt one of contributing editor Mike McGlynn's finest pieces to date.

Over the years, I have built dozens of Greene and Greene pieces, but prior to this project I had never found the opportunity to try my hand at one of their pedestal dining tables. When an old friend decided his card table no longer cut it as a dinner table for four, opportunity knocked.

There are two main examples of Greene and Greene pedestal tables: the Robinson table and the Gamble table. Both have a pedestal that is heavy, with a timber frame and sculptural look; tops that are not quite round, but not square; and massive exposed wood slides. These features are remarkably beautiful, but are also, as I quickly discovered, very challenging to build. My inspiration for this project was the Robinson table. For the top and rim materials I selected even-colored and grained mahogany. The mahogany for the base should be as straight-grained as possible. And

you need to select the wood for the slides extra carefully. If possible, it should all come out of the same plank, so the density is the same throughout all the slide components. As always, purchase your stock and rough-cut it to size well ahead of when you will begin machining, so it has time to adjust to your shop.

Beginning with the Base

Although complex looking, the base is composed entirely of right angles and mortise and tenon joinery. The most difficult aspect of it is shaping the feet, slide rails and brackets.

The first step in constructing the base is to mill all the pieces to their correct dimensions, following the Material Lists on pages 85, 88 and 91. Keep an eye out for any unexpected twisting that may take place at this

The shape of the table's wooden slides is a study in positive and negative space... adding to the sculptural beauty of this dining room piece.

point—especially in the long rail members, as it may interfere with the smooth operation of the slides.

Laying out the joints and plug holes comes next, and it is the most confusing step in the construction of the base. Lay out one part (such as a foot or upright) completely, and then mark out all other like parts with a joint or plug centerline and, if need be, an orientation mark. This method works well for me, as I use a multi-router to cut the majority of these joints. Re-measure at least twice—it can save you a lot of heartache later on. (I incorrectly laid out and cut the lap joint in one of the rails—which I had already shaped—ruining six hours of work.)

Form your tenons and mortises now, while the stock is sticked up. The lap joint between the slide rails and uprights is a simple, yet extremely precise joint requiring patience and a light touch. These joints are easily visible and need to be tight. The best way to ensure precision is to dry-assemble each side

Faux Tenon Routing... Beautiful Trickery

To rout these mortises, use a solid-carbide ¼", downspiral bit with a ⁵⁄₁₆" (³⁄₈" o.d.) rub collar. Like the other plug holes, cut them ³⁄₁₆" deep and clean up the corners with a chisel.

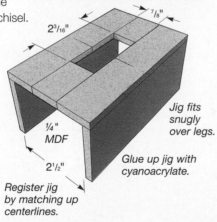

2³⁄₁₆"
⁷⁄₈"
¼" MDF
2½"
Jig fits snugly over legs.
Glue up jig with cyanoacrylate.
Register jig by matching up centerlines.

Make the faux tenon routing jig so it has a nice, tight slip fit over the leg. Precisely mark the centerline on the inside edges so you can line it up with the centerlines on the legs.

Feet

(Top View)   (Side View)

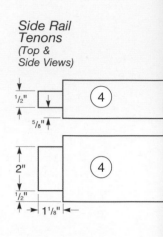

11"   6"   8"
½"   ½"
2"   ½"   ½"
¾"   1¼"
①   13"   ①

Side Rail Tenons
(Top & Side Views)

½"   ④
⁵⁄₈"

2"   ④
½"
1⅛"

1¼"
½"   ⑤
⁵⁄₈"

2"   ⑤
½"

End Rail Tenons
(Side & Top Views)

Uprights

(Side View)   (Front View)

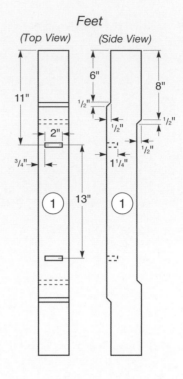

3½"
1¼"
6¾"
9¾"
②   ②
¾"
2"
4¾"
1¼"
2"   ½"
1¾"
½"
1"

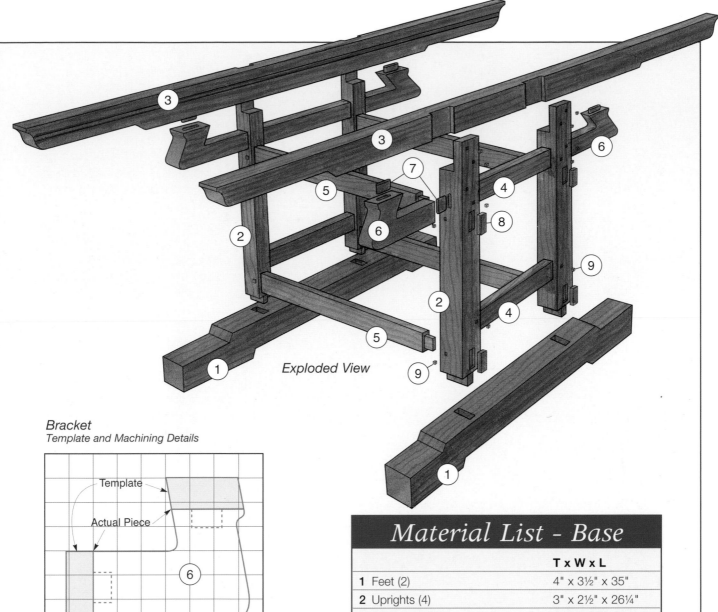

Exploded View

Bracket
Template and Machining Details

Template

Actual Piece

6

Each square = 1"

Attaching the brackets is the one operation where a little slop is acceptable. In order to slide the brackets onto their floating tenons when assembling the base, the tenons need to be just a bit undersized.

Material List - Base

	T x W x L
1 Feet (2)	4" x 3½" x 35"
2 Uprights (4)	3" x 2½" x 26¼"
3 Slide Rails (2)	3½" x 2¾" x 61"
4 Side Rails (4)	3" x 1¾" x 12¾"
5 End Rails (4)	3" x 1¾" x 27"
6 Brackets (4)	1¾" x 4¾" x 6½"
7 Floating Tenons (8)	½" x 1¼" x 1½"
8 Faux Tenons (8)	¾" x 2" x ⅜"
9 Ebony Plugs (60)	⅜" x ⅜" x 5⁄16"

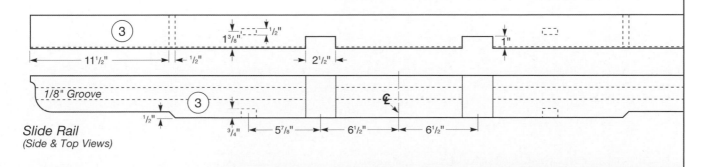

3

1³⁄₈"   ½"

1"

11½"   ½"   2½"

1/8" Groove

3

½"   ¾"   5⅞"   6½"   6½"

Slide Rail
(Side & Top Views)

Taking the Next Step in Template Routing

The feet and a couple of other parts of this table are too thick to be template-routed in a single pass. To solve this problem, the author devised a slick, two-step process. First, attach the template guide to the stock and, using a pattern routing bit (bearing at the shank of the bit), shape the foot, reaching slightly past the centerline of the stock (see drawing below). Next, switch to a flush-trimming bit (bearing at the end of the bit), flip the stock over, and use the already routed shape to guide your cut.

The first cut, using a template as a guide, allows you to shape more than half the thickness of the foot accurately.

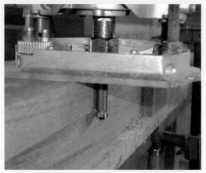

Flip the foot over and switch to a flush-trimming bit, and you can complete the shape of the foot using your previously routed profile to guide the router bit.

---

of the base and take measurements directly at the top of the uprights. First, cut the notches at the top of the uprights, then follow with precision chisel clean-up. Cut the slide notches last, as it is their edges that will show the most where they intersect the uprights. Work carefully on these joints, as it is difficult to get a perfect fit on two lap joints at the same time, which is what is necessary.

Before you begin profiling the base parts, the faux tenon mortises and plug holes need to be cut. Double-check your layout—now is not the time to drill a hole in the wrong place. Cut the plug holes with a mortise chisel in a drill press or mortising machine. Cut the false mortises using the shop-made jig shown on page 84.

Making the Templates

Profiling the feet, slide rails and brackets involves making complicated and precise templates that you will most likely never use again. However, this is the only way to get the multiple parts with the precision required.

Make your templates out of ¼" MDF and use the table saw for as many of the cuts as possible to ensure accuracy. It is critical that all curves be symmetrical, fair and true. Run your finger over the edges to test for bumps or divots. Make all the templates following the Elevation Drawings. Again, these templates ensure your success… take time to build them accurately.

The last step before you proceed to round over and detail the base pieces is to cut a groove in the slide rails. These pieces (as well as eight of the 12 slides)

have a ⅛"-deep groove to accept the back of the T-rails.

Before you start to round over and detail the base pieces, raise the grain of all pieces with water and give them an initial sanding to 120 grit. Pay especially close attention to the template-routed areas, as you must smooth out a bit of unevenness between the passes.

Rounded edges and softened corners are part of the distinctive Greene and Greene look, and it is important to take your time with these details. The first step is to do a complete roundover of all the appropriate edges with a ⅛"-radius roundover bit. Just make sure you don't round over any of the tenon or lap joint shoulders. Once they are done, go over all of them with sandpaper to blend them perfectly.

Before proceeding to assembly, raise the grain once again and carefully sand everything with 220-grit sandpaper. Now is the time to decide whether or not the table will be stained. It is easier to stain the pieces when they are apart than when assembled. I stained this table with one coat of water-based aniline dye stain.

The assembly of the base is very straightforward. Start by bringing together the uprights and the side and end rails with epoxy, checking often for squareness. Next, glue on the feet, and then glue and screw on the slide rails. The final step is to glue the brackets into place, using the floating tenons. Here you'll need just a bit of slop to be able to fit the brackets.

Building the Slides

The main thing to keep in mind as you build the slide assembly is that it needs to slide freely. Every milling operation in its construction is going to release tension in the wood, which will make the parts want to warp minutely. So you must mill and fit, mill and fit, and mill and fit. Patience is indeed a virtue, and you will be rewarded for it.

The bold use of Asian-influenced timber frame construction stands in stark contrast to sparsely placed delicate ebony plugs.

The slides consist of interlocking T-slotted slide members and T-rails, along with stop blocks and closing plates. The best place to start is with the slotted slide members.

Begin by milling the pieces to size, making sure you give them time to adjust before final dimensioning. As I learned the hard way, it is best to profile the ends of the slotted members before you mill out the T-slots. Double-face tape the template into position, and use a template bit in a router table.

Cutting the T-slots into the sliding members comes next. The first step is to waste away most of the center groove with passes on a table saw. Then use a T-slot cutter in a router table, making two passes to complete the shape. There is one vitally important thing to keep in mind during this process: you are making six members with the slot on one side and six with the slot on the other! Mark them with chalk so you don't end up with four slide sets that all work on the same table side.

Once you have shaped the sliding members, flip them over and rout the slight groove in eight of the twelve. The innermost members don't need it because they won't have a T-rail glued to them.

Milling the T-rail is next. Keep in mind that you want a smooth sliding fit. Don't make the T-rail much longer than the necessary length as it will tend to distort. With a piece this small in cross-section, it's difficult to get an accurate cut out of the profile.

After plowing a simple groove *into the slide member, expand the slot with a T-slotting router bit.*

For the best results, rough-cut the T-profile on the table saw to about 1/16" oversized, let it sit overnight to straighten any resulting twist, and cut to size.

You should now have 12 slotted members and T-rails that will fit together with a tapping but not a sliding fit. This is what you need for the next operation: profiling the ends of the T-rails.

When profiling the ends, keep in mind that six are for the left side, and six are for the right side. The T-rail ends are profiled by sliding them into the T-slots, marking the ends with a pencil, trimming them oversize, and reinserting into the T-slot with about 1/16" protruding. Then, clamp them into place and, using the already profiled member as a template (see photo, page 89), rout them to shape with a template bit. To prevent blowout, put a shim between the ends of the T and the slot. After profiling the ends, you can cut the rails to final length, and you're ready for fitting.

In a perfect world, all the members of the slides would be interchangeable. But, wood being what it is, this just

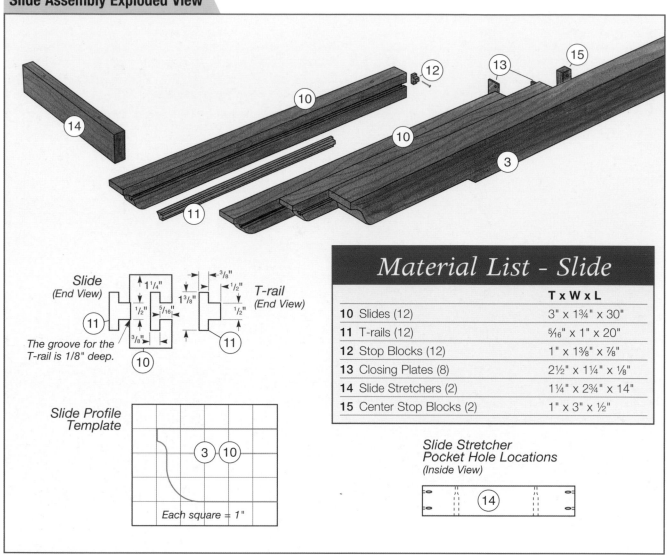

Slide
(End View)

T-rail
(End View)

The groove for the
T-rail is 1/8" deep.

**Slide Profile
Template**

Each square = 1"

Material List - Slide

		T x W x L
10	Slides (12)	3" x 1¾" x 30"
11	T-rails (12)	5⁄16" x 1" x 20"
12	Stop Blocks (12)	1" x 1⅜" x ⅞"
13	Closing Plates (8)	2½" x 1¼" x ⅛"
14	Slide Stretchers (2)	1¼" x 2¾" x 14"
15	Center Stop Blocks (2)	1" x 3" x ½"

**Slide Stretcher
Pocket Hole Locations**
(Inside View)

Brass closing plates are mounted as shown above. Also note the T-shaped stop blocks (pieces 12) secured with screws in the T-slots next to the closing block.

won't happen. Before starting to fit the slides, it is best to match them up into four sets and label them with tape and a marker so you can keep the sets together through final assembly.

The first step of fitting is to pair the T-rails with the ⅛"-deep grooves. This will take a little sanding and scraping of the T-rail sides. The next step is to raise the grain and thoroughly sand everything, including the inside of the T-slot. Sanding the inner faces of the T-slot takes care of any minute vertical warp; sanding the underside faces of the T-rail takes care of any horizontal warp. When testing, it is important to

press-fit the T-rail into its proper groove, as this will show you the true horizontal alignment and spacing. Be patient at this stage. The fit you want is a nice, smooth slide without a hint of binding.

Once you're pleased with the fit of the slides, joint 1⁄16" off the tops of each of the two slide members closest to the slide rails. This clearance allows the top to slide much freer, as the leaves rest entirely on the slide rails and innermost members, which are screwed to the top. To prepare for attaching the top, drill three stepped holes in each of the inner slides for the attachment screws. All the slide pieces can now be rounded over, with either a ⅛" roundover bit or by hand with sandpaper. Before finishing, you should raise the grain again and sand everything with 220-grit paper.

The next pieces to make for the slides are the stop blocks and closing plates. The stop blocks are nothing more than ⅞"-long pieces of T-rail made to fit without slop. As can be seen from the Exploded Drawing on the facing page, they are secured in the T-grooves with countersunk screws. The closing plates are made of brass and attached with countersunk screws.

The final step to making the slides is to glue the T-rails into their appropriate grooves. Before doing this, it's a good idea to go over the fit of the slides one last time; better to catch problems now than when you're finished. Don't forget to glue T-rails to the outer slide rails.

After the glue has dried, slip all the slide members into their proper places on the base, install the stop blocks and closing plates and make sure the slides work well. The slide stretchers join the two banks of slides. They are attached (use pocket-hole joints) to the two innermost slides on each end of the table. Cut and fit them now, and prepare their surfaces as you did the slides. If you plan to stain the table, you can then disassemble all pieces, stain them, and set them aside.

Making the Top

I prefer to have the rough-cut top wood sitting in my shop for at least a month before I mill it to final dimensions for glue-up. The top has very little secondary structure—such as an apron—and it needs to end up as flat as possible.

Your first step is to joint and plane the boards to 1¹⁄₁₆". After thicknessing, lay out your boards on a benchtop and arrange them to achieve both the best grain pattern and even board widths. Then joint, rip, and joint your boards to width.

With your boards cut and jointed to size, lay out the two top halves and the leaves. Mark the leaves and tops for biscuit joints and cut. After cutting the biscuit joints, glue up the top and leaves with epoxy, taking care to equalize the clamping pressure with clamps on both faces. This will help prevent warped panels. Once the glue has dried, sand the tops and leaves to a uniform 1" thickness with a wide belt sander.

As you did with the base, you will now need to spend a bunch of time making very precise templates for the top and the outer and inner rim edges. While they will help you achieve a perfect job, it is likely you will only use them once. The keys to the top templates are symmetry, smoothness, and perfectly interlocking joints. The drawing on the next page will help, but you will still need to carefully smooth the template and check its symmetry by tracing one side onto onion skin and flipping it over to see if it matches the other side. Make minute corrections and check again. It is best to make all three templates at the same time.

All aspects of these templates are very important, but the gapless fit between the top template and the inner rim edge template is the most critical aspect to a good job. To put this into perspective, I spent the better part of

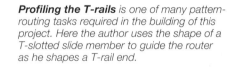

Profiling the T-rails *is one of many pattern-routing tasks required in the building of this project. Here the author uses the shape of a T-slotted slide member to guide the router as he shapes a T-rail end.*

three days making and fitting these templates.

Once you have your templates made, you can rough-cut your tops to shape, double-face tape and clamp your template into place, and rout the top to shape.

It is now time to move on to the rim. Mill the rim stock to 1¹⁄₁₆", taking care to keep the stock as flat as possible. The drawings indicate the sizes and angles of the pieces that make up the rim blanks. When cutting the pieces for the rim blank, take extra care to get the end angles right on, as even a half-degree mistake can make a huge difference. Once satisfied with the fit, you can biscuit joint the ends

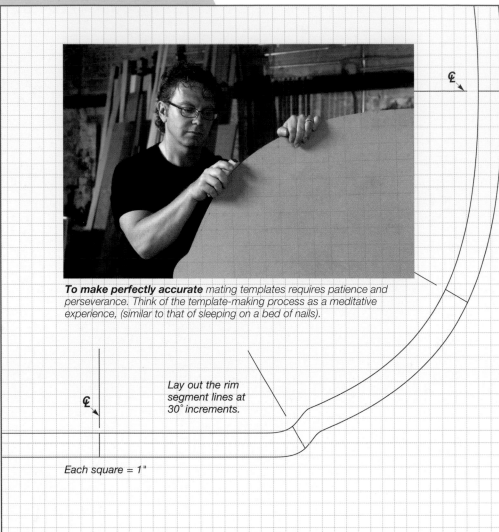

To make perfectly accurate *mating templates requires patience and perseverance. Think of the template-making process as a meditative experience, (similar to that of sleeping on a bed of nails).*

Lay out the rim segment lines at 30° increments.

Each square = 1"

Building the templates used to shape the table's top elements is perhaps the most significant challenge of this project. Use the drawings at left as a starting point for the three templates you'll need: one for the top, one for the inside edge of the rim and one for the rim's outside edge. The top and the inside rim edge template should mate perfectly. This is done by aligning the edges of the templates, marking the areas where they touch (by doing so, they actually hold the templates apart) and then carefully sanding those spots. These areas where the templates touch will get larger and larger as the templates become more accurate. This process took the author the better part of three days to complete.

Clamping the rim *to the tabletop is a significant task. Affixed with epoxy and located horizontally with the aid of multiple small splines, this is the most visible joint on the entire table project.*

and glue them up with epoxy. As is obvious from the drawing, it's critical that you place the biscuits where they won't be exposed when the outside is routed to shape. When the glue has dried, clean up both faces and sand to 120 grit.

Using the two rim templates, trace the inside and outside lines on the blank rims, and then band-saw to within 1⁄16" of the inside line. Leave the outside rough for now. After carefully taping and clamping the inside template down, rout the inside rim edge with a template bit. When both inside edges have been cut, the outside edge can be cut 1⁄16" oversize on the band saw.

I spent quite a bit of time thinking about how to attach and align the rim with the top. I finally decided to use a spline system in conjunction with glue relief grooves to get the strength I wanted without producing any glue squeeze-out at the top surface/rim joint.

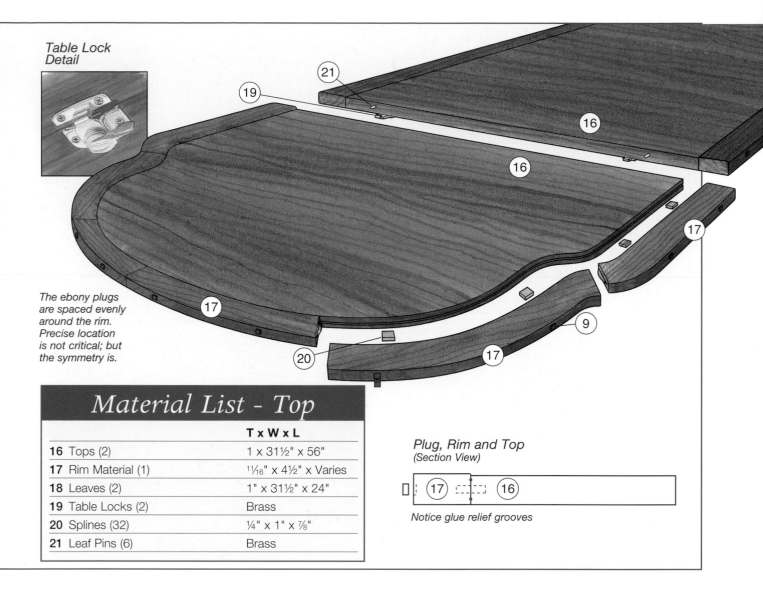

Table Lock Detail

The ebony plugs are spaced evenly around the rim. Precise location is not critical; but the symmetry is.

Material List - Top		
	T x W x L	
16 Tops (2)	1 x 31½" x 56"	
17 Rim Material (1)	¹¹⁄₁₆" x 4½" x Varies	
18 Leaves (2)	1" x 31½" x 24"	
19 Table Locks (2)	Brass	
20 Splines (32)	¼" x 1" x ⅞"	
21 Leaf Pins (6)	Brass	

Plug, Rim and Top
(Section View)

⊓   (17) ⸬⸬⸬   (16)

Notice glue relief grooves

With the help of a scrap piece of rim material to check alignment, rout a groove in the tops with a ¼" three-wing cutter. Then, using the same bit in a router table, rout the rims with a corresponding groove. When used with a spline, the rim should be flush with the bottom and stand ¹⁄₁₆" proud of the top. The groove should stop just short of the center joint.

It is easiest to cut the glue relief grooves now, before you start fitting the rim to the top. Do this—very carefully—with a utility knife and a fresh blade.

To ease the process of fitting the rim, which involves holding the rim against the top a number of times, glue some short pieces of spline material in place so that when you push the rim in place you don't have to worry about holding it up.

The fit between the rim and top must be perfect. My motto for this type of fitting is "slow and cautious." At this point in the process, if you decided to leave your table natural,

The joint between the tabletop and the border *must be without visible gaps. Accurate template work is the only way to achieve such a long, continuous joint.*

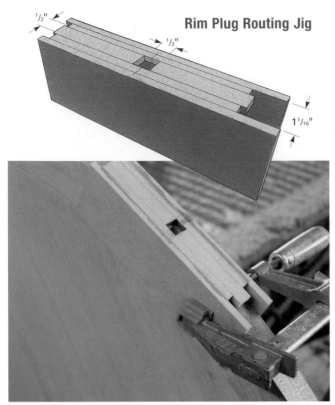

Rim Plug Routing Jig

½"

½"

1 1⁄16"

Routing the mortises into the rim for all the ebony plugs is achieved using a small clamped-on jig. The router is outfitted with a ¼" bit and a ⅜ o.d. rub collar.

QuickTip

Tailpipe Drill Press Extension

If you wish you could extend the spine of your benchtop drill press to expand its capacity, maybe you can. Try using a length of automotive tailpipe as a replacement for the column.

Exhaust pipe

the rims can now be glued on, using the splines, epoxy, and a lot of clamps. If your table is to be stained, it is far better to complete building the rims and stain them, along with the top, before the rim is glued into place. Without the rim glued in place, you will need to temporarily affix it so you can rout the outer edges and cut the plug mortises. The best way to do this is to accurately locate the plug mortises and use those holes to sink #6 screws. The screws need to be sunk at least 5⁄16" below the surface. Only after routing the rims to size should you make the rims for the leaves.

I made the rim plug mortises with a combination of router template, guide-down spiral bit jig and chisel. My jig for the plug mortises (shown in the photo at left) indexes off the centerline for each plug, so you will need to carefully lay out the centerlines. The last steps before staining are to round over the rim edges with a ⅛" roundover bit, flush up the ends of the rims with the top and leaf edges, raise the grain, and give it a pass with 220-grit sandpaper.

When the staining is complete, the rim can be glued into place. The temporary screws can be used to great effect for clamping purposes.

Choosing Finishing Materials

There are two different finishes used on this table: catalyzed lacquer on the majority of the table, and Sam Maloof's oil on the slides. I used three coats of oil, which makes for a slippery finish that can be renewed as needed. The base, top, and leaves are all sprayed with four coats of catalyzed lacquer with careful sanding and buffing between coats. If you don't own spray equipment, you could use a wipe-on gel varnish instead to achieve a similar sheen and durability to lacquer.

After the oil on the slides cures for several days, buff out all the surfaces with a fine Scotchbrite® pad and give all the parts several coats of paste wax.

Conducting the Final Assembly

The final assembly of the table involves four steps: First, install the leaf pins; second, install the table latches; third, install the slides and fourth, screw down the top.

I preferred to install two leaf pins per edge, so that if some seasonal vertical movement occurs the leaves still fit together. I used brass pins and sockets as they look nicer and last longer. Install them using a centerline indexing drill jig.

Lay the tops and leaves upside-down on a padded bench and attach the table latches. It is important that the latches work in all possible leaf configurations and do not interfere with the slides or the base. The slide members can now be slid into place and their stop blocks and closing plates installed.

To attach the top to the slides, lay the top upside-down on a padded surface and latch it together. With the help of

Details, such as exposed end grain on the faux tenons and the mirror-image symmetry of the overall design, join together as a harmonious ode to the Greene brothers' legacy.

a couple of friends, set the base upside-down onto the top. After much measuring, mark the slide screw holes by dropping a screw in each of them and tapping with a hammer. Before removing the base to drill the screw holes, carefully mark the base position with tabs of masking tape. After drilling the screw holes, screw the top to the slides with 3", #8 flathead screws onto which you've threaded a #6 washer. This combination of washer, screw and oversize hole allows the screws to rock slightly with seasonal changes.

Plugs Before Guinness

Now, before you can go and have that celebratory Guinness, there is one last amazingly time-consuming step that needs to be done—making and installing the 72 ebony plugs. I use a similar method for installing plugs in many of my furniture designs. The basics are to mill a ⅜" by ⅜" stick, sand and buff the end to a dome on a low-speed grinder, cut it off, and repeat. To install the plugs, slightly bevel the inside end, put a drop of glue in the hole, and tap it gently into place with a hammer.

After all these plugs are properly installed and you're finally through, the celebration might actually require two Guinnesses!

by Mike McGlynn

GREENE & GREENE INSPIRED DESK

If you've ever dreamed of a signature piece in your home office or den, this handsome mahogany desk could well be it. It has the plug, trim, and drawer pull details that make it pleasing to touch and view. And once you're seated behind it, you'll know you've got a serious desk. So round up some prime mahogany and get started!

With a little investigation, I think you'll agree that this Greene and Greene inspired desk is one of those rare woodworking projects: It manages to be an impressive piece on many levels, yet it's very straightforward to build.

For many years now, I have been tremendously fond of the Greene brothers' style. I once toured the Gamble house, their California masterpiece, and viewed even more examples of their furniture in both the Los Angeles County museum and the Huntington Museum. Seeing the Greenes', (more accurately their builders, the Hall brothers') work up close inspired me and taught me some new tricks. I put this newfound knowledge into the design of this desk.

Stocking Up

With the exception of the many decorative details, this desk's construction is true bread-and-butter woodworking: mortise and tenon joinery, frame and panel construction, pocket hole joints, breadboard ends.

One nice aspect of Greene and Greene furniture is its mahogany construction. In addition to looking nice, it makes wood selection easier, due to

the availability of clear, large-dimension boards. To construct this desk, you'll need some 10/4 stock for the legs and 5/4 for all the other solid parts. In addition, you will need a sheet of ¾" mahogany plywood. You'll also need ½" Baltic birch plywood for the drawer boxes and a small amount of ebony for the accent plugs and top splines.

Making the Drawer Pedestals

The first step to building the drawer pedestals is to mill all the solid-wood parts (pieces 1 through 7) to the dimensions in the Material List, page 98.

After you have your parts dimensioned, but before you taper the feet and profile the bottom rails, cut all the joints and panel grooves. There are essentially two types of joints in these drawer pedestals: mortise and tenon and pocket screw. I use pocket screws in certain areas because I feel they are strong, efficient options.

I cut my mortises and tenons on a Multi-Router, but as all of the mortises and tenons are at right angles, they can be readily cut with a variety of methods. Before you start to cut, make sure you match up your legs into groups of four and mark which faces go together; there

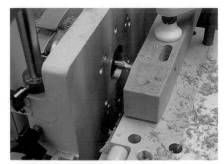

Mike chops his mortises with a Multi-router. This project's mortises are all conventional straight mortises that can be formed just as easily in the traditional manner.

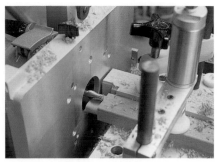

Tenons on the panel dividers are shorter than those on the bottom rails. Test-fit the tenons in their mortises as you make them.

Install a mortising attachment on your drill press to create the square mortise for the legs' decorative ebony plugs.

is nothing worse than completing your mortises and realizing you chopped a set on the outside face of one of your perfectly grain-matched legs.

After matching up your legs completely, lay out the mortises on one front (panel end) leg. (See the Technical Drawings for more construction details.) By drawing centerlines through these mortises and transferring just the centerlines to the other legs you will have your mortise index line without having to completely draw out all the mortises.

Once you've cut the leg mortises, lay out and chop the mortises in the top and bottom side rails. These are quite shallow mortises and are used more for positioning than for strength.

When you have finished all the mortises, lay out the tenons and cut them with your preferred method. To make this project simpler, something I am always in favor of, all the mortises and tenons are the same size (with the exception of the side panel stiles).

Cutting the Panel Grooves

Once your mortises and tenons are cut, get ready to cut the panel retaining grooves in all the appropriate legs, rails and stiles.

You could use solid-wood panels in this desk, but I opted to use ¼" plywood for its lightness and for its book-matched figure. If possible, go to a yard where they will allow you to look through the plywood. Carefully examine

the veneer seams and choose sheets from which you'll be able to cut balanced-looking panels. When you get the plywood to your shop, you'll notice the ¼" plywood is more like ⁷⁄₃₂" or ³⁄₁₆" thick. It's for this reason you don't want to plow the panel grooves before you have your plywood in hand. I cut my grooves on a router table with a fence. You might have to take two passes with a smaller bit to make a properly sized groove, which should be a nice slip fit—not too tight or too loose. (NOTE: set aside the top and bottom rails on the drawer side: these don't need grooves.) Start by grooving the central panel stile, then the top and bottom rails, and finally the legs. This way, you can slip the piece into its mortise and match up the groove in the receiving piece perfectly. Now is the time to cut your plywood panels (pieces 8 and 9) to size, testing their fit as you go.

Before proceeding to the detailing, cut the square mortises for the ebony plugs. As before, do a complete layout on one leg and then use centerlines on all the others. Cut these mortises ³⁄₁₆" deep with a square mortising chisel set-up on your drill press.

Greene and Greene Details

Special design details create this desk's Greene and Greene style. Creating them requires several steps: tapering the bottoms of the legs, cutting the cloud lifts in the rails, and rounding over all the appropriate edges. Taper the

legs on a simple table saw tapering jig and clean them up with a block plane and sandpaper. The cloud lifts are best made by template-shaping on a router table. I usually make a template from ¼" material, draw the pattern on the desk component, cut it out to within ¹⁄₁₆", then tape the template to the part and shape it with a ½" bearing-guided pattern bit in a router table. After routing, square up the inside corners with a sharp chisel.

You also need to ease the outside corner of the cloud lift to a slight curve. The last step before the roundovers is to cut pocket holes in the top rails and the drawer dividers.

To do your roundovers, use a trim router if you have one with a ⅛" roundover bit. You will be rounding over the appropriate edges of the legs, the bottom rails, the top rails, the panel stile and the drawer dividers. Be very careful not to round over the ends of any part other than the leg bottoms.

To prepare for staining, sand all pieces, including the panels, to 120 grit. Raise the grain with a damp cloth and then sand to 220. I prefer to stain the pieces apart because it results in a more even stain job and less time in purgatory for swearing. The stain I use for Greene and Greene mahogany pieces is a water-based aniline dye. It is easily applied, colorfast and doesn't muddy the surface. It's best to experiment and get your technique down before staining the actual parts.

While visiting the Huntington Museum, Mike was powerfully impressed with the level of detail the Greenes included in their furniture pieces. These drawer handles were inspired by observing furniture at the museum. To make the handles, first cut the blanks to size and then create a template to form the handle's subtle curve. Find the template's shape on the Technical Drawings. After you have shaped the curve and relieved the finger-grip cove, step to the table saw and trim the handle's base to match the depth of the cove cut. This creates a base that flows gently into the front aspect of the handle.

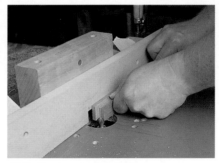

The gentle curve of the drawer pulls only becomes visible as you approach the desk, adding a subtle touch of elegance to a beautiful piece.

Trim the remaining stock away on your table saw to form the drawer pull's final footprint.

Template routing a subtle curve is the first step in making the desk's drawer handles. Use double-sided tape to attach the template—and keep your fingers clear.

With the base to the fence, use a cove bit to relieve a finger grip on the handle. Then step to the table saw to trim the base's footprint.

Substance and style create the Greene and Greene look. The final step in making the handle is boring mortises for the ebony plug accents.

After the stained pieces are dry, there is one final step before assembly: buff all the surfaces with a fine Scotchbrite® pad. It smoothes out any raised grain and will provide you with a much better finish. Be sure to wear rubber gloves when handling the stained parts so that skin moisture doesn't lift or mark the water-soluble dye.

Assembling the Pedestals

The first stage of assembly is to assemble the side subassemblies. In the interest of longevity, I use West System Epoxy for my furniture as it is bombproof and has a long set-up time. Before starting your assembly, gather everything you'll need and be sure the tenon ends and panel edges are slightly eased to aid assembly. Attach the bottom rail to the legs, then the panel stile to the bottom rail, slip the panels into place—in their correct orientation. Clamp everything together and drive home the top rail pocket screws. Although it probably isn't necessary, I also add a screw through the top rail into the end of the panel stile tenon.

Once you have the four side subassemblies done, join them to each other with the top and bottom rails and allow the epoxy to cure. The installation of the drawer dividers is accomplished with the use of two spacer blocks that match the size of the drawer opening. Being that the pocket holes are on the bottom side of the dividers, turn the units upside down and put the top divider in first, resting the spacers on the underside of the top rail. Install the remaining dividers in turn.

The last step in the pedestal assembly is installing the drawer slide supports (pieces 10). They're made of ¾" ply and are screwed in place onto spacers (pieces 11). To ease drawer slide installation, glue small support tabs (pieces 12) to the bottom edge of the slide supports, prior to installing these pieces. When you install the slide supports, use a large combination square to make sure the top face of this tab is in-line and square to the top edge of the drawer dividers.

Making the Drawers

Now you need to build the drawers, drawer faces and drawer pulls (pieces 13 through 24). Since I am more interested in utility than purism, I build my drawers out of ½" Baltic birch plywood with rabbeted corners, with a ¼" mahogany veneered MDF core bottom, nailed directly to the bottom of the drawer box. Purists will cringe at this bottom attachment method, but I challenge any "bottom in a groove" to a strength and longevity test. If you plan to use hanging files in the file drawers, add ⅛" x 1" aluminum rails (see the Technical Drawings).

The drawer faces are made of carefully selected 1"-thick solid wood. For appearance's sake, it is best to get all the drawer fronts—including the pencil drawer—out of one 11"-plus wide board of slightly ribbon striped material. With pieces as wide as the file drawer fronts, be sure to allow them to adjust to equilibrium before their final milling. The pencil drawer front with its cloud lift is machined in the same manner as the bottom rails.

Making the Drawer Pulls

The drawer pulls on this desk were a direct inspiration from some Greene and Greene pieces I viewed at the Huntington Museum. Only up close do you notice the subtle curves of these pulls, but it really adds a delightful touch. See the sidebar on page 97 for instructions on how to build these pulls. One important thing to note is that you should put in plenty of time sanding these to make sure they are smooth, fair and nicely tactile. Stain the pulls and fronts in the same manner as the cabinet.

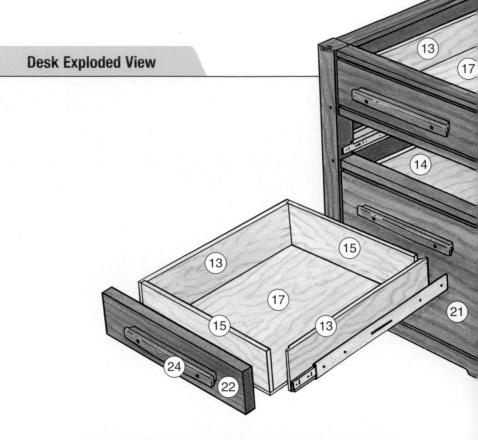

Desk Exploded View

Material List - Case

		T x W x L
1 Legs (8)		2" x 2" x 28"
2 Drawer Dividers (4)		1" x 1⅞" x 14⁵⁄₁₆"
3 Short Bottom Rails (4)		1" x 2" x 16⁵⁄₁₆"
4 Long Bottom Rails (4)		1" x 2" x 31"
5 Short Top Rails (4)		½" x 1⅞" x 14⁵⁄₁₆"
6 Long Top Rails (4)		½" x 1⅞" x 29"
7 Panel Stiles (4)		¾" x 1½" x 23⅞"
8 Pedestal Side Panels (8)		¼" x 14⅛" x 23⅝"
9 Pedestal End Panels (2)		¼" x 14¾" x 23⅝"
10 Drawer Slide Supports (12)		¾" x 3" x 29"
11 Drawer Slide Spacers (8)		¾" x ½" x 20"
12 Drawer Support Tabs (12)		¾" x 1½" x 5"
13 Small Drawer Sides (8)		½" x 4⅝" x 22"
14 Large Drawer Sides (4)		½" x 9⅛" x 22"
15 Small Drawer Fronts & Backs (8)		½" x 4⅝" x 12⁹⁄₁₆"
16 Large Drawer Fronts & Backs (4)		½" x 4⅝" x 12⁹⁄₁₆"
17 Drawer Bottoms (6)		¼" x 13¹⁵⁄₁₆" x 22"
18 Pencil Drawer Sides (2)		½" x 1⅜" x 22"
19 Pencil Drawer Front & Back (2)		½" x 1⅜" x 28¼"
20 Pencil Drawer Bottom (1)		¼" x 22" x 29"

Material List - Drawers & Details

		T x W x L			T x W x L
21	Large Drawer Faces (2)	1" x 10⅜" x 14³⁄₁₆"	29	Top (1)	¹⁵⁄₁₆" x 35¾" x 64"
22	Small Drawer Faces (4)	1" x 5¼" x 14³⁄₁₆"	30	Breadboard Endcaps (2)	1" x 3½" x 36"
23	Pencil Drawer Face (1)	1" x 2¼" x 31¼"	31	Leg and Drawer Ebony Plugs (22)	⅜" x ⅜" x ⁹⁄₃₂"
24	Drawer Pulls (6)	1" x 1" x 10"	32	Small Ebony Plugs (18)	¼" x ¼" x ⁹⁄₃₂"
25	Modesty Panel (1)	¾" x 23¼" x 30⅞"	33	Large End Cap Ebony Plugs (6)	¾" x ⅜" x ⁹⁄₃₂"
26	Modesty Panel Lower Rail (1)	1¼" x 2" x 31⅜"	34	Long End Cap Ebony Plugs (4)	⁹⁄₃₂" x ⅜" x 3¾"
27	Modesty Panel Upper Rail (1)	½" x 1⅞" x 31⅜"	35	Ebony Splines (4)	⅜" x ¹¹⁄₁₆" x 7"
28	Modesty Panel End Stiles (2)	½" x 1¾" x 23¼"	36	Pencil Drawer Trim (1)	½" x 1⅞" x 31⅜"

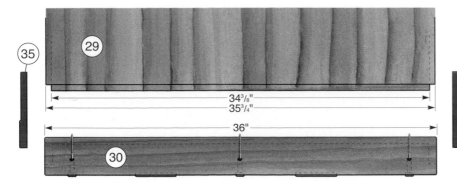

The end caps *are attached with screws but no adhesive. Machine the groove for the top's tongue 1/16" deeper than the tongue itself. The mortises for the ebony spines must allow the splines to float, to accommodate seasonal wood movement.*

For Modesty's Sake...

The next subassembly to tackle is the modesty panel. This is quite simple, as it consists of only five parts. I used ¾" plywood for the center panel (piece 25), and while this may seem like an odd choice, I knew ¼" was too thin and ½" is hard to find.

As with the other panels, cut a piece that has a nicely center-balanced veneer pattern. Once you have the panel in hand, mill up your four surround pieces (pieces 26 through 28) with the appropriately sized grooves in them to receive the panel. Using the same method employed in the bottom rails, form the cloud lift in the bottom rail. After drilling the attachment holes in the side and top rails, round over the edges and stain the parts. Then, using glue, nails and screws, assemble the panel.

Topping It Off

Construction of the top is the last major subassembly. Quite frankly, if the other subassemblies were fairly easy, the top (piece 29) looks deceptively simple, but is in fact quite difficult, especially the floating ebony splines. Because the top is the most visible part of the desk, carefully select the wood with the most pleasing grain match possible. Also, make sure the top boards are milled perfectly flat.

Again, I use epoxy to glue up the top. One quick point: an epoxy glue line will not react with the aniline dye as regular glue will. Once the top is glued up, square it up and cut it to size.

Cutting the tongues on the end of the top and their matching spline grooves is the first real opportunity you have to completely screw up the top—one false move and you have a

lot of nice mahogany for some smaller project. I cut the tongue with a three-wing slot cutter in a hand-held router. Make two to three passes on each side to form the tongue; this will result in a much smoother job. (Clamp a piece of waste stock on each side to prevent blowout.) Now, lay out the spline-mortise (for the ebony spline). Using the same router and bit (reset to the correct depth), rout it and clean up the ends of these slots with a chisel.

The end caps (pieces 30) for the top are also fairly tricky. After milling your parts, plow a groove to match the tongue so the cap and the top are flush on the bottom, but notice that the cap is 1/16" proud of the top (see the Technical Drawings). It's important to take this slowly and get a nice slip fit—not too tight, not too loose. Form the groove 1/16" deeper than the tongue to allow for a year-round tight fit. After cutting the groove, mark out the spline slots and chop them out with a chisel. You'll notice this slot is 5/16" deeper than the mortise in the top's edge. This allows the end cap to be 1/8" proud of the top and creates 3/16" of spline-float room, accommodating seasonal expansion and contraction.

The rectangular plug mortises (see the Technical Drawings) in the cap are cut with a combination of router table and chisels. Under the three 3/8" x ¾" mortises there are countersunk holes for attachment screws. These holes and their oversized pilot holes should be drilled on a drill press, as they must be very accurate.

At this point, you can do the round over/sand/stain routine for the top and cap. Be very careful of the inboard top cap edge, as it needs only a slight roundover—best done by hand. Once you have the parts stained, you can slip the caps in place and, through the attachment holes, mark the tongue, drill it and screw the caps in place.

Mike used a waterbased aniline dye *for this project. He prefers to stain the pieces apart because it results in a more even stain job and less time in purgatory for swearing.*

Begin assembling the pedestal's side subassemblies *as shown above. Note the top rails' orientation and pocket screw joints.*

Durable Finish and Ebony Plugs

When you have all your subassemblies stained and ready, it's time for finishing. I spray three to four coats of medium rubbed-effect catalyzed lacquer, but you can achieve just as good a finish by hand with a semigloss varnish and patience.

The final construction step, before assembly, is to make all the ebony plugs and splines (pieces 31 through 35). For the ¼" x ¼" plugs and the ⅜" x ⅜" plugs, I generally mill up a stick of that dimension, sand and polish the end to a slight dome, then cut off the plug to the proper length. I repeat this until I have enough plugs. After easing the inside corners a bit to facilitate insertion, these plugs can be driven home with a touch of silicone caulk on their back sides to hold them if the wood should ever shrink enough to loosen them. The splines are a bit time-consuming because of their shape. I cut them out on a bandsaw and complete them with a combination of files, sandpaper and buffing. You must make sure that they are a slightly loose slip-fit so the cap can expand and contract past them freely. They are glued to the top only. The last ebony parts are the rectangular plugs in the end cap. They are again sawn, sanded and polished to size. The plugs covering the attachment screws are glued in place with silicone adhesive to facilitate possible future removal, and the others are simply glued in place.

Final Assembly

Before starting the assembly, it's best to turn the top upside down, on a padded surface, and lay out the positions of the base pedestals, pencil drawer side mounting and modesty panel. By doing this, you can accurately position the small recesses you have to rout for the tabletop fasteners. While you've got the top turned upside down, attach the trim strip (piece 36) just above the pencil drawer and the

It's All in the Details

Cloud lift horizontal elements, plugs of contrasting colors and accentuating shapes. Simple lines repeated and amplified… strong Asian influences creating subtle yet striking visual effects. The Greene brothers succeeded in developing a recognizable yet fresh style. Their plugs are especially easy to make; just cut a stick to size, round over the top, buff and trim.

It takes a little longer, but getting done in a hurry wasn't one of the Greene brothers' design goals.

pencil drawer slides. It's also a good time to set the modesty panel in place and mark its mounting holes on the underside of the top.

The drawer, drawer front and pull installation is very straightforward, if tedious. For the top drawers, I use K.V. 8500 slides and for the file drawers, K.V. 8505, 22". The pulls are screwed to the drawer faces from inside, and then the faces are attached to the drawer boxes with washer-head screws and oversize holes to allow some positioning for any final adjustments.

With this, your four subassemblies are complete and can be put together. This is done by attaching the top to the drawer pedestals with the tabletop fasteners and then attaching the

modesty panel to the top, drilling the side pilot holes, and screwing the modesty panel to the legs. It should be noted that this assembly must take place wherever you want the desk, because it will need to be taken apart to move from one room to another.

Well, that's it! Now sit back, enjoy your new desk, and dream about your hostile takeover of Microsoft. Well, at least you have the desk for it.

Greene and Greene Desk Top
(Top View)

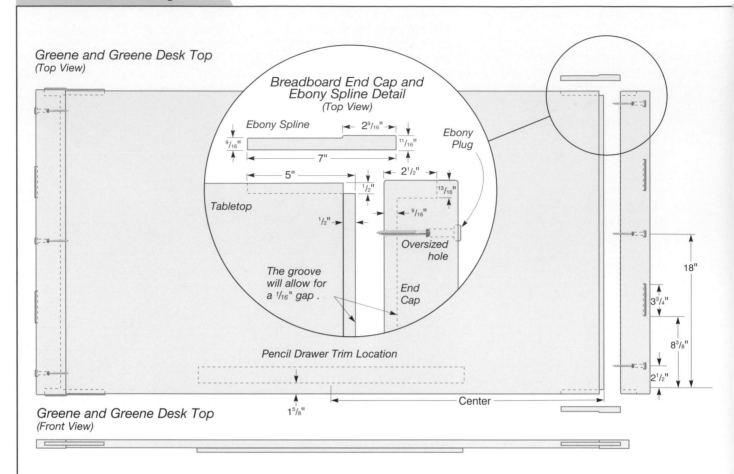

Breadboard End Cap and Ebony Spline Detail
(Top View)

Ebony Spline

2⁹/₁₆"

⁹/₁₆"

¹¹/₁₆"

7"

Ebony Plug

5"

2¹/₂"

Tabletop

¹/₂"

¹³/₁₆"

¹/₂"

⁹/₁₆"

The groove will allow for a ¹/₁₆" gap .

Oversized hole

End Cap

Pencil Drawer Trim Location

1⁵/₈"

Center

18"

3³/₄"

8³/₈"

2¹/₂"

Greene and Greene Desk Top
(Front View)

Greene and Greene Desk
(Side View)

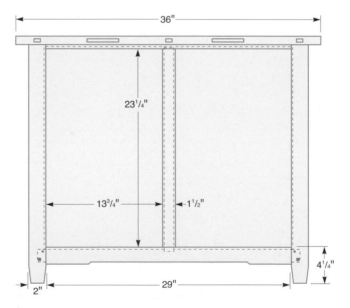

36"

23¹/₄"

13³/₄"

1¹/₂"

4¹/₄"

2"

29"

Greene and Greene Desk
(Front View)

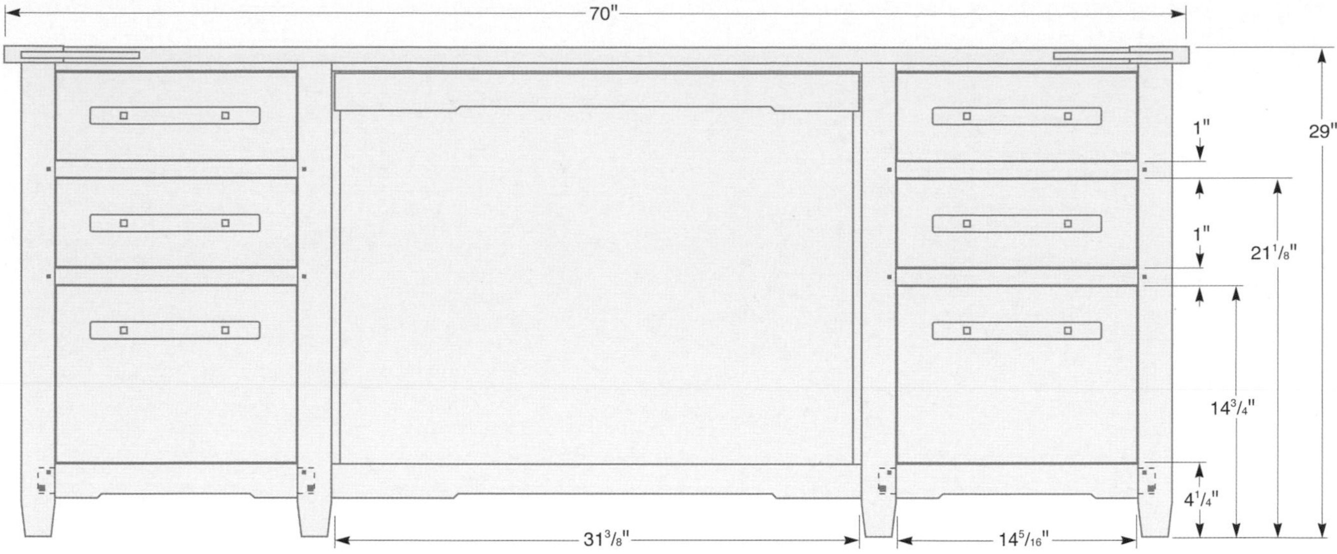

70"

1"

29"

1"

21 1/8"

14 3/4"

4 1/4"

31 3/8"

14 5/16"

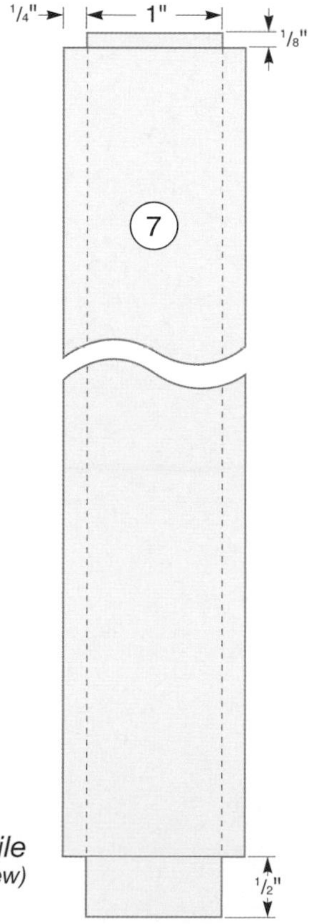

1/4"

1"

1/8"

7

Panel Stile
(Front View)

1/2"

1/2"

1/8"

7

1/8"

1/2"

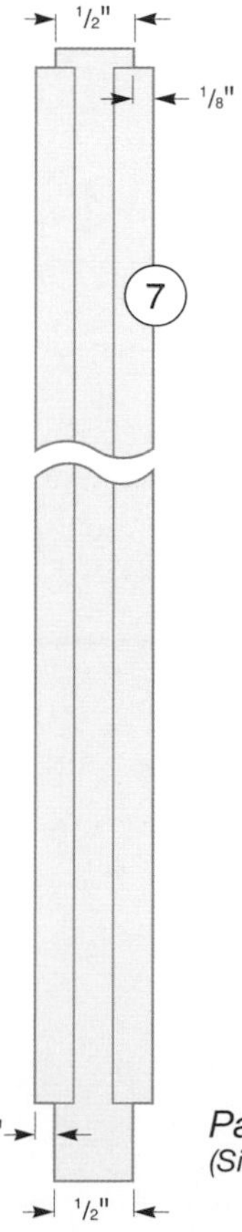

Panel Stile
(Side View)

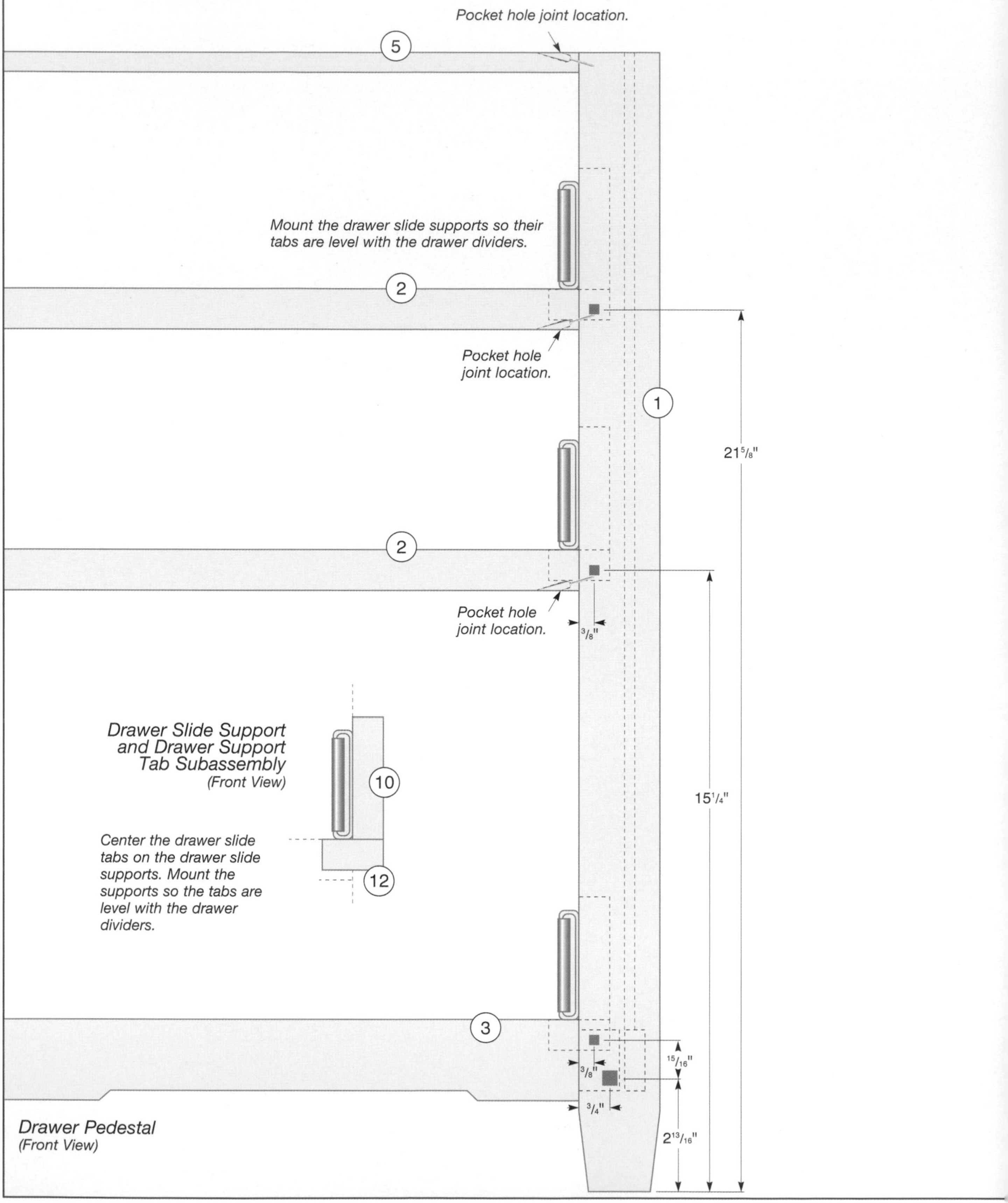

Pocket hole joint location.

⑤

Mount the drawer slide supports so their tabs are level with the drawer dividers.

②

Pocket hole joint location.

①

$21^{5}/_{8}$"

②

Pocket hole joint location.

$^{3}/_{8}$"

Drawer Slide Support and Drawer Support Tab Subassembly
(Front View)

⑩

Center the drawer slide tabs on the drawer slide supports. Mount the supports so the tabs are level with the drawer dividers.

⑫

$15^{1}/_{4}$"

③

$^{15}/_{16}$"

$^{3}/_{8}$"

$^{3}/_{4}$"

Drawer Pedestal
(Front View)

$2^{13}/_{16}$"

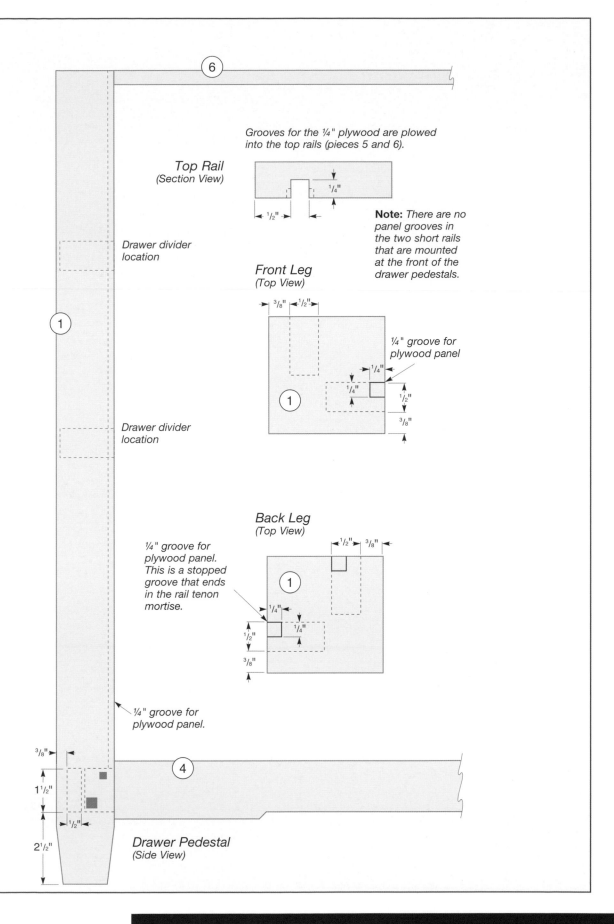

Grooves for the ¼" plywood are plowed into the top rails (pieces 5 and 6).

Top Rail
(Section View)

¼"

½"

Note: There are no panel grooves in the two short rails that are mounted at the front of the drawer pedestals.

Drawer divider location

Front Leg
(Top View)

³⁄₈" ½"

¼" groove for plywood panel

¼"

¼"

½"

³⁄₈"

Drawer divider location

Back Leg
(Top View)

½" ³⁄₈"

¼" groove for plywood panel. This is a stopped groove that ends in the rail tenon mortise.

¼"

¼"

½"

³⁄₈"

¼" groove for plywood panel.

³⁄₈"

1½"

½"

2½"

Drawer Pedestal
(Side View)

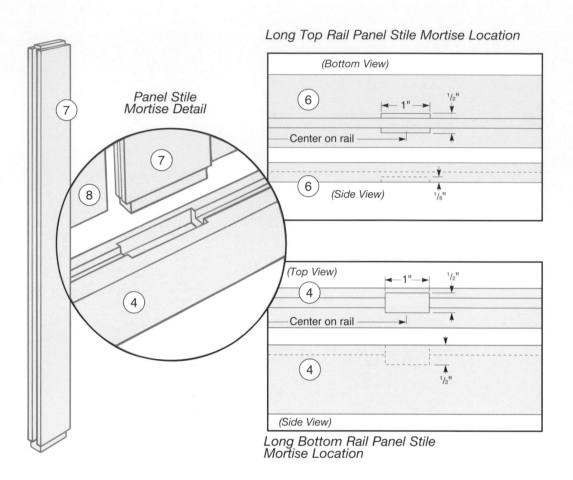

Long Top Rail Panel Stile Mortise Location

(Bottom View)

6

1"   ¹/₂"

Center on rail

6   (Side View)   ¹/₈"

Panel Stile
Mortise Detail

(Top View)   1"   ¹/₂"

4

Center on rail

4   ¹/₂"

(Side View)

Long Bottom Rail Panel Stile
Mortise Location

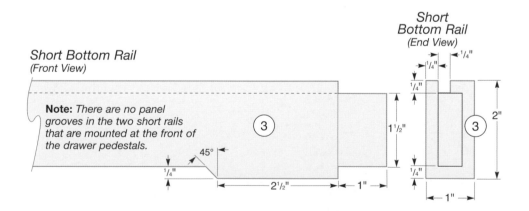

Short Bottom Rail
(Front View)

Note: There are no panel grooves in the two short rails that are mounted at the front of the drawer pedestals.

45°

¹/₄"   2¹/₂"   1"

3   1¹/₂"

Short
Bottom Rail
(End View)

¹/₄"   ¹/₄"
¹/₄"

3   2"

¹/₄"
1"

Long Bottom Rail
(Front View)

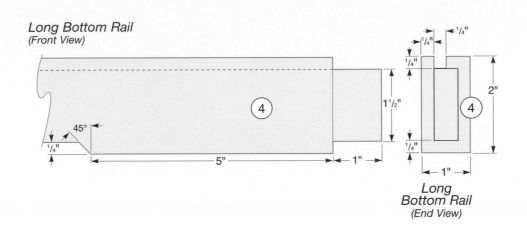

45°

¼"

¼"

1½"

5"

1"

Long Bottom Rail
(End View)

¼"

¼"

¼"

¼"

2"

1"

Drawer Pedestal
(Top View)

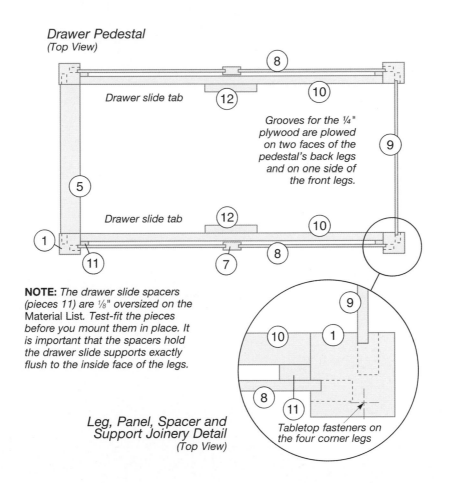

Drawer slide tab

Drawer slide tab

Grooves for the ¼"
plywood are plowed
on two faces of the
pedestal's back legs
and on one side of
the front legs.

NOTE: *The drawer slide spacers
(pieces 11) are ⅛" oversized on the
Material List. Test-fit the pieces
before you mount them in place. It
is important that the spacers hold
the drawer slide supports exactly
flush to the inside face of the legs.*

Tabletop fasteners on
the four corner legs

Leg, Panel, Spacer and Support Joinery Detail
(Top View)

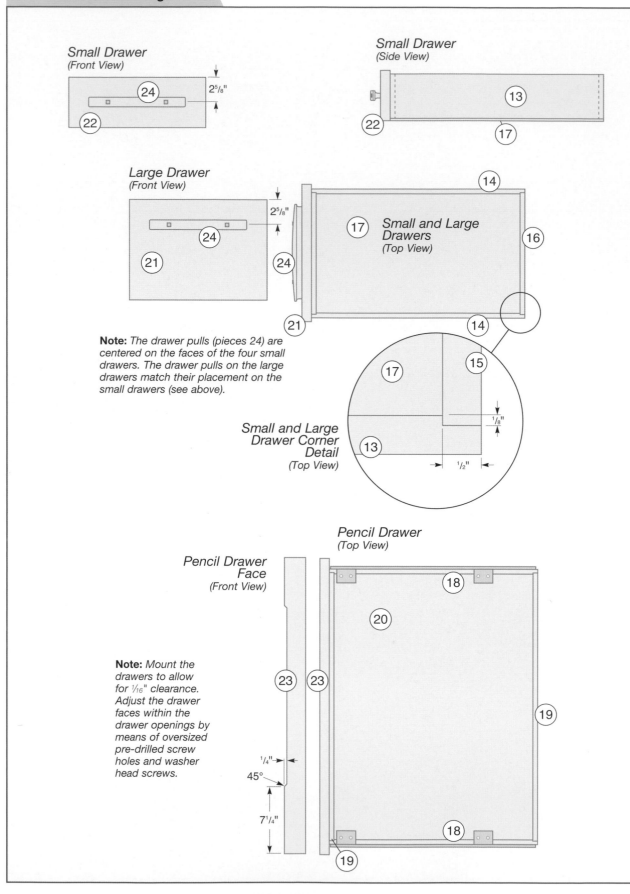

Small Drawer
(Front View)

2⁵/₈"

Small Drawer
(Side View)

Large Drawer
(Front View)

2⁵/₈"

Small and Large Drawers
(Top View)

Note: *The drawer pulls (pieces 24) are centered on the faces of the four small drawers. The drawer pulls on the large drawers match their placement on the small drawers (see above).*

Small and Large Drawer Corner Detail
(Top View)

¹/₈"

¹/₂"

Pencil Drawer
(Top View)

Pencil Drawer Face
(Front View)

Note: *Mount the drawers to allow for ¹/₁₆" clearance. Adjust the drawer faces within the drawer openings by means of oversized pre-drilled screw holes and washer head screws.*

¹/₄"

45°

7¹/₄"

Drawer Handle
(Top View)

1" ³/₄"

Drawer Handle
(Front View)

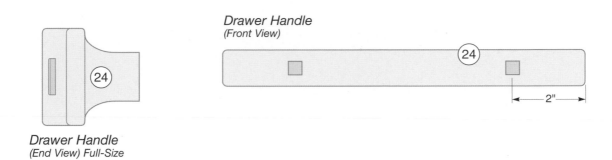

24

2"

Drawer Handle
(End View) Full-Size

24

Modesty Panel Details

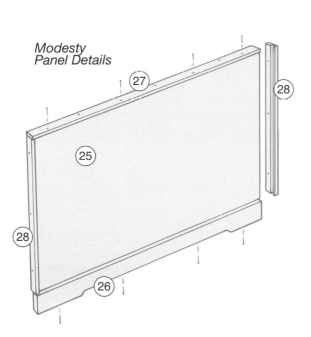

27

28

25

28

26

Modesty Panel Assembly Details
(Section View)

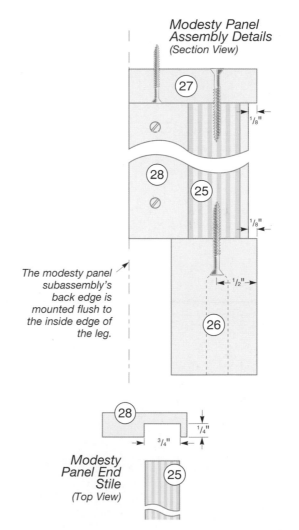

27

¹/₈"

28

25

¹/₈"

The modesty panel subassembly's back edge is mounted flush to the inside edge of the leg.

¹/₂"

26

Note: *The upper and lower modesty panel rails are simple butt joints secured with glue and screws. The modesty panel end stiles are grooved and then glued and clamped in place. The modesty panel subassembly is mounted to the desk with screws only, at the time the desk is assembled (where it will be used).*

28

¹/₄"

³/₄"

Modesty Panel End Stile
(Top View)

25

by Rick White

ARTS & CRAFTS HUTCH

A large piece of authentic Arts & Crafts furniture like this one could set you back thousands of dollars, and you'd never have the satisfaction of building it yourself. From a construction standpoint, our hutch project is every bit as genuine as something Stickley would have built. It's far more affordable these days, and a lot of fun to build.

Few woodworkers have had more impact on furniture design in this century than the Stickley brothers. Their work emphasized simplicity, sturdiness and exposed joinery—what Gustav Stickley liked to call the "structural style." Even though the popularity of their furniture had faded by 1920, the innovations they introduced set the tone for the next several generations of furnituremaking. These days, Stickley designs are showing up everywhere, and prices for their originals have skyrocketed. For instance, I recently saw a Gustav Stickley bookcase (without drawers) selling for $5,500 "firm."

If an original Stickley china hutch is out of your price range, why not try to build your own? Gustav Stickley liked to have his designs built by hobbyists and even wrote articles for amateur woodworkers outlining his construction and finishing techniques. Using examples from old Stickley catalogs, I've combined features from several

cabinets to come up with this hutch design. It's not technically too complex if you have moderate woodworking skills, but you'll need a full gamut of shop machinery.

It's important for a reproduction project like this to have hardware that looks appropriate. Luckily, Arts & Crafts door and drawer pulls are now available that look just like the originals. They're not cheap, but I think they're important for the overall success of the project. In the long run, you probably won't regret the extra expense to have solid, hammered copper hardware adorning your hand-made hutch.

The Stickleys built nearly all their furniture out of quartersawn white oak, and I've stuck with this tradition. The distinctive ray patterns give the project a look that just can't be equalled with plain-sawn oak. As for the glass, look in your phone book for a local supplier. For a small additional charge, they'll usually cut panes exactly to your specifications.

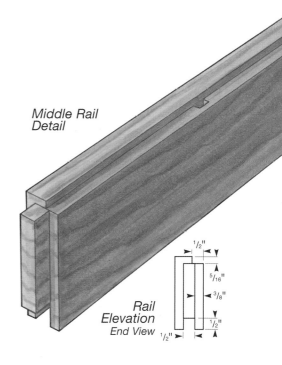

Middle Rail Detail

Rail Elevation
End View

Building the Framework

One of the definitive features of Stickley furniture is the use of thick lumber, which contributes to its sturdiness and long life. Sort through your 1¼" stock and select some highly figured material for the side stiles and rails (pieces 1 through 5), and use less interesting wood for the dust panel rails (pieces 6). Make sure the

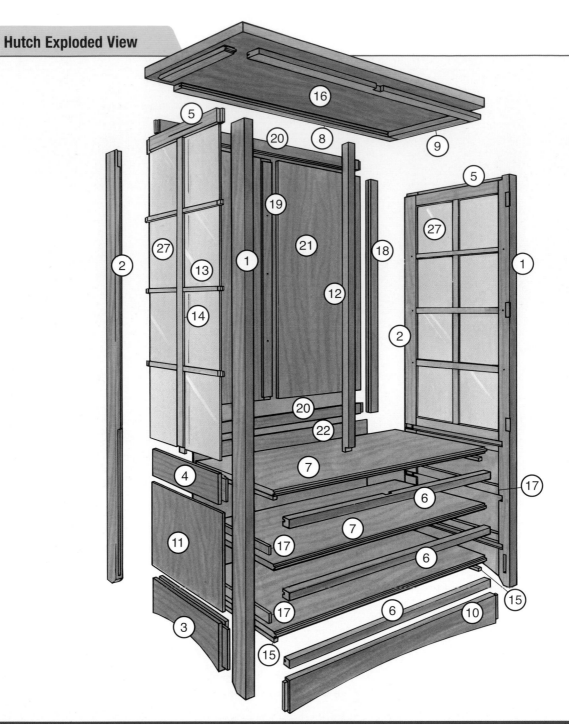

Material List - Carcass

		T x W x L			T x W x L
1	Front Side Stiles (2)	1¼" x 2½" x 69"	**9**	Subtop Rails (2)	¾" x 1¾" x 12⅜"
2	Rear Side Stiles (2)	1¼" x 2½" x 69"	**10**	Apron (1)	¾" x 3¼" x 45¼"
3	Bottom Side Rails (2)	1¼" x 4½" x 12½"	**11**	Side Panels (2)	½" x 12⁵⁄₁₆" x 15⅝"
4	Middle Side Rails (2)	1¼" x 3¼" x 12½"	**12**	Center Divider (1)	1" x 1¼" x 48³⁄₁₆"
5	Top Side Rails (2)	1¼" x 2" x 12½"	**13**	Side Horizontal Muntins (6)	1¼" x 1" x 13⅛"
6	Dust Panel Rails (3)	1¼" x 1¼" x 44½"	**14**	Side Vertical Muntins (2)	1¼" x 1" x 44⅝"
7	Dust Panels (3)	¾" x 15⅛" x 45¼"	**15**	Support Cleats (4)	½" x ½" x 14⅛"
8	Subtop Stiles (2)	¾" x 1¾" x 45¼"	**16**	Top (1)	1¼" x 17" x 49"

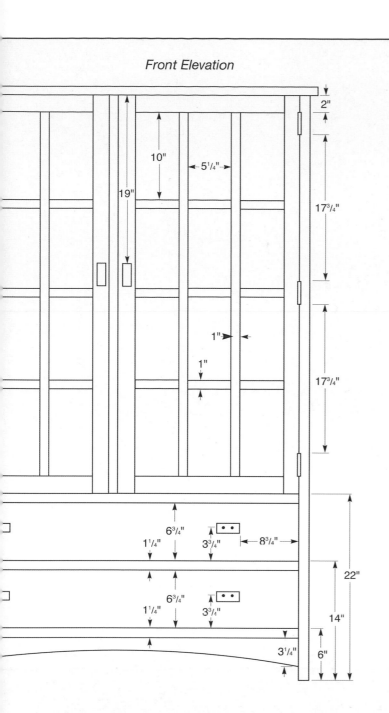

Front Elevation

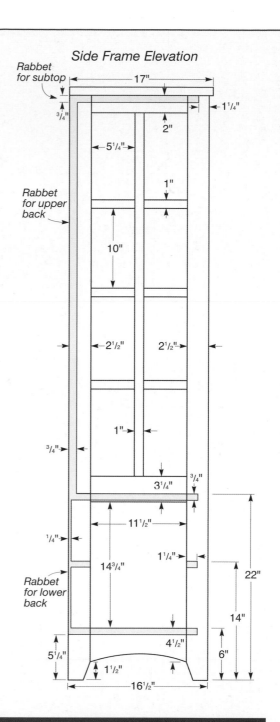

Side Frame Elevation

Material List - Carcass

		T x W x L			T x W x L
17	Drawer Slide Shims (4)	⅜" x 1¾" x 11½"	23	Ball Catches (4)	¼" x 1¾" Brass
18	Upper Back Stiles (2)	¾" x 2½" x 47¼"	24	Shelves (3)	¾" x 13⅝" x 44⅜"
19	U. B. Center Stile (1)	¾" x 2½" x 43"	25	Shelf Banding (3)	¾" x ¾" x 44⅜"
20	Upper Back Rails (2)	¾" x 2½" x 43¼"	26	Glass Retaining Strips (16)	⁵⁄₁₆" x ⁵⁄₁₆" x 96"
21	Upper Back Panels (2)	¼" x 19⅞" x 43"	27	Side Frame Glass (16)	⅛" x 5¾" x 10½"
22	Lower Back Panel (1)	¼" x 16¼" x 45¼"	28	Shelf Supports (18)	¼" Peg (brass)

lumber is straight and flat, then joint one edge and rip the pieces to width. As long as you're at the table saw and jointer, size plywood for the dust panels (pieces 7), cut ¾" stock for the subtop frame and apron (pieces 8, 9 and 10), and machine some figured ½" stock and glue it into the side panels (pieces 11).

Now lay out the mortises, grooves and rabbets on the side stiles and rails after studying the Elevation Drawings on pages 116 and 117. Begin machining the pieces by installing a ½" straight bit in your router table and routing the ½"-deep grooves in the stiles, middle rails and bottom rails for holding the side panels, then adjust your fence and rout the ⁵⁄₁₆"-deep x ½"-wide rabbets in the stiles, the middle rails and top rails for holding the glass. Square the ends of any stopped grooves and rabbets now with a sharp chisel.

To form the ½"-deep mortises in the middle and top rails (see the detail drawing on page 113) and stiles (see Technical Drawings on page 116), use a mortising attachment and your drill press (see Figure 1). If you don't have a mortising attachment, use a drill bit to remove most of the waste and clean up the rest with a chisel.

After forming the mortises, switch to a ¼" straight bit in your router table and rout ¼"-deep grooves in the dust panel rails, as shown in the Dust Panel Elevation on page 116. In addition, rout ½"-deep grooves in the subtop stiles (see elevation on page 116). Select the nicest dust panel for use as the shelf above the top drawer and rout a ½"-wide by ⅜"-deep rabbet along its top back edge for holding the upper back frame in place.

To form all the tenons in this project, use your table saw, a ½" dado blade and your miter gauge. Make sure the miter gauge is square to the blade and, for safety, clamp a set-up block to

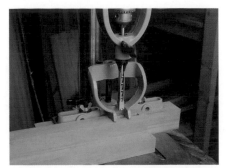

Figure 1: *A mortising attachment equipped with a ¼" hollow-point chisel will form all the mortises for the carcass and doors.*

Figure 2: *It's easy to cut tenons with a table saw using a miter gauge to support the stock and a set-up block to establish the length of the tenon.*

your fence so the stock can't bind as it passes through the blade (see Figure 2). Cut the tenons on the side rails, subtop rails and apron, as shown in the elevations. Next, flip one subtop stile and one dust panel rail on edge and cut the notches (see elevations) for the center door divider (piece 12). Glue the subtop frame together.

Now mount a ¼" dado blade in your table saw and form a tongue on the front edge of each dust panel (see Dust Panel Joint Elevation on page 116). Glue the dust panels to the rails, making sure to glue the notched rail to the top dust panel. (Chop the tongue out of the notch with a chisel. Note: the panels should extend ⅜" beyond each end of the rails.) Sand the side panels and cut them to size, then dry-fit all the parts for the side assemblies to check the fit of the joints. Now is the time to refine the fit, if needed.

Stickley Muntins

Muntins are one of the most distinctive features on many Stickley pieces, giving cabinets like this one a stately, well-constructed appearance. Step-by-step instructions for making the muntins are given in the *sidebar* on the next page. Make two extra muntins to use as test pieces for cutting the joints.

Once the muntins are completed, assemble the muntin frames without glue to check the fit of the half laps, then slip the muntin frames into the side frame assemblies to check the overall fit. If everything fits properly, take the side assemblies apart and spread glue on the joints. Work on one side at a time, first putting the muntin frame together and then building the rails, stiles and panel around it. Don't forget to check each assembly for squareness.

Connecting the Side Frames

Believe it or not, you're close to seeing your cabinet come together, but first you need to rout several dadoes and rabbets in the side frames in preparation for the assembly. Lay out the stopped dadoes for the dust panels, as shown in the Side Frame Elevation, and chuck a ¾" straight bit in your router. Clamp a straightedge jig like the one shown in Figure 3 on page 119 along each layout line, and rout ⅜"-deep dadoes (avoid cutting into the side panels). Follow the same routing procedure to cut a ¾"-wide rabbet at the top of each side assembly for joining the subtop frame to the sides. Use a chisel to square the stopped ends of all the dadoes.

Rabbet the back edge of each side frame for installing the back assemblies (see Side Frame Elevation, page 113). Since the upper back assembly is ¾" thick and the lower back is ¼" thick, the ⅜"-wide rabbets must be cut at two different depths—an easy job for your router and its accessory fence. Be sure to square the stopped end of the deeper rabbets with a chisel.

To reinforce the top and bottom dust panels, I installed support cleats (pieces 15) under each one, as shown in the Exploded View on page 112. Cut your cleats to size and set them aside until you're ready to assemble the cabinet.

Now cut out the full-size patterns of the apron and bottom side rails as found in the Technical Drawings, and trace the shapes onto your stock. Use a jigsaw to cut the gradual curves, and smooth the cuts with your drill and a drum sander. Now you are ready for some major assembly.

Assembling the Cabinet

Since this assembly is so large you might want help putting it all together. First, have your helper hold the side frames on their back edge while you clamp the top dust panel into its dadoes. Next, hold the cleats in position so you can drill pilot holes for screwing them to the dust panel and side rail. Once the pilot holes are drilled, spread glue on the cleats, in the dadoes and in the apron mortises, slip the apron and top dust panel into place and screw the cleats to the assembly. At this point I recommend clamping the subtop frame to the sides, without glue, to keep the assembly square. Now glue the middle dust panel to the sides, then add the bottom dust panel and two more cleats (be sure to glue the top edge of the apron to the bottom dust panel). Check the structure for squareness.

Measure your cabinet for the center divider (piece 12) and cut a piece to fit. Form a 1"-long tenon on its lower end and slip the divider into the top dust panel mortise. Now drill a countersunk pilot hole through the subtop's front stile and into the divider (see Subtop Elevation on page 116), and drill several angled pilot holes through the subtop into the side frames. Remove the subtop frame and drill the counterbored pilot holes for screwing the top (piece 16) to the carcass. Drill standard pilot holes in the subtop's back stile and elongated holes in the front stile (see Subtop Elevation) to allow for wood expansion.

Glue the center divider and subtop frame into the cabinet, and drive screws to secure the subtop to the side frames and the divider.

There's one more item to take care of while you're still dealing with the main carcass. The drawer slides must be mounted flush with the inside edges of the stiles, so you'll need a shim (pieces 17) for each slide. Cut the stock to fit against the side panels in your cabinet, then drill oversized holes in the shims for mounting them to the panels. Go ahead and screw them into place, but don't use any glue or you'll restrict the movement of the panels.

Adding the Top, Back and Doors

Joint and glue up several 1¼"-thick boards for the top (piece 16). While the top is in the clamps, build the back assemblies. I made the upper back assembly a frame and panel structure

Making the Muntins

Begin making the side frame muntins (pieces 13 and 14) by ripping rabbets along two edges of your stock, as shown in the elevation at right.

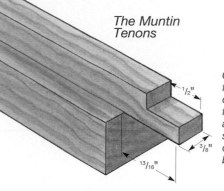

The Muntin Tenons

Cut all the front faces of the tenons first, then adjust the set-up and cut all the back faces.

After cutting the rabbets, measure your side assemblies to get the muntin lengths you actually need, making sure to include the tenons. Cut your muntins to length, then form the tenons, as shown in the *detail* above.

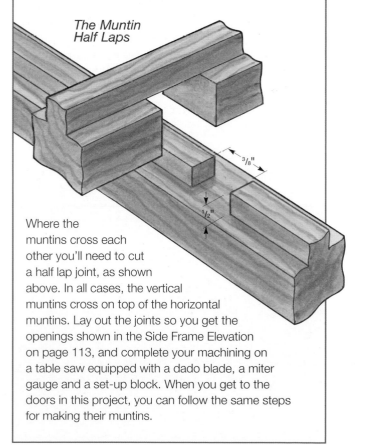

The Muntin Half Laps

Where the muntins cross each other you'll need to cut a half lap joint, as shown above. In all cases, the vertical muntins cross on top of the horizontal muntins. Lay out the joints so you get the openings shown in the Side Frame Elevation on page 113, and complete your machining on a table saw equipped with a dado blade, a miter gauge and a set-up block. When you get to the doors in this project, you can follow the same steps for making their muntins.

Technical Drawings

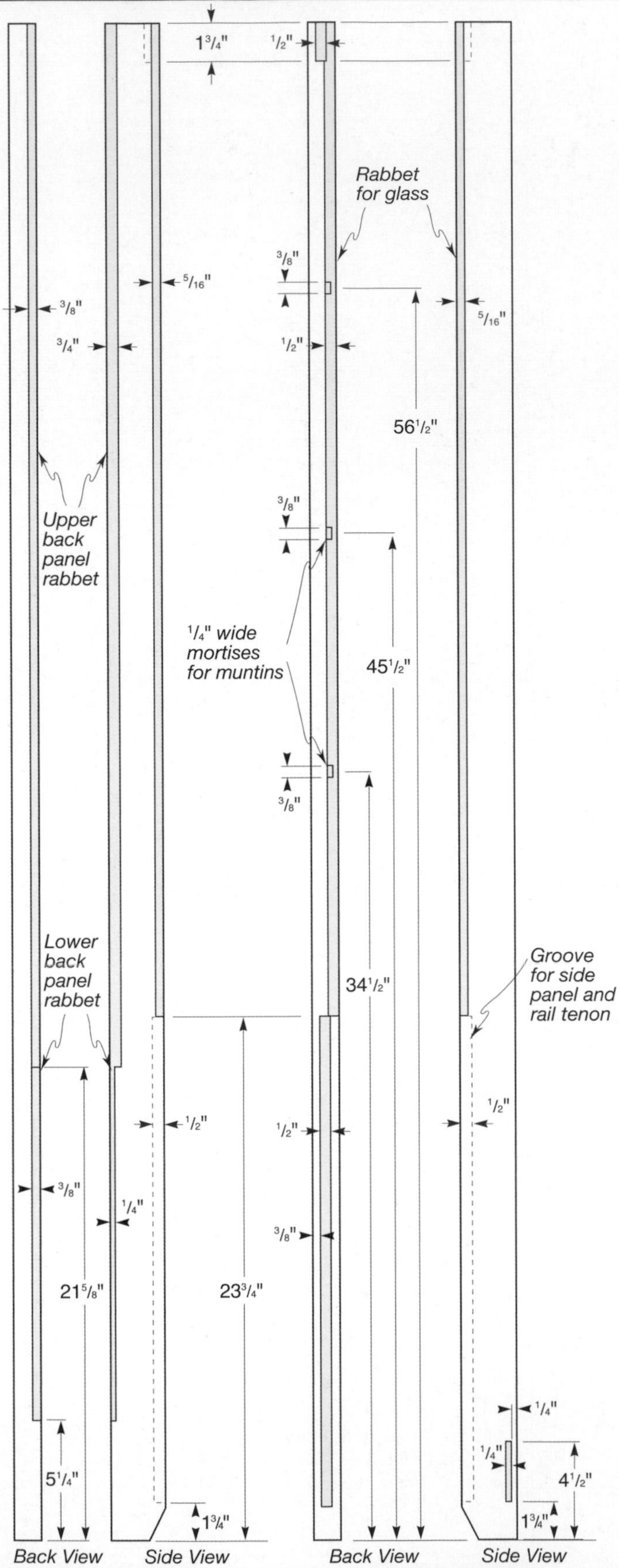

1 3/4"
1/2"
Rabbet for glass
3/8"
5/16"
3/4"
1/2"
56 1/2"
Upper back panel rabbet
1/4" wide mortises for muntins
45 1/2"
34 1/2"
Groove for side panel and rail tenon
Lower back panel rabbet
1/4"
21 5/8"
23 3/4"
5 1/4"
4 1/2"
Back View
Side View

Rear Side Stile

Front Side Stile

Subtop Elevation

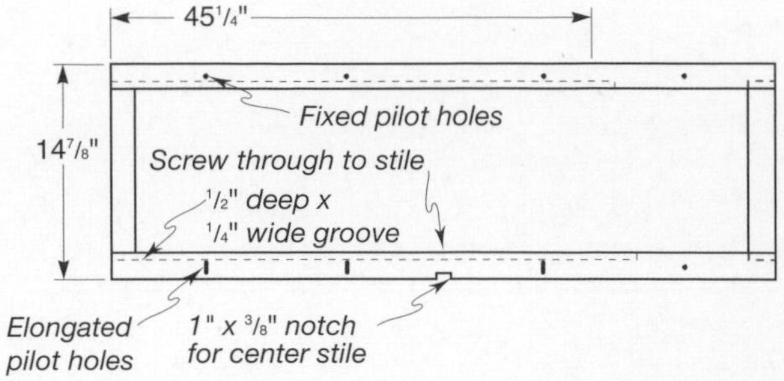

45 1/4"
14 7/8"
Fixed pilot holes
Screw through to stile
1/2" deep x 1/4" wide groove
Elongated pilot holes
1" x 3/8" notch for center stile

Upper Back Elevation

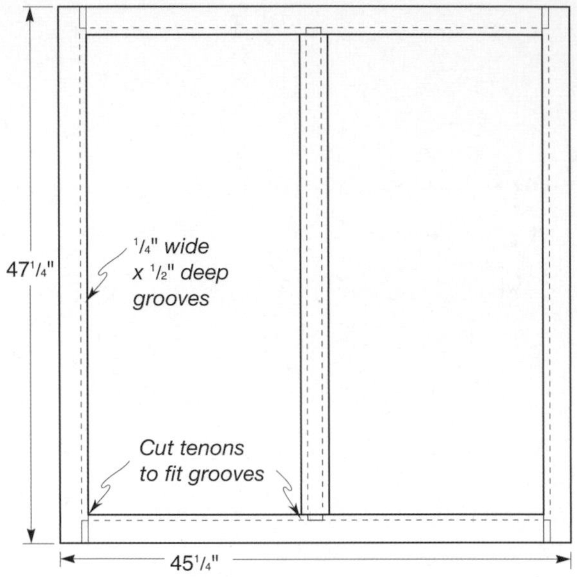

47 1/4"
1/4" wide x 1/2" deep grooves
Cut tenons to fit grooves
45 1/4"

Dust Panel Elevation

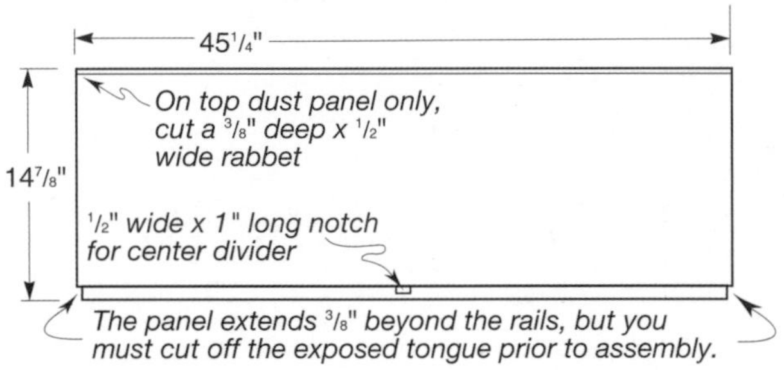

45 1/4"
14 7/8"
On top dust panel only, cut a 3/8" deep x 1/2" wide rabbet
1/2" wide x 1" long notch for center divider
The panel extends 3/8" beyond the rails, but you must cut off the exposed tongue prior to assembly.

Dust Panel Joint Elevation

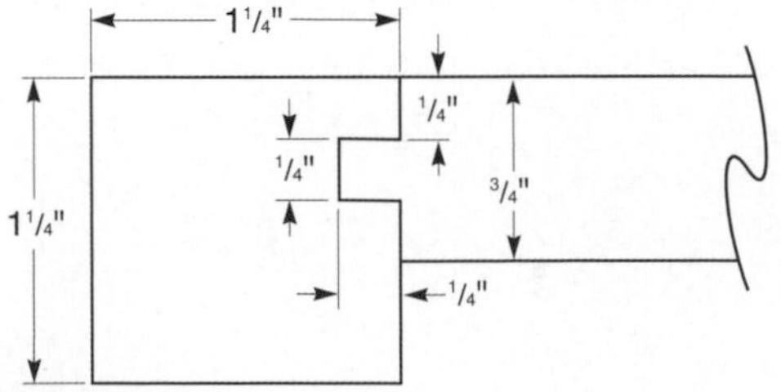

1 1/4"
1/4"
3/4"
1 1/4"

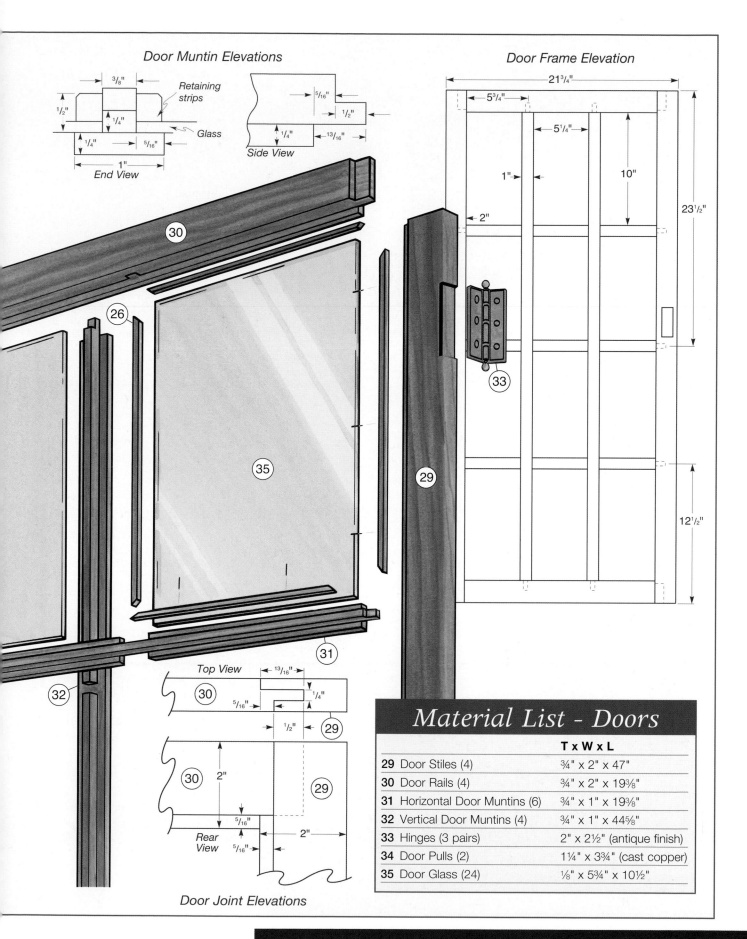

Door Muntin Elevations

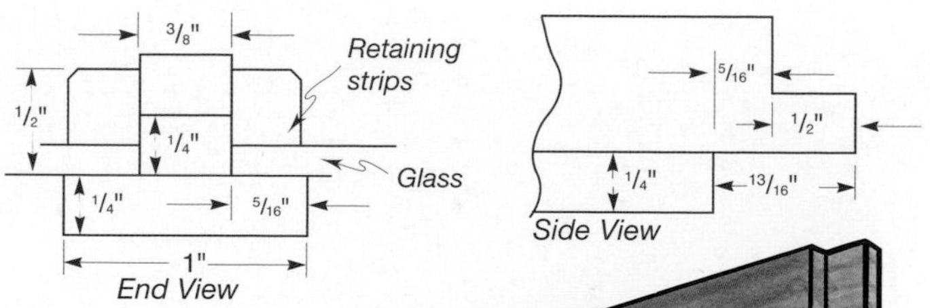
3/8"
Retaining strips
1/2"
1/4"
Glass
1/4"
5/16"
1"
End View
5/16"
1/2"
1/4"
13/16"
Side View

30
26
35
29
33
31
32

Door Frame Elevation

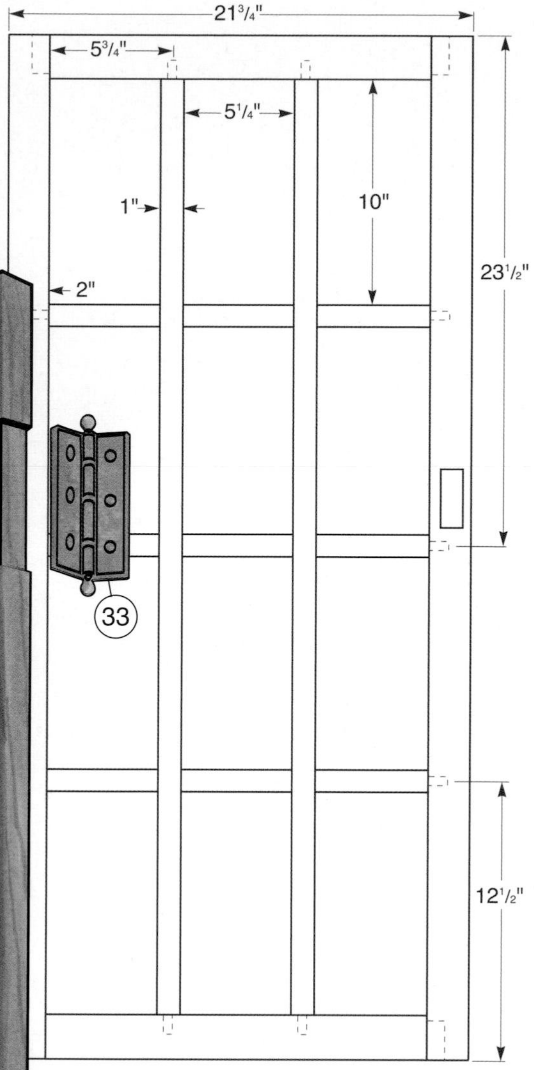
21 3/4"
5 3/4"
5 1/4"
1"
10"
2"
23 1/2"
12 1/2"

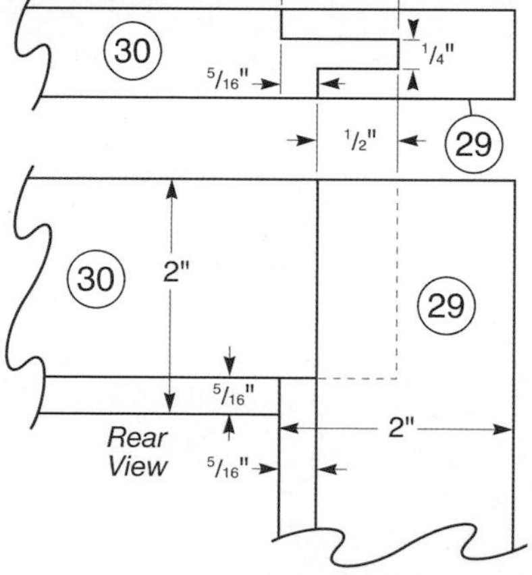
Top View
13/16"
30
1/4"
5/16"
1/2"
29
30
2"
29
5/16"
Rear View
5/16"
2"

Door Joint Elevations

Material List - Doors

		T x W x L
29	Door Stiles (4)	¾" x 2" x 47"
30	Door Rails (4)	¾" x 2" x 19⅜"
31	Horizontal Door Muntins (6)	¾" x 1" x 19⅜"
32	Vertical Door Muntins (4)	¾" x 1" x 44⅝"
33	Hinges (3 pairs)	2" x 2½" (antique finish)
34	Door Pulls (2)	1¼" x 3¾" (cast copper)
35	Door Glass (24)	⅛" x 5¾" x 10½"

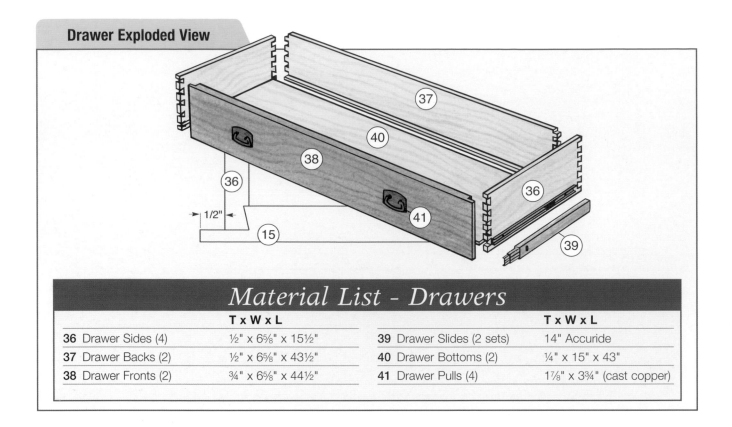

Drawer Exploded View

Material List - Drawers

		T x W x L			T x W x L
36	Drawer Sides (4)	½" x 6⅝" x 15½"	39	Drawer Slides (2 sets)	14" Accuride
37	Drawer Backs (2)	½" x 6⅝" x 43½"	40	Drawer Bottoms (2)	¼" x 15" x 43"
38	Drawer Fronts (2)	¾" x 6⅝" x 44½"	41	Drawer Pulls (4)	1⅞" x 3¾" (cast copper)

because you can see it though the glass doors. A piece of ¼" plywood is adequate for the lower back since this piece is hidden.

Rip the stiles and rails for the upper back (pieces 18, 19 and 20) and cut ¼" plain-sawn white oak plywood for the two upper panels and the lower back (pieces 21 and 22). Next, rout ¼" x ½" grooves in the appropriate edges of the upper back frame pieces and form tenons on the ends of the rails and center stile, as shown in the Upper Back Elevation on page 116. Glue the pieces together for the upper back and fit the frame into the cabinet.

By now the top panel is ready for planing and sanding. Once this is completed, position the top on the carcass with a ½" overhang on the front and 1" overhangs on the sides. Extend the pilot holes from the subtop into the top and screw the top to the cabinet.

Constructing the doors is much like making the sides, except that they call for 3/4" stock instead of the heftier 11/4" material. Rip nicely figured oak for the door stiles, rails and muntins (pieces 29, 30, 31 and 32), and cut the rails and stiles to length. Next, rabbet the inside edge of the rails and stiles and lay out the mortises, as shown in the Door Elevations on page 117. This includes both the rail-to-stile mortises and the muntin-to-frame mortises. Form the mortises with your drill press mortising attachment and cut the tenons on the rail ends with your table saw.

Put the door frames together without glue and measure for the muntin lengths (remember to add the tenons). Cut your muntins to length, then rabbet the edges and form the tenons just like you did earlier on the side frame muntins (see Door Muntin Elevations).

Glue the door parts together, making sure each assembly remains square and perfectly flat. Clean up the glue just after it sets and, once the glue dries completely, sand the frames smooth. Fit the doors to the cabinet and lay out the mortises for the hinges (pieces 33), as shown in the Front Elevation Drawing on page 113.

Carefully chop out the mortises with a chisel and install the doors in the hutch.

Constructing the Drawers

The best drawers are constructed with dovetail joints, and this is certainly what the Stickleys would expect. I used a Leigh jig that makes the dovetails quickly, but they're easy enough to cut by hand if you don't have a jig.

Cut ½"-thick secondary wood, like pine or poplar, for the drawer backs and sides (pieces 36 and 37), and select highly figured ¾"-thick white oak for the drawer fronts (pieces 38). Cut the fronts and rabbet their ends for accommodating the drawer slides (pieces 39), as shown in the Drawer Exploded View, above.

Now use your jig to rout the dovetails, then chuck a ¼" straight bit in your router table and rout the grooves for the bottom panels (pieces 40). Cut the bottoms to size and dry-assemble the drawers to check the fit of the joints. If everything looks good, glue the dovetails together to make the boxes.

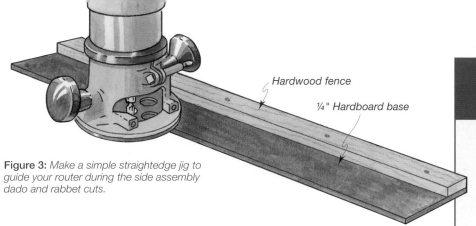

Figure 3: *Make a simple straightedge jig to guide your router during the side assembly dado and rabbet cuts.*

Hardwood fence

¼" Hardboard base

Stickley's Inspiration

William Morris

The Arts & Crafts movement of the late 1800s developed as a rejection of Victorian values and decorating tastes. In Britain, movement leaders like John Ruskin and his disciple, William Morris, struggled to improve the oppressive factory conditions and railed against the ornate, poorly made goods they produced. As an alternative, they advocated the revival of medieval guilds, or cooperatives, made up of skilled artisans turning out high-quality, functional objects for use by the middle class. Morris, an architect, poet, and prolific designer of fabric, wallpaper and furniture, emphasized the wise use of machinery in combination with handwork—an idea that was very appealing to a young American woodworker named Gustav Stickley. Working from Morris' model, Stickley began building "sensible" furniture for the common man. His simple designs relied on the beauty of the wood and exposed joinery for their adornment. Despite the short-lived success of his businesses, this approach to furnituremaking continues to be Stickley's legacy.

Install the drawer slides in the cabinet and on the sides of the drawers. For consistent positioning of the slides in the cabinet, rip a narrow strip of wood (in this case about ⅛" thick) and slip it between the dust panels and each slide while you drill the pilot holes.

Drill the mounting holes for the door and drawer pulls (pieces 34 and 41), as shown in the Front Elevation on page 113. Install this hardware before doing the finishing, just to make sure the doors and drawers operate properly. Hopefully, this will save you from unexpected problems later.

Cut ¾" oak plywood for the three shelves (pieces 24) and glue banding (piece 25) to their front edges. After the glue dries, plane the banding flush with the plywood and sand the shelves smooth.

Before moving on to the finishing stage, cut plenty of retaining strips (pieces 26) for holding the glass in the cabinet and door frames. To make the retaining strips, first cut a small chamfer on all four corners of four ¾" x 3" x 96" boards, then kerf the edges on-center using a table saw. Next, rip off the edges of the board to yield strips roughly ⁵⁄₁₆" square. Finish the strips now, just like you do the rest of the cabinet. Later, after the varnish dries, miter the strips to length for each glass frame in the hutch.

Finishing Up

You can get as complicated as you want when finishing Stickley-style pieces. I simply used a quart of Bartley's walnut gel stain. One coat gave the look I was after; then, I followed it with a coat of sanding sealer and two coats of satin varnish. Remember to sand lightly with 400-grit silicon carbide paper between each coat of varnish.

A couple of days after the last coat of varnish dries, begin installing the glass (pieces 27 and 35). Miter the retaining strips for the glass and nail them to the frames with brads. If any raw wood remains exposed after the installation, use a cotton swab to dab on a little stain and it will blend into the rest of the hutch.

Remount the hinges, pulls and slides, and screw the two backs to the cabinet. Next, drill the ¼" holes for the shelf supports (pieces 28) in the side stiles, the center divider and the center stile on the upper back assembly. To position the holes, make a simple lay out jig. Cut a 1"-wide by 38"-long strip of scrapwood and drill a ¼" hole 34³⁄₁₆" from one end. Now hold this strip against each of the cabinet members listed above and drill the holes for the top shelf supports. Next, cut 11" off the undrilled end of the jig and drill the middle shelf support holes, then cut another 11" off and drill the lower holes. The shelf supports are positioned so the shelves line up behind the muntins in the doors and sides.

Install the ball catches (pieces 23) for holding the doors shut and set the shelves into the cabinet. This completes your Stickley reproduction. While your china hutch may not command the high price tag of the originals, it didn't cost you a year's salary to make either. And who knows? With time your piece may appreciate in value, too!

by Chris Marshall

ARTS & CRAFTS WINE CABINET

Here's an exercise in case construction that will test your furniture-building skills. This is a huge cabinet: the upper unit provides loads of shelf space for storing and displaying glassware, while the bottom stows a substantial collection of wine. If you have other needs for this project, it easily converts to a conventional hutch by simply omitting the lower shelf dividers or flipping the shelves over.

We'll never know if Gustav Stickley would approve of an Arts & Crafts wine cabinet, but the style lends itself well here, both in terms of form and function. The base cabinet discreetly stores more than five dozen bottles of wine, while the divided glass doors above show off a full collection of stemware.

If you've never worked with quartersawn white oak, here's a fitting opportunity to select some top-quality stock from a reputable supplier. For a vibrant and authentic look, choose boards with a wide flake pattern. It's also a good idea to splurge for plywood laid up with quartersawn face veneer so the plywood components blend in well with the solid-wood parts. Quartersawn oak veneered plywood can be difficult to find. If you can't locate it, riftsawn veneered plywood is a good substitute. It looks more appropriate than common rotary-cut veneer for this project.

Building the Upper Carcass

The upper cabinet has a pair of frame-and-panel ends made of solid wood, but the rest of the carcass is mostly plywood. Start building the carcass by choosing the best plywood veneer for the back panel. As you can see in the Exploded Drawing on page 122, the cabinet back consists of three plywood panels (pieces 1 and 2) joined

Removable shelves *in the base cabinet are outfitted with divider strips to keep the bottles stationary and evenly spaced. The shelves could be flipped over onto their flat faces for storing other items as well.*

with biscuits. Here's why: In order to orient the plywood veneer so the grain pattern runs vertically—a visual necessity here—you'll need a panel nearly five feet wide and four feet long. I chose the most dazzling veneer for the center panel, since it shows through in the end.

Cut the three back panels to size and mill #20 biscuit joints along the mating edges, then glue the panels up.

Cut the rails (pieces 3) now, too. The rails stiffen the fragile biscuit joints, and the bottom rail forms a finished edge where the two cabinets meet. The back panel and rails are joined with ¼" x ½" tongue and groove joints. I used a piloted slot cutter to cut the long panel grooves. Stain and finish the completed panel now, while all its surfaces are fully accessible.

Follow the Material List dimensions to cut plywood parts for the subtop, horizontal divider, side panels and bottoms (pieces 4, 5, 6 and 7). Rout slotted holes through the subtop so the solid-wood top can expand and contract with the seasons. Cut the side panel bottom rails (pieces 8), and join these to the sides the same way you did with the back panel rails. Complete the sides at this stage by cutting ⅜" x ¾" dadoes across their inside faces for the horizontal divider.

Next, make the solid-wood end frames (pieces 9, 10, 11 and 12). The rails and stiles are joined with more tongues and grooves (see Elevation Drawings, page 123). Cut a wide rabbet along the back edge of the rear stiles to house the back panel. Carefully choose your stock for the panels that float inside these frames. Quartersawn flakes are hard to match up if you need to prepare the panels from more than

Upper Carcass Exploded View

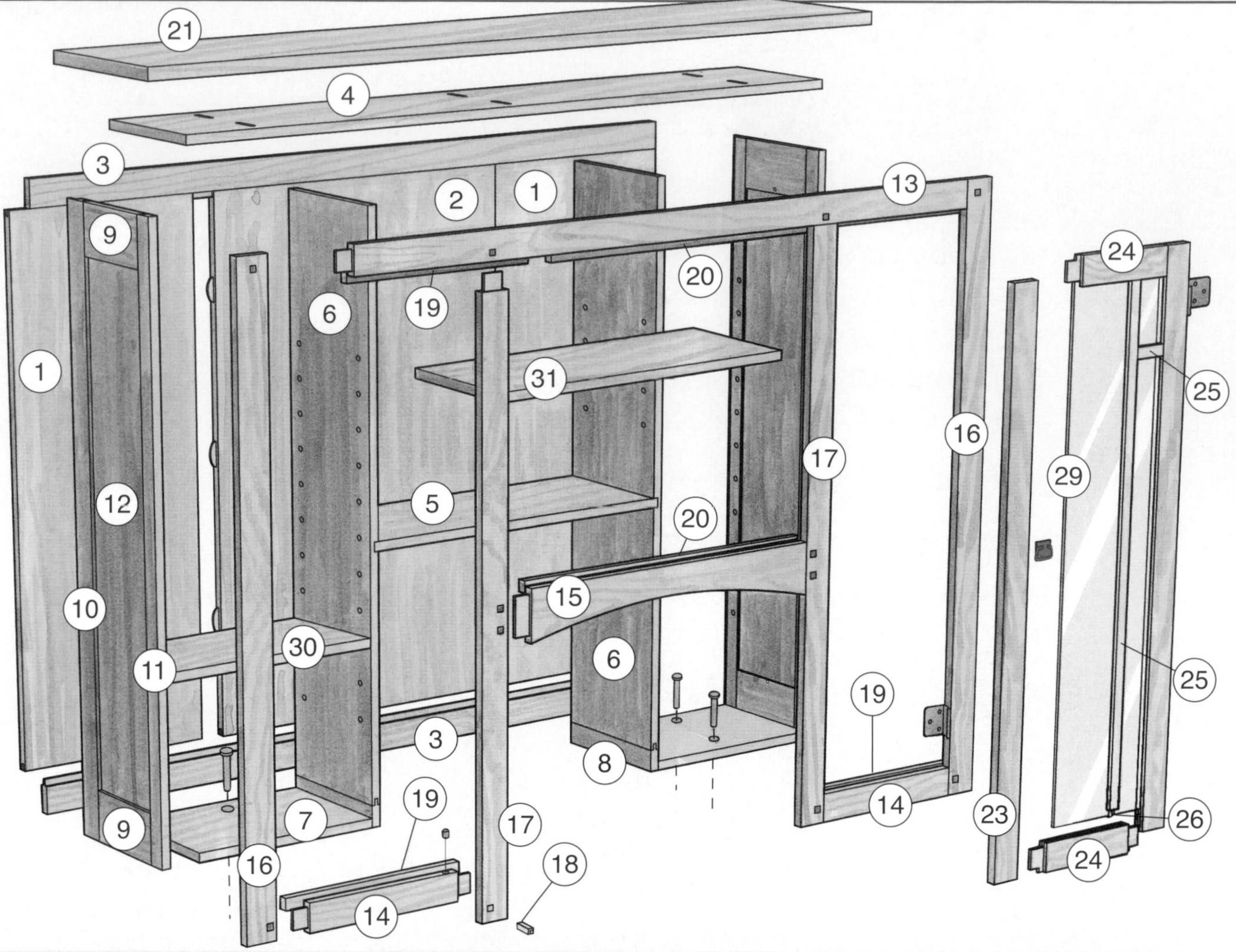

Material List - Wine Cabinet

	T x W x L		T x W x L
1 Back End Panels (2)	¾" x 16⅜" x 44½"	16 Outer Face Frame Stiles (2)	¾" x 2½" x 48"
2 Back Center Panel (1)	¾" x 26¾" x 44½"	17 Inner Face Frame Stiles (2)	¾" x 2¼" x 47"
3 Back Panel Rails (2)	¾" x 2¼" x 59½"	18 Face Frame Pegs (12)	⅜" x ⅜ x ¾"
4 Subtop (1)	¾" x 10½" x 58½"	19 Large Door Stops (4)	½" x 1" x 15½"
5 Horizontal Divider (1)	¾" x 10½" x 26¾"	20 Small Door Stops (2)	½" x 1" x 26"
6 Side Panels (2)	¾" x 10½" x 45½"	21 Top (1)	1" x 13" x 66"
7 Bottoms (2)	¾" x 10½" x 15½"	22 Short Door Stiles (4)	¾" x 2¼" x 23¾"
8 Side Panel Bottom Rails (2)	¾" x 2¼" x 10½"	23 Tall Door Stiles (4)	¾" x 2¼" x 43½"
9 End Frame Rails (4)	¾" x 4" x 8½"	24 Door Rails (8)	¾" x 2¼" x 10¾"
10 Rear End Frame Stiles (2)	¾" x 2¼" x 48"	25 Muntins (8)	¼" x ⅞" x Varies
11 Front End Frame Stiles (2)	¾" x 1½" x 48"	26 Muntin Backer Strips (8)	⅜" x ½" x Varies
12 End Frame Panels (2)	½" x 8¼" x 41"	27 Small Glass Retainer Strips* (20)	¼" x ⅜" x Varies
13 Face Frame Top Rail (1)	¾" x 2¼" x 58"	28 Large Glass Retainer Strips* (28)	⅜" x ½" x Varies
14 Face Frame Bottom Rails (2)	¾" x 2¼" x 15¼"	29 Glass* (12)	⅛" x Varies
15 Face Frame Arched Rail (1)	¾" x 4" x 28"	30 Side Shelves (6)	¾" x 10⅜" x 15¼"

**Measure and cut after doors are assembled*

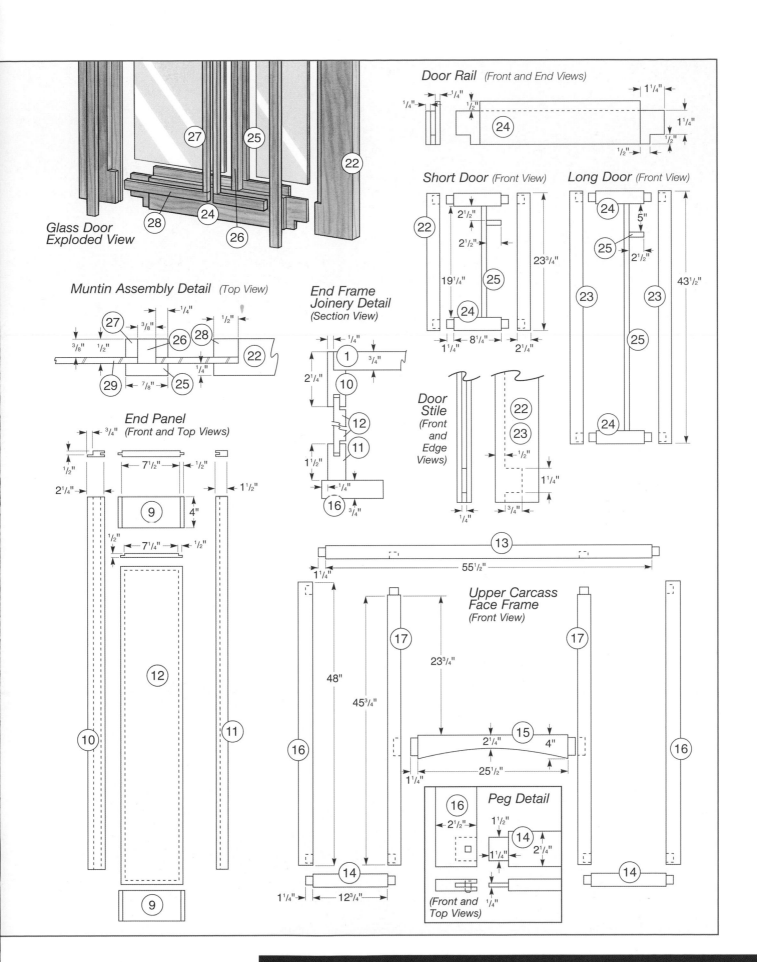

Door Rail *(Front and End Views)*

Glass Door Exploded View

Muntin Assembly Detail *(Top View)*

End Frame Joinery Detail *(Section View)*

Short Door *(Front View)*

Long Door *(Front View)*

Door Stile *(Front and Edge Views)*

End Panel *(Front and Top Views)*

Upper Carcass Face Frame *(Front View)*

Peg Detail *(Front and Top Views)*

Tongue-and-groove joints connect the upper cabinet end frame parts. Finish the floating panels before assembly.

one board. My stock was too thin to resaw for a book-matched look, so I made each panel from two widths of single boards to help blend the random grain pattern.

Once you've got your panel blanks planed and trimmed to size, mill a rabbet around the inside faces (see Elevation Drawings). When you fit the frames and panels together, you'll notice that the panels are undersized ¼" across their width to accommodate wood movement. You should pre-finish the panels now, including the topcoat. This way, bare wood can't show if the panels shrink. Assemble the frames and panels with the panel rabbets facing inward, and lock the panels to the rails with a centered dowel, top and bottom. This keeps the rabbet reveals even if the panels shift inside the frames.

Before you assemble the rest of the carcass, drill rows of shelf pin holes in the side panels and end frame stiles. Remember that the side panels require shelf pin holes on both faces—two columns for shelving in the long cabinets and another set for the center cabinet shelves. Now, assemble the carcass by joining the end frames, side panels, subtop and bottoms with #20 biscuits and glue. Drive countersunk screws down through the subtop and into the side panels instead

of using biscuits here—it's easier. Slip the horizontal divider into its dadoes and pin it in place with 18-gauge finish nails.

Making the Face Frame

Following the Material List, cut all the face frame parts (pieces 13 through 17) to size. The rail and stile joints are straightforward mortises and tenons. The tenons are all ¼" thick, 1½" wide and 1¼" long, except for those on the arched rail (piece 15), which are 3" wide. Mill these joints using whatever machining techniques you prefer. Cut the curve in the arched rail, sand it smooth on a drum sander, and glue up the face frame. Connect the parts, starting with the arched rail and working toward the outer stiles. Chamfer the outer edges with a block plane or a chamfer bit in your router for a more finished look.

To break up the flat plane of the face frame and doors, I locked the face frame joints with square oak pegs (pieces 18). If you've got a mortising machine, simply lay out the peg locations and chop square holes using a ⅜" hollow-chisel bit. Otherwise, you could pull off this technique by drilling slightly undersized round holes and tapping in the square pegs. Once the holes are chopped, plane down some oak scrap into ⅜" x ⅜" strips and cut

them into pegs (pieces 18). Chamfer the "show" ends of the pegs (see top photo on the next page) before gluing them in.

With the face frame and carcass construction behind you, apply finish to these parts before attaching them. I used the face frame to square up the carcass instead of following the usual convention of installing the back to pull things into square. The face frame is oversized to provide ¼" of overhang where it meets the end frames, horizontal divider and side panels. By installing the face frame first, you'll be able to square the carcass in relation to the face frame and keep the overhangs even all around. Nail on the face frame and, while the back is still off, cut and attach pairs of door stops (pieces 19 and 20) to the back of the face frame at each door opening with short countersunk wood screws. Then fasten the back into its rabbets with more screws.

Make a blank for the top (piece 21). I glued ours up from several pieces of 5/4 stock planed to 1" thickness. Pre-finish the top on all surfaces and attach it to the subtop with #10 panhead or washerhead wood screws. Drive these up through slotted holes in the subtop so the top can expand and contract widthwise.

Cut ⅝" deep square holes for the face frame pegs using a mortising machine. Support the face frame with blocking and line up the bit carefully. You may need to raise the mortiser's table with additional blocking (as I did) to get full throw of the lever arm on ¾" thick stock.

Make the face frame pegs from longer strips, chamfering each on a sander before cutting it to length. A simple angle jig helps maintain even chamfers. Press the pegs into their square face frame holes with a C-clamp to avoid marring them.

Making Door and Muntin Assemblies

Now, on to the doors. Spend some extra time at the jointer when preparing your door frame stock to ensure the part surfaces are dead flat and square. Build all the door frames at once to economize your machining sequences. Once the rails and stiles (pieces 22, 23 and 24) are cut to size, mill ¼"-wide, ½"-deep centered grooves along one edge of these parts. These grooves will house the glass, muntin assemblies (pieces 25 and 26) and retainer strips (pieces 27 and 28). Follow the sidebar at right to make the corner joints. Glue up the door frames and complete them by trimming off the back lip of the rail and stile grooves to form a ½" x ½" rabbet. I used a router and piloted rabbeting bit for this task, then squared up the rounded corners where the bit couldn't reach with a chisel.

Rather than employing a single large piece of glass in the doors and dividing it with faux muntins, these doors feature working muntins and individual panes of glass (pieces 29). Essentially, the muntins are "stick built" into the door frames. They're easy as pie, and you don't need cope-and-stick bits. To make the dividers, mill long strips of both backers and muntins. Follow the three photos on the top of page 128 to install the muntin parts. Slip the glass panes into the rabbets formed by the muntins and backers, and then cut and fit four retainer strips around each glass pane. Mount the retainers to the door frames with hot-melt glue or silicone caulk; this way, the strips are easy to remove in the event a glass pane breaks someday.

Now comes a moment of truth: hanging the doors. If you've sized the doors and face frame openings carefully, a couple passes over the jointer should shave the doors down just enough to fit in their openings. Aim for about ¹⁄₁₆" of clear space all around to allow room for the hinge leaf thickness and swing clearance.

Haunched Tenons for Solid Corner Joints

These door frames are joined by rock-solid haunched tenons and mortises. Cut the mortises in the stiles first with a plunge router, drill press or mortising machine. Start the 1¼" long mortises a ½" in from the ends of the stiles, and cut them a bit deeper than necessary to allow extra room for glue to pool. Then set up your table saw and dado blade to cut 1¾" wide, 1¼" long tenons on the ends of the door rails.

Trim the haunch from the outside edge of the tenons to complete them. Index the haunches off the ends of the tenons with a ½"-thick stop block clamped to your rip fence. Once the joint parts are cut, refine their fit with a hand plane and chisel.

Keep trimming and test fitting until there's just a bit of friction between the mortises and tenons. Otherwise, an overly tight joint can introduce a twist into an otherwise flat frame, which is the last thing you'll want when hanging these flush-fitting doors.

Haunches on these door tenons add more glue surface area, which strengthens the joint. They also fill the ends of the full-length grooves in the stiles.

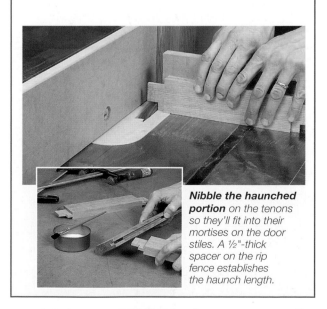

Nibble the haunched portion on the tenons so they'll fit into their mortises on the door stiles. A ½"-thick spacer on the rip fence establishes the haunch length.

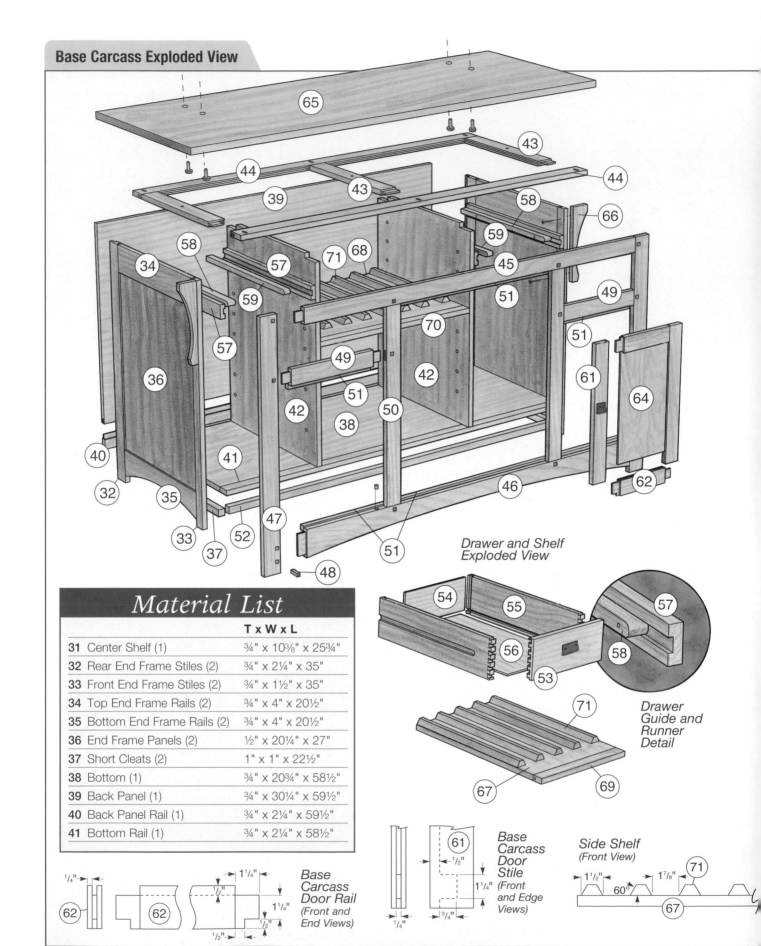

Drawer and Shelf Exploded View

Drawer Guide and Runner Detail

Material List

		T x W x L
31	Center Shelf (1)	¾" x 10⅜" x 25¾"
32	Rear End Frame Stiles (2)	¾" x 2¼" x 35"
33	Front End Frame Stiles (2)	¾" x 1½" x 35"
34	Top End Frame Rails (2)	¾" x 4" x 20½"
35	Bottom End Frame Rails (2)	¾" x 4" x 20½"
36	End Frame Panels (2)	½" x 20¼" x 27"
37	Short Cleats (2)	1" x 1" x 22½"
38	Bottom (1)	¾" x 20¾" x 58½"
39	Back Panel (1)	¾" x 30¼" x 59½"
40	Back Panel Rail (1)	¾" x 2¼" x 59½"
41	Bottom Rail (1)	¾" x 2¼" x 58½"

Base Carcass Door Rail (Front and End Views)

Base Carcass Door Stile (Front and Edge Views)

Side Shelf (Front View)

Material List

		T x W x L
42	Dividers (2)	¾" x 22½" x 30¼"
43	Support Frame Stiles (3)	¾" x 2½" x 19½"
44	Support Frame Rails (2)	¾" x 2½" x 58½"
45	Face Frame Top Rail (1)	¾" x 2¼" x 58"
46	Face Frame Bottom Rail (1)	¾" x 4" x 58"
47	Outer Face Frame Stiles (2)	¾" x 2½" x 35"
48	Face Frame Pegs (14)	⅜" x ⅜" x ¾"
49	Face Frame Drawer Rails (2)	¾" x 2¼" x 15¼"
50	Inner Face Frame Stiles (2)	¾" x 2¼" x 30¼"
51	Door Stops** (1)	½" x 1" x 120"
52	Long Cleat (1)	1" x 1" x 56½"
53	Drawer Fronts (2)	¾" x 5⅜" x 12⅝"
54	Drawer Backs (2)	¾" x 4⅝" x 11⅞"
55	Drawer Sides (4)	¾" x 5⅜" x 20"
56	Drawer Bottoms (2)	¼" x 11¾" x 19⅞"
57	Drawer Guides (4)	¾" x 2" x 22½"
58	Wide Drawer Runners (2)	¾" x 1¼" x 20¼"
59	Narrow Drawer Runners (2)	¾" x 1" x 20¼"
60	Tall Door Stiles (4)	¾" x 2¼" x 27¾"
61	Short Door Stiles (4)	¾" x 2¼" x 20"
62	Door Rails (8)	¾" x 2¼" x 10¾"
63	Tall Door Panels (2)	½" x 9" x 24"
64	Short Door Panels (2)	½" x 9" x 16¼"
65	Top (1)	1" x 25" x 68"
66	Corbels (2)	1" x 3" x 12"
67	Side Shelves (8)	¾" x 15¼" x 21¼"
68	Center Shelves (5)	¾" x 21¼" x 25¾"
69	Shelf Edging (8)	¾" x 1½" x 15¼"
70	Long Shelf Edging (5)	¾" x 1½" x 25¾"
71	Bottle Divider Strips (80)	¾" x 1½" x 18"

***Cut to fit.*

Base Carcass Support Frame
(Top View)

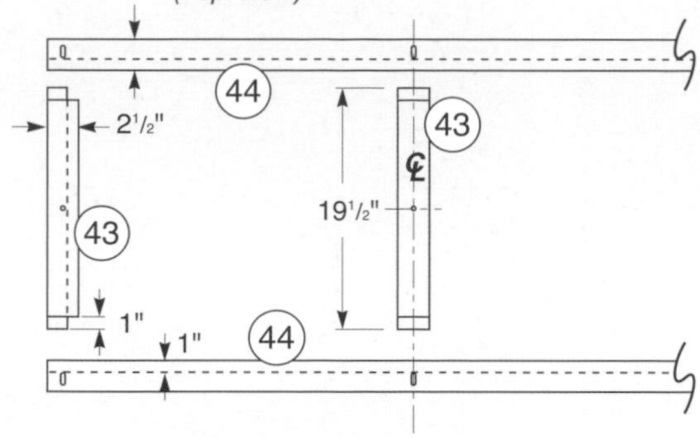

Base Carcass Face Frame
(Front View)

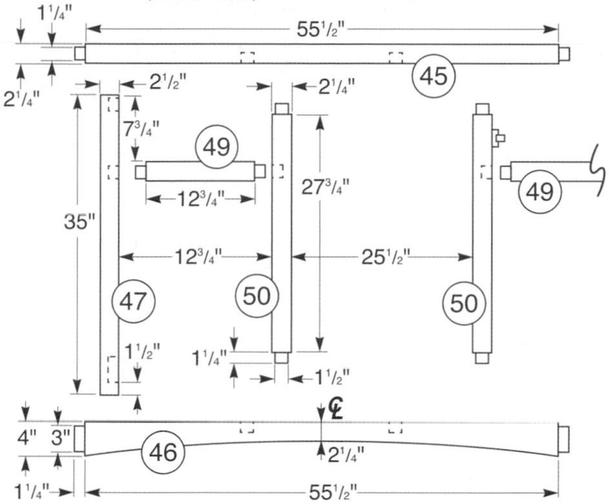

Corbel
(Front View)

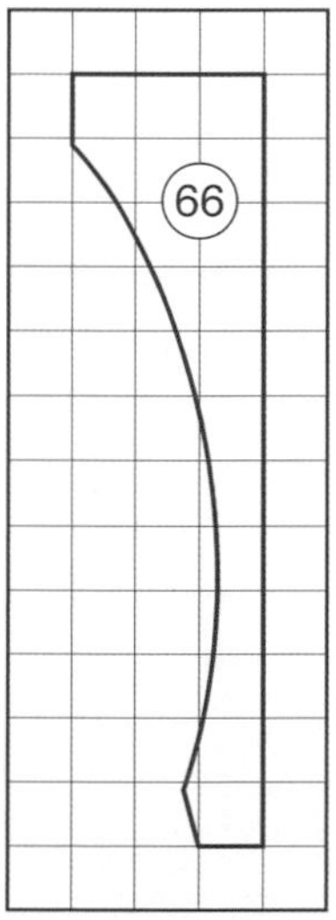

Each square equals 1"

Base Carcass Assembly Detail
(Top View)

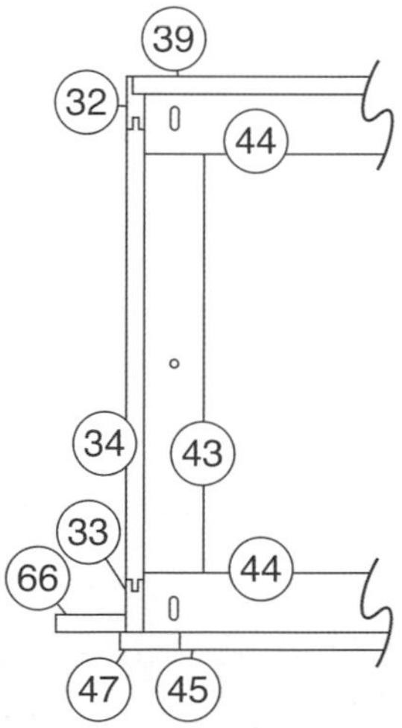

Base Carcass End Panel
(Front View)

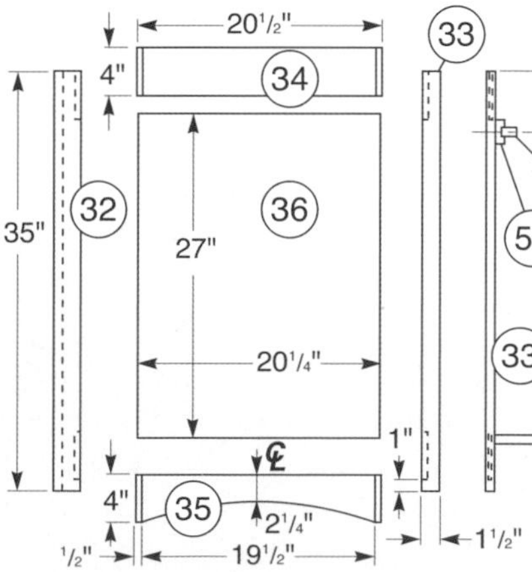

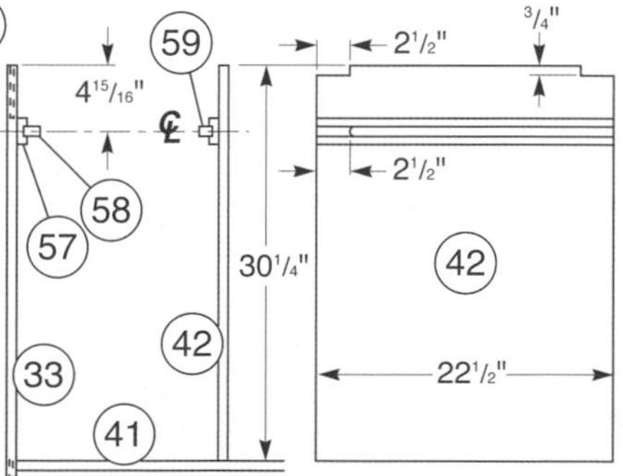

Base Carcass
Drawer Guide Locations
(Front and Side Views)

Cut, fit and glue *the vertical backer pieces into the door frame rabbets first, locating the backers so they'll be centered behind the long muntins (left photo). Flip the doors, then cut and glue the long, vertical muntin strips to these backers (right photo). Flip again to install the short horizontal backer pieces, followed by the short muntin strips. With enough spring clamps, you'll be able to assemble the muntins for an entire door or two at once without waiting for glue to dry.*

Drive 2" screws *through the support frame stiles to attach this frame to the end frames. Mount the support frame just shy of flush with the upper end frame rails. The offset will enable the support frame to pull the cabinet top down flat and hold it under tension.*

If you end up with a door that twists slightly or discover an out-of-square face frame opening (it happens to the best of us!), take a few shavings off the backs of the door frames or the edges and ends with a sharp low-angle block plane to improve the fit. The hinges you use may allow for some adjustment as well. You'll save yourself door hanging headaches and the effort of cutting all those hinge mortises if you use non-mortising hinges. Wrap up the assembly by making the side and center shelves (pieces 30 and 31).

Turning to the Base Carcass

Except for a few design details (and a couple of drawers), building the base cabinet is similar to constructing the upper cabinet. It's actually even easier. Start by cutting and assembling pieces 32 through 36 to create your end frames. The joinery for the frames and floating panels is the same as for the end frames on the upper cabinet, but this time stop the grooves in the stiles 1½" from the bottom ends. This will position the bottom curved rails 1" up from the floor.

Also, don't forget to cut the rabbet along the back edge of the back stiles.

Tackle the glue-ups for the wide, thin floating panels in two stages. First, glue up a couple of narrower blanks from thicker stock and mill them down to ½", then join these together to form the wide panels. It makes the thin, wide stock easier to clamp, and you'll have far fewer wet joints to manage during final clamping. Apply finish to the wide panels before assembling and pegging the end frames. Attach short cleats (pieces 37) with screws and glue to the bottom arched rails.

Make the bottom assembly, back panel assembly and dividers (pieces 38 through 42) and the support frame (pieces 43 and 44) next. You'll see in the Exploded Drawing, page 126, that the bottom and back panels have solid-wood rails along one edge joined to the plywood with tongues and grooves. Notch the top corners of the dividers so they'll fit around the support frame rails. The support frame rails and stiles are joined by deeper ¼" x 1" centered tongues and grooves. Cut three groups

of round and slotted holes in this frame for attaching the cabinet top later.

Time for some assembly. Drive screws up through the end frame cleats to attach these frames to the cabinet bottom. Fasten the support frame to the end frames with screws (see photo, above). Slip the divider panels in place and fasten these with more screws. Drill all the shelf support holes at this point, taking into account where the drawers will hang when you lay out your hole locations—no need for shelf supports there.

Build the base cabinet face frame (pieces 45 through 50) with the same joinery you used for the upper face frame. This time, however, bore holes for the pegs that secure the drawer rails to the inner face frame stiles before you assemble the full face frame. Otherwise, your mortiser might not reach these locations once the face frame is glued up. Cut the large arch in the bottom face frame rail prior to assembling the face frame but after tenoning the ends. Sand the curve smooth. Screw the door stops (pieces 51) behind the face frame openings, and nail the face frame to the cabinet. As an added measure of support, fasten a long cleat (piece 52) to the face frame and cabinet bottom with glue and countersunk screws.

Making the Drawers, Doors & Top

Refer to the Drawings on page 126 to construct the drawers (pieces 53, 54, 55 and 56) and mill the stopped dadoes in the drawer sides. These grooves fit over drawer runner assemblies (pieces 58 and 59) and keep the drawers tracking straight. Make the drawer guides and runners, rounding the front corners of the runners to fit the curved ends of the drawer dadoes. Screw together two pairs of runners

Slip the loose guide/runner assemblies into the drawer dadoes and slide the drawers and guides into their face frame openings to position them. Support the guides and drawers temporarily from below with clamps and scraps as you tack the guides in place. Test the drawer action, then fix the guides permanently with countersunk screws.

and drawer guides with the back ends of the parts held flush. Mount these inside the carcass to the end frames and dividers so they're centered on the drawer openings in the face frame (see photo below). The guides holding the wide runners fit against the end frames, and the narrow runners with their guides belong on the dividers (as shown in the Exploded View).

You're in the home stretch now, believe it or not! Build the four base cabinet doors (pieces 60 through 64), employing the same haunched tenon joinery as the upper glass doors and swapping wood panels for glass. Leave both lips of the tongue-and-groove joints intact this time. Hang the doors on their hinges. Apply finish to all the interior cabinet surfaces, drawers and doors before installing the back panel.

Glue up 5/4 stock in several subassemblies to make the base cabinet top (piece 65), then apply finish to all its surfaces. Mill the corbels to shape (pieces 66) and mount them flush against the face frame overhangs on the end frame stiles with screws. Fasten the top to the support frame with #10 panhead or washerhead screws.

Time for More Shelving

Cut plywood blanks (pieces 67 and 68) according to the Material List dimensions, and attach solid-wood edging (pieces 69 and 70) to the front edges with tongue-and-groove joints. Wrap the other exposed edges and end of each shelf with iron-on veneer edge tape to give the shelving a finished look. Bevel-rip the bottle divider (pieces 71) strips (yes, there are 80 in all!), and cut them to length. Nail five dividers to each side shelf and eight dividers to the center shelves. It helps to make a bevel-edged spacer block for separating the dividers evenly.

Dress this cabinet project with hammered copper Arts & Crafts door and drawer pulls. They may cost more than cheap imitations, but you won't regret the investment when you see how good they look.

Finishing Up

Apply the stain of your choice and follow up with several coats of satin varnish. Gel varnish is a good choice here: you can rub it on with a rag and avoid all the annoying drips and sags that happen when brushing varnish on vertical surfaces. Then rub some paste wax on the drawer runners. Install the door catches as well as the drawer and door pull hardware. To keep the upper cabinet safely upright on the base, run pairs of connector bolts and cap screws through the upper cabinet bottoms and the top of the base cabinet, or attach the cabinets with metal strapping and screws driven into the backs. Install shelf supports and slide in the shelving. Then take a well-deserved rest with a bottle of your best vintage…after all, this unit holds 67 of 'em!

by Rick White

SET OF ARTS & CRAFTS DINING ROOM CHAIRS

This Gustav Stickley-inspired set of chairs incorporates several elements of his Craftsman style: quartersawn oak, housed tenons, pyramid plugs and leather upholstery.

There's a well-founded belief among woodworkers that chairs are the most challenging projects to build. While that's true, the simple lines of these classic Craftsman-inspired pieces are well within the scope of most hobbyists' abilities. That's due, in large part, to the overriding philosophy behind their original inspiration, the Arts & Crafts movement. In the early 1900s, the Arts & Crafts philosophy swept Britain and the Americas, inspiring woodworkers to recreate the simplicity and function of medieval craftsmanship while adapting it to modern living.

My chair is a prime example of the pieces Gustav Stickley created after 1905, under the influence of noted architect Harvey Ellis. For a brief bit of time, Ellis worked for Stickley's *The Craftsman* magazine. During that short period, these two friends refined the earlier versions of Craftsman furniture and developed the look the world has come to admire: taller, more slender pieces that combine style and function.

Selecting Stock

While Gustav Stickley almost exclusively used quartersawn white oak, the same cut of red oak is quite acceptable. I settled on quartersawn red oak here because the lumber supplier had some excellent stock featuring dramatic ribbon effects.

The grain in a standard plain sawn board is tight at the edges and can be quite wide down the center. A quartersawn board, on the other hand, features tight grain across its entire width. This makes for a very stable piece of lumber. Whichever species you choose, let it acclimate to the humidity of your shop for at least a week before milling it to size.

Begin with the Back

The first step in construction is to lay out and cut the back legs (pieces 1) to size and shape. The legs are cut from 1½" thick by 3" wide stock. If possible, start with 8/4 rough stock and plane it until you reach the correct thickness.

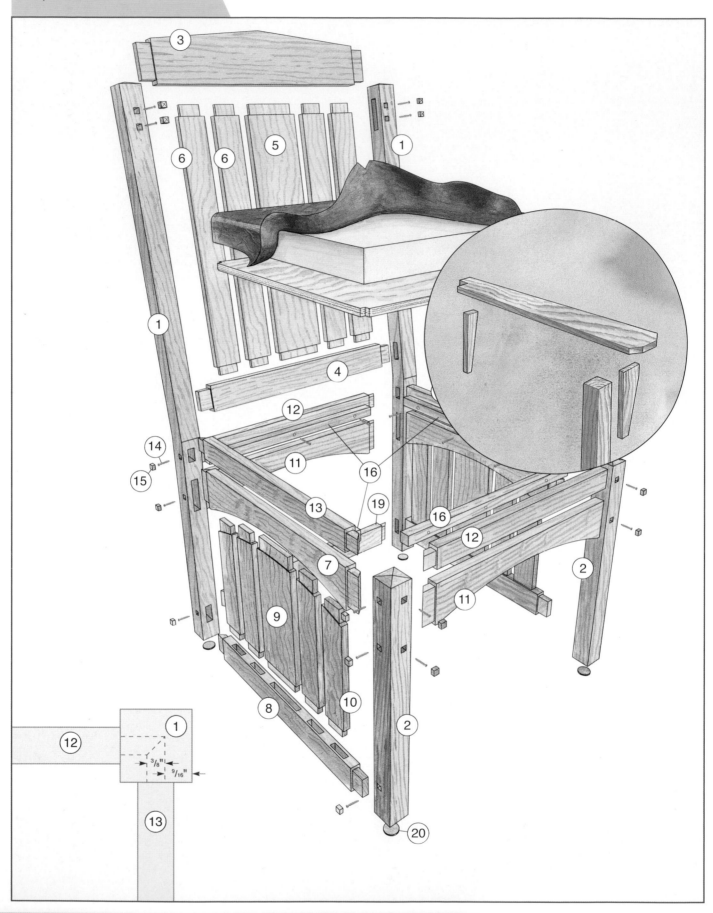

Material List - Dining Room Chairs

		T x W x L			T x W x L
1	Back Legs (2)	1½" x 3" x 42¼"	**11**	Front and Back Arched Rails (2)	¾" x 3" x 18⅝"
2	Front Legs (2)	1½" x 1½" x 17⅝"	**12**	Front and Back Seat Rails (2)	¾" x 1½" x 18⅝"
3	Backrest Top Rail (1)	¾" x 3½" x 18⅝"	**13**	Side Seat Rails (2)	¾" x 1½" x 18⅝"
4	Backrest Bottom Rail (1)	¾" x 2" x 18⅝"	**14**	Tenon Screws (20)	#6 x ⅝"
5	Backrest Center Slat (1)	½" x 4" x 18⅝"	**15**	Tenon Screw Pegs (20)	⅜" x ⅜" x ½"
6	Backrest Exterior Slats (4)	½" x 2" x 18⅝"	**16**	Seat Support Cleats (4)	¾" x ¾" x 15⅝"
7	Side Arched Rails (2)	¾" x 3" x 18⅝"	**17**	Plywood Seat (1)	¾" x 17¼" x 17¼"
8	Side Bottom Rails (2)	¾" x 2" x 18⅝"	**18**	Cleat Screws (12)	#6 x 1¼"
9	Side Center Slats (2)	½" x 4" x 10¹⁄₁₆"	**19**	Back Bottom Rail (1)	¾" x 2" x 18⅝"
10	Side Exterior Slats (8)	½" x 2" x 10¹⁄₁₆"	**20**	Leg Pads (4)	1" Dia.

Making Mortises Mechanically

There's no great secret to cutting the stopped mortises used in this project. Since the dawn of the 20th century, advances in power tools have made the process a whole lot easier. The original Arts & Crafts builders would have bored out most of the mortise with a bit and brace, or chopped them with a stout mortiising chisel, then finished the cuts with finely sharpened chisels. Now there is a new generation of easy-to-use mortising machines. Once you count the number of mortises in each chair and multiply by four, perhaps you'll conclude there is a new mortising machine in your future.

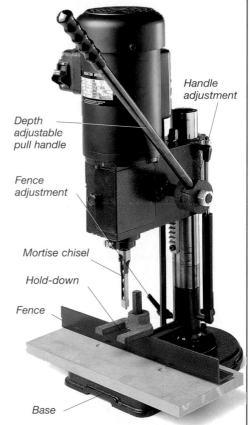

Handle adjustment

Depth adjustable pull handle

Fence adjustment

Mortise chisel

Hold-down

Fence

Base

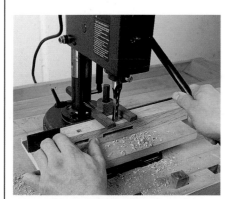

Drilling square holes *is a snap with a mortising machine. Here's how it works: an auger-like drill bit is housed inside of a square hollow chisel. Available in many standard sizes — and able to form mortises in hard and soft wood — these machines are true time savers.*

A lever locks the fence *on this model in place. A hex nut secures the U-shaped hold-down. The key advantage of a mortising machine over a mortise attachment on your drill press is the longer stroke of the machine, allowing for deeper one-step mortises.*

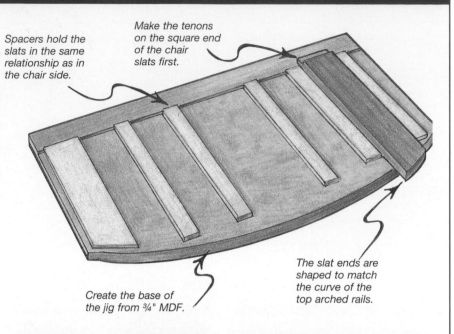

Spacers hold the slats in the same relationship as in the chair side.

Make the tenons on the square end of the chair slats first.

The slat ends are shaped to match the curve of the top arched rails.

Create the base of the jig from ¾" MDF.

Use a routing jig and a flush trimming bearing bit to cut the gentle arc onto each chair slat, as shown at left. To start the tenons on the curved tops of the side slats, use a ⅜" piloted rabbeting bit, as shown at right.

We made the curved tops of the side slats with this simple jig. The spacers hold the slats in position while you form the curves on their tops. Before clamping them into the jig, cut the tenons on the bottom end of each slat on your table saw. Now run a flush trimming bearing bit around the curved end of the jig to create the gentle arc on the top of each slat. Move to your router table and use a ⅜" piloted rabbeting bit to form the cheeks on the curved ends of the slats. Finish the tenons by notching their shoulders on the bandsaw.

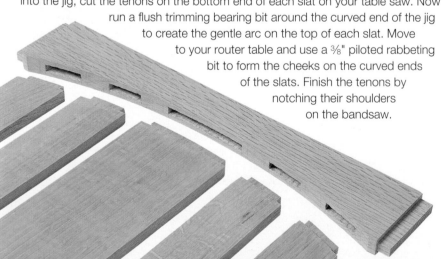

Follow the profile on the Technical Drawings, page 136, to lay out the back legs, then bandsaw them to shape. Next, slice the front legs (pieces 2) from the same 1½" stock. Belt-sand all four faces of each leg, then refer to the Elevation Drawings to establish and mark the locations of the leg mortises. These mortise locations (see Figure 1) create right and left chair pieces. Now is the time to make the pyramid details on the top of the legs. See the sidebar on the next page to learn the technique.

The backrest of the chair is comprised of two rails (pieces 3 and 4) and five vertical slats (pieces 5 and 6). The rails are joined to the back legs with mortise and tenon joinery, just as the slats are joined to the rails. Cut these pieces to size. Form mortises and tenons as required, following the Technical Drawings.

Building the First Subassembly

With the backrest rails and slats milled, there's only one detail to address before you can complete your first subassembly. Following the profile shown on the Technical Drawings, lay out the angular cut on the top edge of the backrest

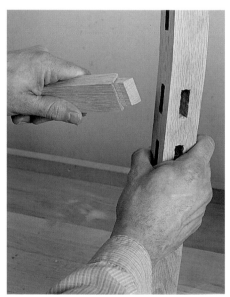

Figure 1: *Mortise and tenon joinery is the key to this chair's durability. Different mortise locations create right and left chair parts. Some of the tenons are mitered to meet inside the uprights.*

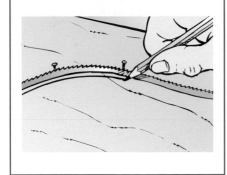
Pyramids: The Great ... and the Small

In a reflection of the medieval origins of his style, Stickley often softened the tops of his chair legs by milling mild chamfers that met to form a four-sided pyramid. You can duplicate this effect by setting a sharp, fine tooth, crosscut blade to 15°, then using your table saw's miter gauge to help you make these cuts. If your saw table is too big for the crooked back leg to lie flat, simply raise the blade, reverse the piece, and run the gauge in the opposite slot. To make the small pyramid plugs, sand long thin pieces of stock on your stationary sander with the miter gauge set at 15°. Then trim them to length with your bandsaw.

top rail, then trim it to shape on your bandsaw. Belt-sand the saw marks until they are gone, then give the rails and slats a thorough sanding to 180 grit.

Dry fit the slat tenons in the rail mortises and, when everything fits perfectly, glue and clamp them together (see Figure 2, page 138). Make sure the subassembly is perfectly flat and square when you tighten the clamps, then set the backrest aside to dry.

The Four Arched Rails

Perhaps the most challenging aspect of this chair is forming the side subassemblies. Each of these is composed of an arched top rail (pieces 7), a flat bottom rail (pieces 8) and five slats (pieces 9 and 10).

After cutting these parts, along with the final two arched rails (pieces 11) to the dimensions shown on the Material List, follow the Technical Drawings to lay out the mortises in the side arched rails. Chop these mortises, then make a full-sized pattern for the arched profile. Trace the shape onto all four of the chair's curved rails, and band saw them to shape. Clean up the cuts with a drum sander chucked in your drill press.

It's essential that assembly takes place on a flat, stable surface and that each component is checked for squareness and plumb as the clamps are tightened.

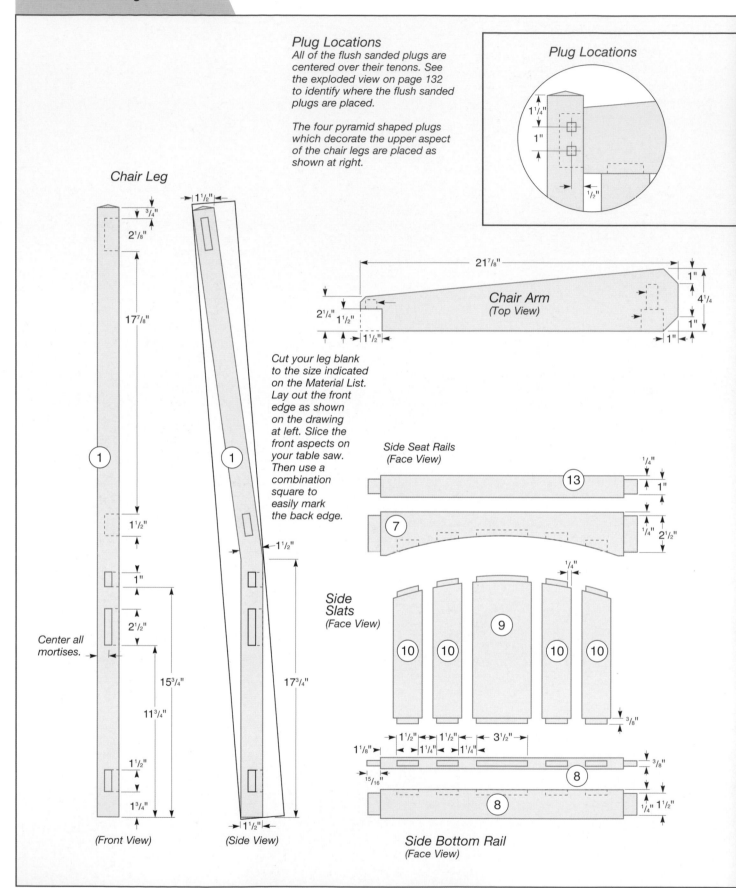

Plug Locations

All of the flush sanded plugs are centered over their tenons. See the exploded view on page 132 to identify where the flush sanded plugs are placed.

The four pyramid shaped plugs which decorate the upper aspect of the chair legs are placed as shown at right.

Plug Locations

Chair Leg

Cut your leg blank to the size indicated on the Material List. Lay out the front edge as shown on the drawing at left. Slice the front aspects on your table saw. Then use a combination square to easily mark the back edge.

Center all mortises.

(Front View)

(Side View)

Chair Arm
(Top View)

Side Seat Rails
(Face View)

Side Slats
(Face View)

Side Bottom Rail
(Face View)

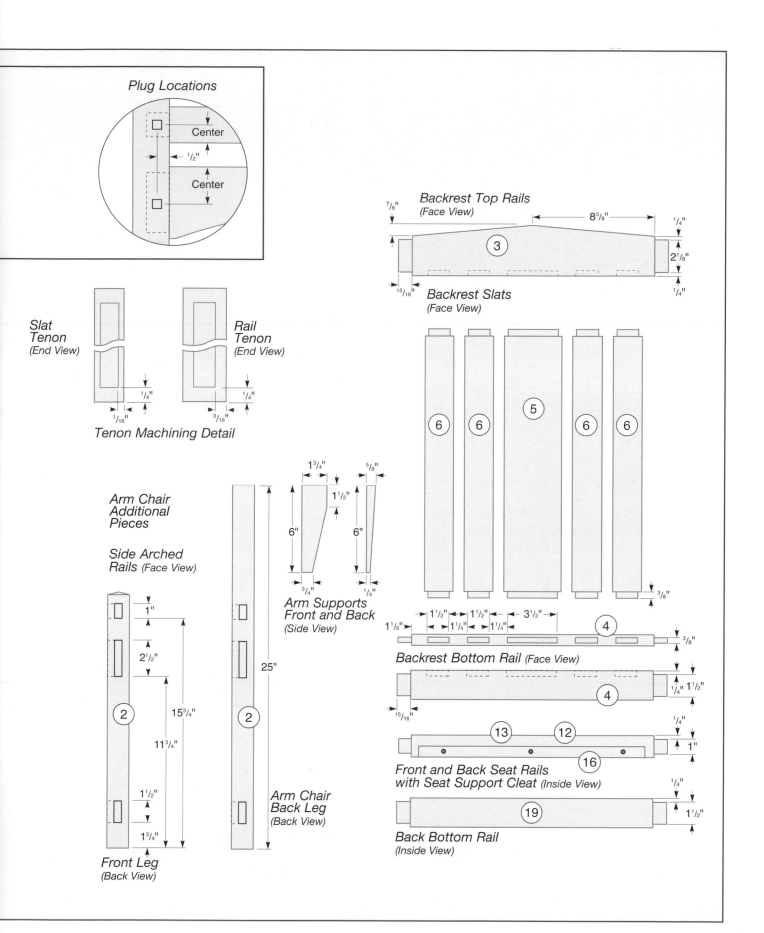

Plug Locations

Center

$^{1}/_{2}$"

Center

Slat
Tenon
(End View)

Rail
Tenon
(End View)

$^{1}/_{4}$"

$^{1}/_{16}$"

$^{1}/_{4}$"

$^{3}/_{16}$"

Tenon Machining Detail

Backrest Top Rails
(Face View)

$^{7}/_{8}$"

$8^{3}/_{8}$"

$^{1}/_{4}$"

③

$2^{1}/_{8}$"

$^{15}/_{16}$"

$^{1}/_{4}$"

Backrest Slats
(Face View)

⑥ ⑥ ⑤ ⑥ ⑥

Arm Chair
Additional
Pieces

Side Arched
Rails (Face View)

$1^{3}/_{4}$"

$^{5}/_{8}$"

$1^{1}/_{2}$"

6"

6"

25"

$^{3}/_{4}$"

$^{1}/_{4}$"

Arm Supports
Front and Back
(Side View)

$^{3}/_{8}$"

$1^{1}/_{2}$" $1^{1}/_{2}$" $3^{1}/_{2}$"

$1^{1}/_{8}$" $1^{1}/_{4}$" $1^{1}/_{4}$"

④

$^{3}/_{8}$"

1"

$2^{1}/_{2}$"

Backrest Bottom Rail (Face View)

②

②

$15^{3}/_{4}$"

$11^{3}/_{4}$"

④

$^{1}/_{4}$" $1^{1}/_{2}$"

$^{15}/_{16}$"

$1^{1}/_{2}$"

⑬ ⑫

$^{1}/_{4}$"

1"

$1^{3}/_{4}$"

⑯

Front and Back Seat Rails
with Seat Support Cleat (Inside View)

Front Leg
(Back View)

Arm Chair
Back Leg
(Back View)

$^{1}/_{4}$"

⑲

$1^{1}/_{2}$"

Back Bottom Rail
(Inside View)

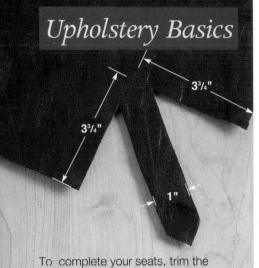

To complete your seats, trim the leather to a 24"x 24" square. Then, on the rough side of the leather, mark a 3¾" square in each corner. Next, mark a 1" strip diagonally from the inside marked corner to the outside edge of the leather. Trim on your lines to create the shape shown above.

Cut 2" thick high density foam *on your bandsaw with the table set at 30°. The smaller face of the foam should match the size of the plywood. Round over the plywood edges.*

Gently pull the side flaps *up and secure the leather with staples. Keep the tension across the seat even. Pull the strip up snugly and staple as shown below. If the corner is too bulky, you may need to trim a bit of foam.*

Follow the procedure shown on page 68 to mill the curved tenons on the top of the side slats. Create the bottom rails and arched rails with mitered tenons as indicated on the Drawings. The tenons on the bottom rail penetrating the front leg are not mitered. When they fit snugly, glue and clamp them together, checking to be sure they are flat and square. While the glue dries, mill mitered tenons on the final two arched rails and the four seat rails (pieces 12 and 13).

Preassembly Details

While mortise and tenon joinery is extremely strong, a dining chair is subject to a lot of use and movement. To help prevent the joinery from ever loosening up, most of the tenons are locked into their mortises with short screws driven through the shoulders into the mortise walls. These screws (pieces 14) are set below the surface in their own small mortises, then plugged with square hardwood pegs (pieces 15). Locate all 20 of these small mortises on the Exploded Drawings, page 132, then chop them to size.

Four cleats (pieces 16) support the plywood seat (piece 17). Cut these to size, then refer to the Technical Drawings for the locations of the screws (pieces 18) that will hold them in place. Predrill countersunk pilot holes for these screws, then cut the back bottom rail (piece 19) to size and mill mitered tenons on its ends (see Technical Drawings). Sand all the chair elements to 180 grit before starting the final assembly procedure.

Assembling the Chair

There's a logical order to the assembly process: you'll work from the back to the front. Begin by laying out all the parts and subassemblies, so you're not searching for pieces while reaching for clamps. Dry-fit everything to make sure there are no problems before you start gluing. If you need a hammer to close any joints, they're fitting too tightly. Refine them as needed before going on with assembly.

Lay one of the back legs on its side, then glue the seat back subassembly, the

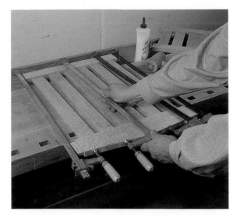

Figure 2: *Glue up the subassemblies of the back and chair sides. Make sure they are flat and square. After the glue has cured, move on to the final assembly.*

back seat rail, the back arched rail and the back bottom rail snugly in place. Turn them upside down and glue their tenons into the mortises in the other back leg, clamping the entire subassembly so it is flat and square. Drive home the four small screws in the top, front screw mortises. Let the glue cure before moving ahead.

When the glue is dry, lay the back subassembly on its back and glue the two side subassemblies in place, along with the two side seat rails. Working quickly now, glue the front seat rail and arched rail into the front legs, then glue and clamp the front subassembly to the sides. Snug up your clamps and stand the chair on a flat, level surface before tightening them. Make sure that

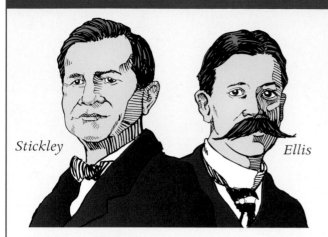
everything is square and true as you apply pressure, then drive home the rest of the small tenon screws.

After the glue dries, plug all the screw holes. The easiest way to do this is to rip a long piece of stock to the thickness and width of the plugs, then trim them a little longer than you need them. Four of the plugs are sanded to small pyramids and glued in place. The rest are glued in place and sanded flush. Level the legs if needed (see below) and move on to finishing.

Finishing Thoughts

After a final sanding, I applied Bartley's dark walnut stain, then sealed it with three coats of a compatible low luster finish. Polyurethane is a good choice, because it's rugged enough to endure the constant handling and use of a dining room chair. Another good topcoat would be lacquer, if you're set up to spray it.

Stickley's seats were often upholstered in soft, brown leather. After all this hard work on the chair frames, it would be a fitting final touch for your chairs, too. For instructions on completing that task, refer to the sidebar on the preceding page. When you're done, screw the seat support cleats in place and attach the plywood seat to them with screws. Stick a felt pad (piece 20) to the bottom of each leg, and you're ready to start seating guests at your celebration dinner party.

On a level surface, *check to see if your chair rocks. If it does, make a line exactly the same distance up from the surface on all four chair legs. Sand carefully to the lines, and your chair will sit flat.*

by Mike McGlynn

WRIGHT-INSPIRED STOOL

Chairs can be a little intimidating to build, but the knowledge you'll gain
from trying is as sweet as the project you'll end up with if you work carefully.
Mike McGlynn, our designer here, says take the plunge: If you can build a few
jigs, template-rout and cut mortise and tenon joints, you're well suited for this job.

This chair project was adapted from a Frank Lloyd Wright design first included in the Husser House (1899): one of the first to show elements of what would later become known as the Prairie style. For my client, the design had to be modified into a bar-height stool, so I added rails to the base to strengthen the structure (which wasn't necessarily one of Wright's typical design elements).

This is not an easy project, and many woodworkers shy away from building chairs. But while this design calls for some difficult joinery, if you take it step by step, you'll do fine. The underlying principle behind all of these joinery choices is strength. No piece of furniture takes as much abuse as a chair: if you don't make it bombproof, it will soon become loose and fall apart.

Selecting Suitable Stock

You'll need some ⁸⁄₄ stock for the legs and ⁵⁄₄ for the other parts. Select straight-grained stock, which lessens the chances of warping and looks better with Wright's designs. The wood should be well-dried with even moisture content, and you should let the boards sit in your shop for a week or two before starting, so they can acclimate.

While you are letting the wood adjust, get started by making the leg templates. These templates will not only help you lay out your parts, but they will also be used as shaping templates later on. I like to make my templates out of ½" baltic birch plywood; it stays straight and has solid edges. Lay out your templates as shown in the Technical Drawings, on pages 148 and 149, then

saw them out with a combination of your band and table saws. It is important that you do an accurate job on these templates. Make sure all the straight lines are true, all the curves are fair and the edges are square. Now lay out and drill the attachment holes and dowel marking holes (for the crest rail). Find their locations in the drawings.

The author has a large professional shaper to use for template-shaping. A router table equipped with a piloted flush-trim bit is a more likely small shop alternative. Shape the long planes of the legs with the setup shown at right—then shape the curved ends and feet by hand.

Build an Angled Tenon Ramp

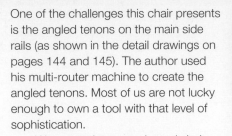

One of the challenges this chair presents is the angled tenons on the main side rails (as shown in the detail drawings on pages 144 and 145). The author used his multi-router machine to create the angled tenons. Most of us are not lucky enough to own a tool with that level of sophistication.

We created a ramp-shaped sled, secured to the miter gauge, to form the angled tenons. Because the lower and upper tenons are located on the legs at different positions (again see the detail drawings), you will need to create two ramps, at slightly different angles. See the drawing and instructions on page 145 for more details.

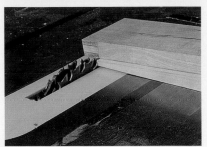

Flop the ramp to form the angled tenons for each rail. Secure the ramp to the miter gauge with screws. It's a slick solution to a tricky problem.

As soon as you're comfortable that your stock has acclimated, mill your leg stock. Face-joint one side, then plane the stock to the 1⁷⁄₁₆" dimension. Sand the faces of your planks after planing—it's easier to sand milling marks off a nice, wide board. Lay out the legs (pieces 1 and 2) using the templates. It's fine and dandy to nestle the legs to get more pieces out of each board, just remember you're going to have to cut them slightly oversize, so leave a bit of room to maneuver.

Cut the leg blanks out with your band saw. Leave between ¹⁄₁₆" and ⅛" extra to mill off when you template-shape them. Don't leave more than ⅛" because it results in chipping, especially if you do the shaping on a router table.

Template-shaping is a great way to ensure that multiple pieces match perfectly. It's also a great way to destroy parts and injure yourself if you are not careful. The keys to safe template-shaping are: Leave no more than ⅛", and preferably ¹⁄₁₆", to mill off. You must keep your hands well away from the cutter. Your template must be attached to your stock so it can't flex and you must know which way the cutter is rotating and how it will interact with the wood grain.

When you're wrapping up this project, you don't want to be filling screw holes on the outside of the legs. That's why you should attach your templates to the inside faces—so the screws can be strategically driven into the areas that will later become mortises.

Use a shaper if possible, as it's more stable and you can use a bigger cutter. If not, a router table will work fine if you are careful. Have a piece of scrap wood to practice on before you start with your actual parts.

When you're finished shaping all the legs, clean up your milling marks with a sharp scraper and some sandpaper. Note: The faces you are cleaning up must remain square and flat because some will be joint faces. Then move to the table saw to cut any excess off the feet, to ensure all the legs are the exact same length.

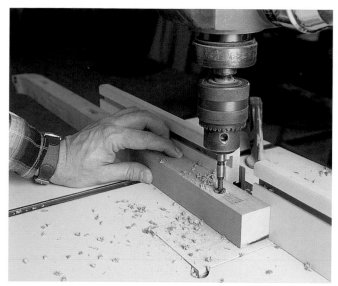

The mortises on the legs are the same size, but they are asymmetrically placed. Use a sharp Forstner bit to rough them out, then clean out the remaining waste with chisels.

The author's multi-router allowed him to create angled tenons with ease. We designed a tapered ramp (see facing page) to help you achieve the same results with a table saw.

Mortise and Tenon Joinery

Now we come to the heart and soul of chairmaking: the joints. Many of these mortise and tenon joints are angled, which makes them more difficult (see the sidebar, left). However you cut the mortise and tenons, the mortises should be cut first. As you will notice in the drawings on pages 148 and 149, all the mortises are the same size: ½" x 1½". Completely lay out all the mortises on one front and back leg to use for the drill press setup (shown above), then just mark the centerline of all other mortises on the rest of the legs. Sort your legs into matching pairs and complete the boring. After the mortises

are chopped, cut all the rails (pieces 3 through 10), except the crest rail, from 1" stock. Lay out your tenons with as much accuracy as you can muster, using scrap lumber to check your setups as you go. When all these joints are done, there is the matter of the mortises for the back slats. Make a pair of slat receivers (pieces 11) and cut notches into them as shown in the right photo, below. Don't forget to plow a groove in the bottom back rail for one of these receivers.

There are a couple more steps before you can move on to the crest rail. The first procedure is to form the angle on the front legs (see left photo, 146). Here again it pays to have

Notched Slat Receivers

Rather than chop a series of small mortises, cut two slat receivers and notch them on your table saw. If your layout is off by just a little bit, the regimented orientation of the slats will make your error noticeable.

The author used his multi-router to create tiny round tenons on the ends of the slats. Our alternate method is "notched slat receivers" (see page 148).

Lay out and notch the slat receivers in matched pairs on your table saw. In this operation, accuracy is critical, so work carefully for best results.

Material List - Stool

		T x W x L
1	Back Legs (2)	1⁷⁄₁₆" x 2⅛" x 54"
2	Front Legs (2)	1⁷⁄₁₆" x 2⅛" x 31"
3	Upper Side Rails (2)	1" x 3½" x 17"
4	Middle Side Rails (2)	1" x 2" x 17¼"
5	Lower Side Rails (2)	1" x 2" x 17¼"
6	Lower Front Rail (1)	1" x 2" x 16"
7	Lower Back Rail (1)	1" x 2" x 14⅜"
8	Middle Front Rail (1)	1" x 2" x 16"
9	Upper Back Rail (1)	1" x 2" x 14¼"
10	Upper Front Rail (1)	1" x 3½" x 16⅛"
11	Slat Receivers (2)	⅜" x ¾" x 12⅛"
12	Crest Rail (1)	¾" x 6" x 12⅛"
13	Corner Blocks (2)	1⁷⁄₁₆" x 2⅛" x 3⅛"
14	Trim Cap (1)	½" x 1³⁄₁₆" x 54"
15	Trim (1)	¼" x ½" x 54"
16	Slats (11)	⅜" x ⅝" x 43½"

*Upper Rails
Tenon Detail*
(Top View)

*Middle and Lower
Rails Tenon Detail*
(Top View)

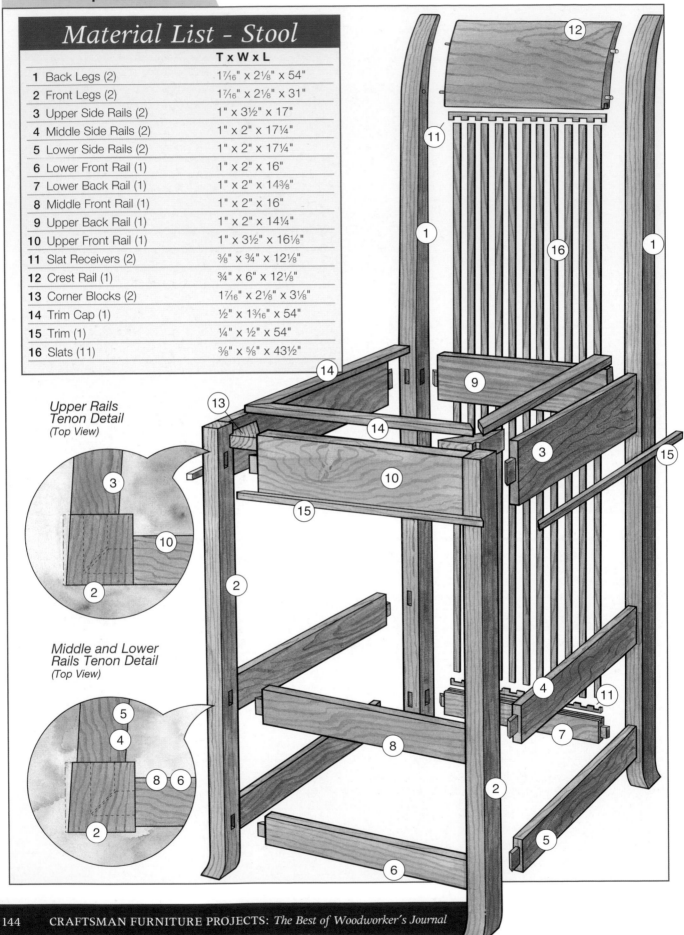

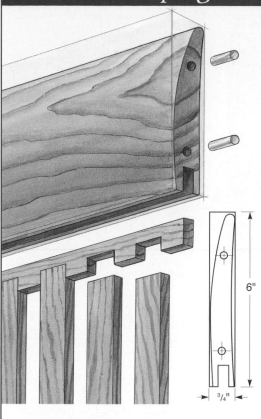

The layout for this doweling jig appears on page 149.

Cut your stock 27" long so you can shape two rails at once (assuming you're making more than one chair), and then step to the table saw to plow the groove for the slat receiver.

The next step is to shape the front and back faces of the crest rails. Mike made a round-bottom wooden plane for this step, shaping the back (concave) face by planing on a marked line and gradually flaring out from there. The same task could be accomplished with chisels and scrapers, but it will just take longer. Shaping the front (convex) face is much easier, because you can use a regular flat-bottomed plane. Once again, you should mark a center line—in this case the high point—but, in addition, you should mark both the edges and ends for how much material you need to take off. When both faces are shaped, you will need to sand them smooth and round over the top edge. This can be done with a light, sure touch and a random orbit sander. Cut the rails to length on your table saw with the concave side down. It is also a good idea to put masking tape over the outline on the concave side to prevent chipping.

an extra blank to test your set-up. Now move on to mitering the tenons. Even though you want as much gluing surface as possible, allow $\frac{1}{32}$" to $\frac{1}{16}$" between the mitered tenon faces for glue squeeze-out.

A Defining Element: The Crest Rail

The crest rail (piece 12) is complex, time-consuming and one of the truly defining elements of this design. Work very carefully as you shape it, referring to the sidebar above for the procedure to create the concave and convex shapes.

Once you've got the shape right, the last step on the crest rail is the dowel joints. Like everything else about the crest rail, this is a rather complex job and requires a well-made jig. The positions of the dowel holes in the legs are marked by

lightly tapping a small brad through the appropriately sized holes previously drilled in your template. A detailed drawing of the doweling jig for the crest rail is shown on page 149. Build the jig starting with a base cut to $\frac{3}{4}$" x 8" x 13$\frac{5}{8}$". Rip a $\frac{1}{2}$" x 1" x 13$\frac{5}{8}$" cleat. Attach it flush to one long base edge. Now cut two $\frac{3}{4}$" x 2" x 8" jig ends. Glue and nail them in place and locate the holes as shown in the drawing. Test the jig with scrap lumber. You must be very accurate in the drilling of the dowel holes in the legs and crest rail. They must line up perfectly, so the jig needs to be dead-on.

Now comes the fun part—sanding everything up to 220 grit. Note: Be very careful about not rounding the wrong edges as you work.

Simple Upholstery

While not exactly woodworking, upholstery (as done here) is an easily mastered skill. Two tools will make upholstering much easier: A power staple gun of some sort and a webbing stretcher. Follow the steps below to top off your chair.

Use 3" nylon webbing: fold over a small flap and staple it, stretch and staple again. Weave the webbing to increase strength and durability. The webbing must be evenly spaced on the frame.

Cut the foam to size and bevel its edges. Start the upholstery process by wrapping the frame and foam with muslin cloth. You don't have to remove every single wrinkle during the muslin-wrapping step.

Wrap and staple the cover (cloth or leather) in place, taking care to keep it wrinkle-free. Pay special attention to the corners. Complete the upholstery by stapling on a bottom cloth.

Moving on to Assembly

I prefer to assemble the sides of the chairs first, then assemble the sides to one another. I also use West System epoxy for the adhesive. If you want these chairs to last one or two lifetimes, this is the glue that will do it. Before you start to assemble, do two more things that will help prevent foul language. First, ease all sharp tenon corners; this will prevent the tenons from catching as they're inserted. Second, start with a clean, padded bench surface with all the equipment and supplies that will be required—there's nothing worse than having something half-assembled and precariously balanced and then realizing you don't have the right clamp at hand!

The assembly itself is pretty straightforward. With a glue brush, apply glue to all appropriate mortises on the back leg. Slip in the rails. Apply glue to the front leg mortises, slip it in place and clamp this subassembly with bar clamps. Epoxy usually takes eight to twelve hours to cure, so you may have to complete one side in the morning and the other in the evening.

Once each of the sides have cured, they can be assembled to each other, just as before, with one exception: Before inserting your tenons, check each mortise for hardened glue and clean it out with a chisel.

When these assemblies have cured, there are several small items to take care of before you can apply finish. Fabricate and install the corner blocks (pieces 13). Glue them in place with spring clamps or a bar clamp and notched caul. Before you can get to the next step—installation of seat rail trim—you need to be sure the seat rails and front legs are perfectly flush with one another. Despite your best efforts, there may be some subtle misalignments here—trust me.

With utmost patience, a sharp scraper, block plane and a hard sanding block, true up any discrepancies. The seat rail trim cap (piece 14) is the easier of the two trim strips to install. Miter, trim to fit,

After the mortises are chopped, the front legs are sliced to match the angled shape of the chair's footprint.

Be sure to gather all the supplies and equipment you'll need for the glue-up before you start the process.

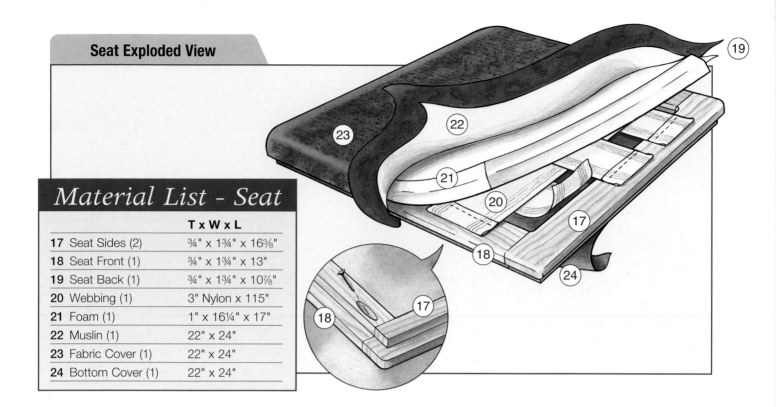

Seat Exploded View

Material List - Seat

	T x W x L
17 Seat Sides (2)	¾" x 1¾" x 16⅜"
18 Seat Front (1)	¾" x 1¾" x 13"
19 Seat Back (1)	¾" x 1¾" x 10⅞"
20 Webbing (1)	3" Nylon x 115"
21 Foam (1)	1" x 16¼" x 17"
22 Muslin (1)	22" x 24"
23 Fabric Cover (1)	22" x 24"
24 Bottom Cover (1)	22" x 24"

tack and glue it in place. The trim strip (piece 15) on the bottom of the rails is a little more complex, as it has to be applied with glue only. It is best to do the two side pieces first and the face piece last. The front miter must land exactly on the corner as you glue the strips on. The last step is to install the back slats (pieces 16). These slats are simple to make and install. Snap the slats into place by inserting one end and gently flexing each slat; you'll be able to pop the other end right in. (Don't forget to glue them first.) Lastly, attach the slats to the back seat rail with two small nails apiece. Use a temporary spacer block so they don't end up crooked.

Before finishing, there are a couple of prep steps to complete. First fill and sand the nail holes in the slats and the uncovered template screw holes on the legs. Choose a putty that, when finished, will be somewhat darker than the wood itself. This will allow for the natural wood darkening that occurs with age.

Applying Finish

There are many choices of finish that could be used on these chairs. I recommend Deft Oil: it's easy to apply, goes a long way and enhances the look of most woods. The drawback to oil is that it is not very durable. So after the oil has completely cured, follow it up with polyurethane. Apply three coats, smoothing between each application with extra-fine steel wool.

Making the Upholstered Seat

There is only one thing left to complete your chair: the upholstered seat. Many people might feel it best to farm this job out to an upholstery shop, but it is not a difficult task. The first step is to build the frames (pieces 17 through 19). Most upholstery frames are made of a medium-density hardwood that is strong but not so hard that it is difficult to staple into. Poplar is a good choice. The dimensions of the frame are shown on page 149. As you can see, the joinery is simple— glued butt joints and pocket screws. After you have glued up the frame, cut a rabbet around the outside. This is easily done on a table saw. Next, round over the outside and inside top edge with a ⅜" roundover bit. This roundover provides a smooth edge to the seat and eliminates sharp edges that might bear against the webbing. Break any sharp edges with sandpaper to reduce wear on the cloth. Follow the steps in the sidebar, left, if you do the upholstery yourself.

I don't attach a seat like this to the chair frame; it sits nicely in place, and it's a nice convenience to be able to just lift it out of the frame when somebody spills something on it. So, that's it! You've completed a master class in woodworking…take a load off and enjoy. It just so happens you've got a good-looking place to do just that.

Slat Receiver (Side View)

⊄

⑪

3/8"

To mill the slat receivers, put a 5/8" dado head in your table saw. Form the center dado first and work your way out to the ends.

7/16" 5/8" 3/8"

Upper Back and Side Rail Detail
(Top View)

① ⑨ ③
1 1/16" 1/8"
1/2" 1/8" 11/16"
1/2" 4°

⑫

⑯

①

Upper Rail Subassembly
(Top View)

⑨

Right Back Leg

③ ③

⑬

Right Front Leg

⑩

Upper Front and Side Rail Detail
(Top View)

⑬ ③
4°
1/4"
1/2" 1 1/8"
⑩ 1/2"
1/4" ②
1"

Tenon Detail
(Side View)

③ ⑨
⑩
1"
1 1/2"
1"

⑭
⑩
⑮
②

Lower and Middle Side Rail Detail
(Top View)

1 3/32"
1/4" ①
1/2" 1 1/8"
⑦ 3/32"
1/2" ④
3°

Middle and Lower Rail Subassembly
(Top View)

⑦
5/16" 3/8"
15"
12 1/8"

④ ④
⑤ ⑤

⑥ ⑧
14 1/8"

Note: The lower back rail (piece 7) joins the back legs as shown at right. There is no corresponding middle back rail. See the Exploded View on page 144.

⑧

⑥

(Front View)

Lower and Middle Front Rail Detail
(Top View)

④ ⑤
3°
1/8"
⑥ 1/2" 1 1/16"
⑧ 1/2"
1/4" ②
15/16"

Tenon Detail (Side View)

④ ⑤ ⑦ ⑥ ⑧
1/4"
1 1/2"
1/4"

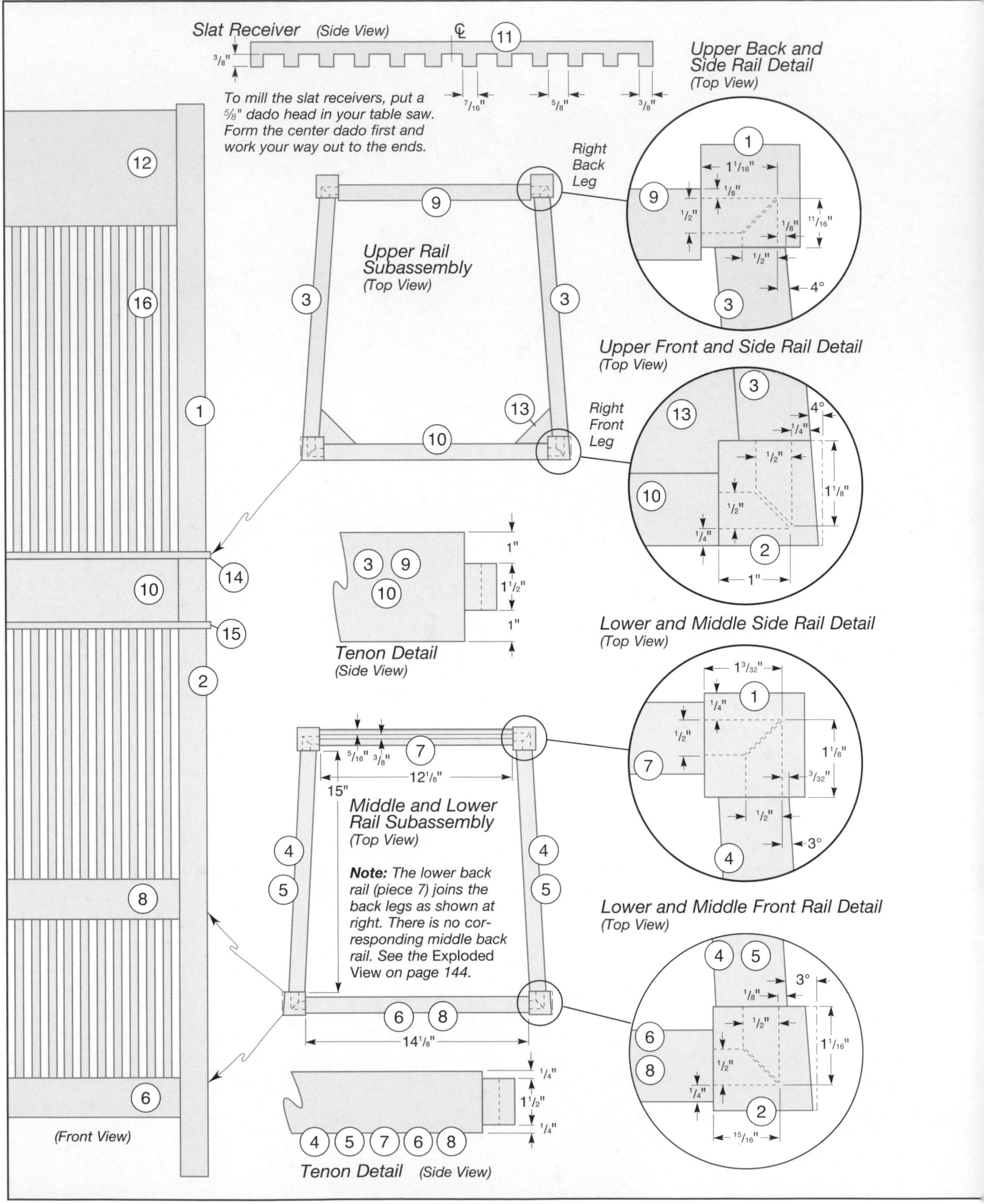

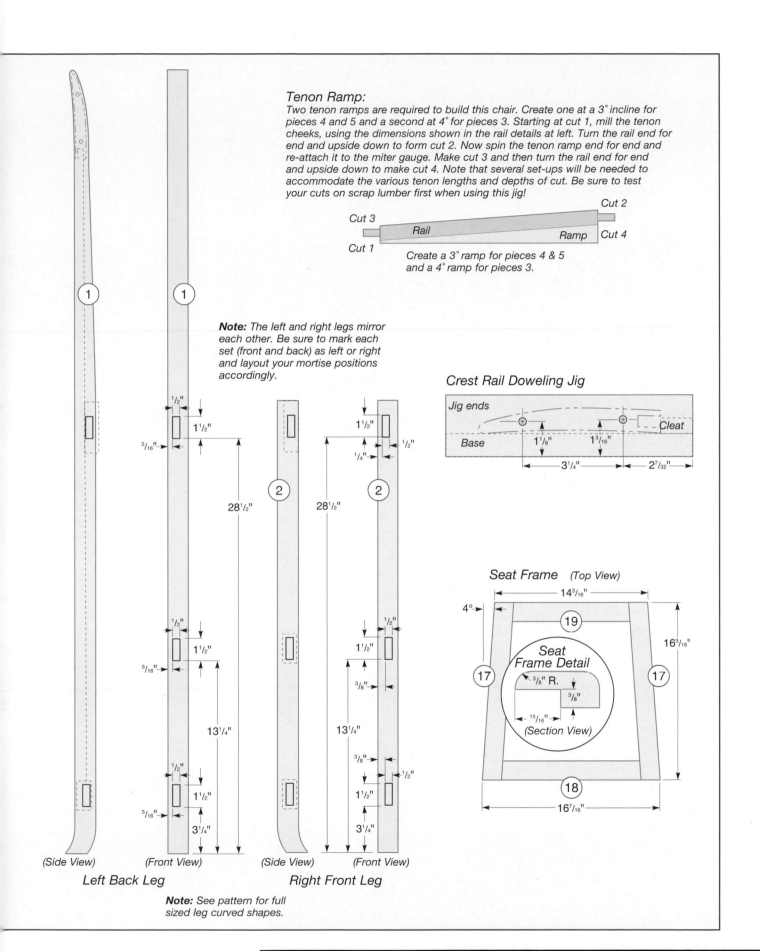

Tenon Ramp:

Two tenon ramps are required to build this chair. Create one at a 3° incline for pieces 4 and 5 and a second at 4° for pieces 3. Starting at cut 1, mill the tenon cheeks, using the dimensions shown in the rail details at left. Turn the rail end for end and upside down to form cut 2. Now spin the tenon ramp end for end and re-attach it to the miter gauge. Make cut 3 and then turn the rail end for end and upside down to make cut 4. Note that several set-ups will be needed to accommodate the various tenon lengths and depths of cut. Be sure to test your cuts on scrap lumber first when using this jig!

Cut 3   Cut 2

Rail   Ramp   Cut 4

Cut 1

Create a 3° ramp for pieces 4 & 5 and a 4° ramp for pieces 3.

Note: *The left and right legs mirror each other. Be sure to mark each set (front and back) as left or right and layout your mortise positions accordingly.*

Crest Rail Doweling Jig

Jig ends

Base

Cleat

$1^{1}/_{8}$" $1^{3}/_{16}$"

$3^{1}/_{4}$" $2^{7}/_{32}$"

Left Back Leg (Side View) (Front View)

$^{1}/_{2}$" $1^{1}/_{2}$"

$^{5}/_{16}$"

$28^{1}/_{2}$"

$13^{1}/_{4}$"

$3^{1}/_{4}$"

Right Front Leg (Side View) (Front View)

$1^{1}/_{2}$" $^{1}/_{2}$"

$^{1}/_{4}$"

$28^{1}/_{2}$"

$1^{1}/_{2}$"

$^{3}/_{8}$"

$13^{1}/_{4}$"

$^{3}/_{8}$"

$1^{1}/_{2}$" $^{1}/_{2}$"

$3^{1}/_{4}$"

Seat Frame (Top View)

$14^{3}/_{16}$"

4°

19

17   17

Seat Frame Detail

$^{3}/_{8}$" R.

$^{3}/_{8}$"

$^{15}/_{16}$"

(Section View)

$16^{3}/_{16}$"

18

$16^{7}/_{16}$"

Note: *See pattern for full sized leg curved shapes.*

by Chris Inman

CRAFTSMAN STYLE ROCKING CHAIR

Start with a classic design, meld fine machine joinery with a few hand tool operations, and you have a beautiful introduction to Arts & Crafts chairmaking. This will be an involved project, but there's no reason to fear its construction. Most of the joint cutting can be done by ordinary shop machines with excellent results, and the handwork amounts to fine paring and fitting.

Arts & Crafts style furniture developed in the late nineteenth century, beginning in England and migrating to America where it became better known as the Craftsman style. Other names, such as Mission furniture, were also commonly used to market this style of furniture. Craftsman designs were characterized by simple, economical lines, dramatically diverging from the Victorian frilliness of the previous era. By 1900 the Arts & Crafts Movement was a dominant force in American furniture and lighting design, pottery, architecture and the decorative arts.

Gustav Stickley became the standard bearer of the Arts & Crafts Movement in the United States, developing a line of furniture that exemplified the ideals of simplicity and quality craftsmanship, while remaining within economic reach of the middle class. Other notable American figures in this movement were architects Frank Lloyd Wright, Louis Sullivan and Charles and Henry Greene and lighting artist Louis C. Tiffany.

Understated Artistry

In reaction to the cruel industrial practices of the 1800s, Craftsman artisans strived to maintain the finest elements of creative handwork while selectively using modern machinery to best advantage. Blending the two methods relieved workers of repetitious, unskilled work so they had time for more individualized, expressive woodworking tasks.

The rocking chair detailed in this article is a hybrid of several arts and crafts designs that were popular at the turn of the century. The lines are less severe than the originals, and the various components in the chair aren't as heavy. All these changes make the chair more pleasant to sit in.

Cutting and Mortising the Legs

Chairs are subject to incredible stress from all the movement a person goes through while sitting. People lean, tip back, swivel and manage other contortions that make designing chairs difficult and risky. All of this makes chair design and construction a specialized branch of woodworking.

The main structural components of this rocking chair are the back legs. These are the heaviest pieces in the design and support the rest of the chair. All the legs receive a number of mortises which, in this design, are square to the leg profiles. The legs also have tenons on their ends for joining them with the arms and rockers.

Following the scale drawings on page 154, cut the back legs (pieces 1) out of wide 1¼"-thick stock and then clamp them together to belt-sand their front edges to a smoothly matching profile. To sand the back edges of the legs, install a 3" diameter drum sander in your drill press and clamp a pivot block 1¹³⁄₁₆" away from the drum (see Figure 1). Slowly feed the legs into the gap between the sander and the pivot block to reduce the stock to its finished size and to make the two edges of each leg parallel. Make sure you feed the wood against the rotation direction of the drum to maintain control.

Once the back legs are sanded, lay out the six mortises in each back leg and the four mortises in the front legs (pieces 11) as shown in the Back and Front Leg Elevations on page 154. The mortises include joints for the crest rail (piece 2), the lower rail (piece 3), the

Figure 1: *Create uniformly sized and smoothed curves by pushing the stock between a V-block and a sanding drum mounted in a drill press.*

seat support rails (pieces 4, 5 and 6) and the stretchers (pieces 8, 9 and 10). Don't lay out the mortises for the arms until later, when the front tenons are made and the exact slope of the arms is apparent. The ½"-deep mortises are

cut squarely into the legs with a router, a ½" straight bit and an edge guide, and then the rounded ends of the mortises are squared with a ½" chisel. With one exception, the mortises for the rails and stretchers are centered on the legs, but be sure to note that the legs are 1¼" by 1¾", requiring two settings of your edge guide to keep the bit centered. The exceptions are the two mortises for the back seat support rail. For these, the center of the router bit is positioned ½" in from the back edge of the two back legs.

After all the mortises are routed, begin cutting the through tenons on the top of the front legs. The arms slope from the front legs to the back legs at a 5° angle, so you must cut the tenon shoulders to establish this angle. Lay out the tenons' side shoulders at a 5° angle, and then connect these lines across the front and back leg faces.

QuickTip

Holder for a Drafting Lamp

Here's a great way to add some task lighting to virtually any workbench equipped with bench dog holes. Just take a piece of 2 x 4 and drill two holes several inches apart. One should fit the lamp base, while the other should be the same diameter as a bench dog. Glue a dowel into the second hole and you can mount an articulated desk lamp anywhere on the benchtop. The hinged arm on the lamp allows you to adjust the light right where you need it most.

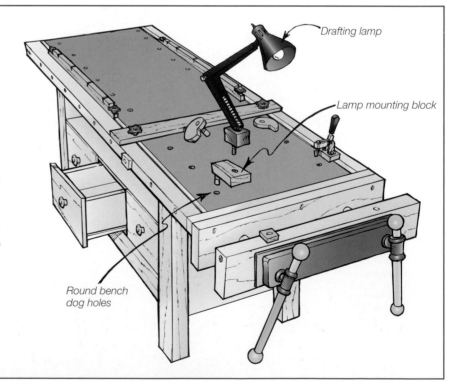

Drafting lamp

Lamp mounting block

Round bench dog holes

Pivot your table saw's miter gauge to 85° for cutting on the left side of the blade, and raise the blade ⅛" above the table surface. Cut one sloped shoulder on each leg, and follow this with multiple passes over the blade to remove the waste for the tenon. Now swing the miter gauge to its opposite 85° setting and repeat the tenon cutting process on the other side of the stock. To cut the remaining two shoulders on each leg, straighten the miter gauge to 90° and tilt the blade to 85°. Cut one set of shoulders with the miter gauge on the left side of the blade and the other set on the right side of the blade. In both cases repeatedly pass the stock over the blade to complete the tenon in side-by-side passes. Clean off the saw marks on the tenons with a wide chisel.

The front leg tenons pass through the arms and are topped with a pyramid design. This design, intended to highlight the skill of Stickley craftsmen, became a trademark during the Arts & Crafts era. The pyramid can be cut with a sharp handsaw and a wide chisel. Lay out a line on all four sides of both front legs ¼" down from the top and center a line on the top of the legs from the front edge to the back. Use your handsaw to rough in the angled cuts from the line on top of the legs to the line on the long sides. Now begin paring thin shavings off the four sides of the pyramid to get the desired shape.

Forgo cutting the bottom tenons on both the front and back legs for now. Later, you can scribe the tenon shoulders to the specific curve of the rockers. This technique will be described in detail later.

Making the Crest and Lower Rails

The next major chair components are the crest rail (piece 2) and the lower rail (piece 3). Rip the rails to their finished

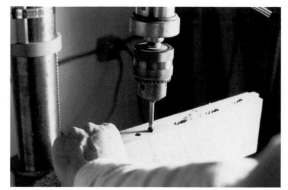

Figure 2: *Use the drawing below to lay out all the angled tenons in the project. Hollow out the rail mortises with a ⅜" drill bit, then clean up the mortises with sharp chisels.*

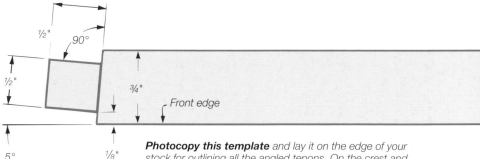

Photocopy this template *and lay it on the edge of your stock for outlining all the angled tenons. On the crest and lower rails, align the template with the front of the stock and cut the tenons prior to band-sawing the curve.*

width from 1½"-thick stock. Lay out the curves and the mortises for the slats (pieces 12) on the bottom edge of the crest rail and on the top edge of the lower rail as shown in the Crest Rail Drawing on page 155, and lay out the angled tenons at each end of these pieces using the template shown above. Be sure to align the front edge of the template with the front edge of the stock.

Chuck a ⅜" Forstner bit in your drill press and adjust the drill to bore ½" into the bottom edge of the crest rail (see Figure 2). Now drill four holes into each mortise area to remove the bulk of the waste, then readjust the drill press bed to perform this same operation on the narrower lower rail. Once the drilling is complete, square the ends of each mortise with a sharp ⅜" chisel and pare the mortise walls clean.

Due to the widening of the chair from back to front, the pieces connecting the back legs or the front legs join the legs at a 5° angle. Since all the mortises

Figure 3: *Align the arm mortise with the front leg tenon and rest the arm on the shoulder. Lay out the rear joint where the arm intersects the back leg.*

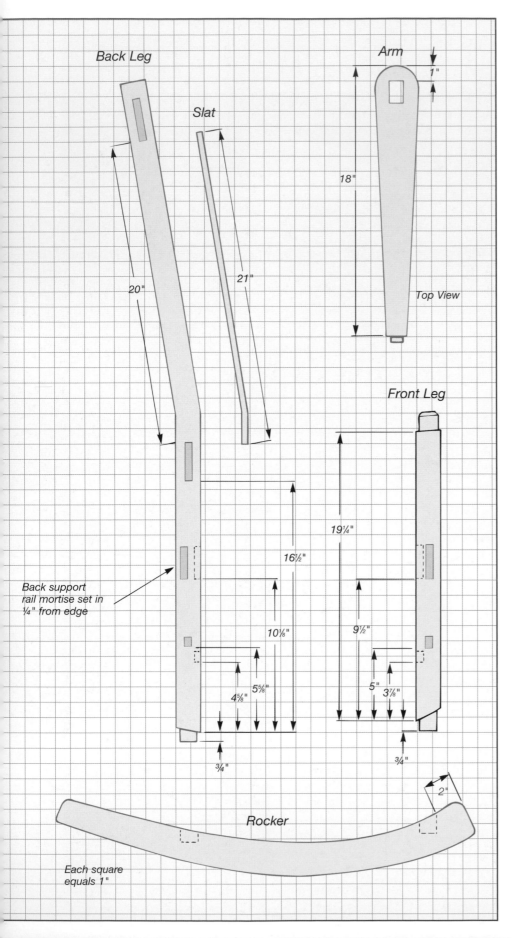

Back Leg

Slat

Arm

1"

18"

Top View

20"

21"

Front Leg

19¼"

16½"

Back support
rail mortise set in
¼" from edge

10⅛"

9½"

5⅝"

5"

3⅞"

4⅝"

¾"

¾"

2"

Rocker

Each square
equals 1"

are routed squarely into the legs, the 5°
angle must be accommodated by the
tenons, and the first step in this process
is cutting the tenon shoulders.

Cutting the angled shoulders on
the crest rail and lower rail is easily done
on the table saw. Attach a 16"-long
scrapwood auxiliary fence to your miter
gauge and set your blade to a 5° angle.
Put your miter gauge in the slot to the left
of the blade and cut off the end of the
wood fence at a 5° angle, then repeat
this process on the right side of the blade
to cut the other end of the fence. The
ends of the fence now serve as guides
for cutting the tenon shoulders.

With the back side of the crest rail
facing down, line up the right tenon
shoulder line with the cut-off end of the
fence (with the fence on the left side
of the blade). Adjust the height of the
blade so the teeth just reach the cheek
line on the rail stock and pass the rail
over the blade. Flip the stock around
and cut the matching shoulder on the
other end. Now make these two cuts on
the lower rail.

Cut the shoulders on the front face
of the rails by lowering the blade so the
teeth just reach the cheek, and then
follow the procedure you just used for
the first set of shoulders.

The next step in forming the tenons
is cutting the cheeks on the band saw.
Set the rail stock on edge and feed
the wood slowly into the blade, staying
just outside the layout lines. Be careful
to stop cutting when you reach the
shoulder kerf. Cut both cheeks on each
tenon, and then nip off the pointed bit of
waste material that remains at the end
of the tenon.

Now cut the shoulders on the top
and bottom edges of all the tenons
using a handsaw and chisel. Remember
that these cuts follow the 5° angle of the
shoulders. With a handsaw, cut into the

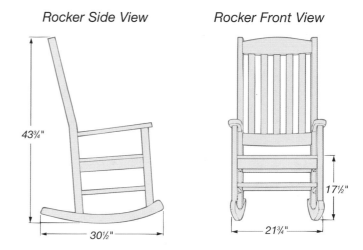

Rocker Side View

43¾"

30½"

Rocker Front View

17½"

21¾"

stock ⅛" and then remove the waste with a chisel. Once the edge shoulders are formed on each tenon, smooth the tenon cheeks with a sharp 1" chisel. Check the fit of the tenons in their mortises occasionally as you work.

Cut the rail curves on the band saw using a medium-toothed ½"-wide blade. Cut just outside the layout lines, then belt-sand the backs of the pieces smooth. Chuck a drum sander in the drill press and clamp a V-block to the bed to uniformly smooth the inside curves of the rails.

The top edge of the crest rail can now be cut on the band saw to its curved profile. Lay out the curve (shown at right) and cut just outside the layout line. Carefully remove the ridges with a belt sander.

Creating Seat Supports and Stretchers

Rip all the seat support rails (pieces 4, 5 and 6) and the lower stretchers (pieces 8, 9 and 10) to width on the table saw, and then cut them to length.

On the rails and stretchers crossing between the back or front pairs of legs (pieces 4, 5, 8 and 9), lay out the angled tenons using the template on page 153. Cut the shoulders on these pieces just as you did earlier on the crest rail and lower rail. Cut the cheeks on the band saw, and use a handsaw and chisel to cut the edge shoulders. Fit the tenons in their mortises after smoothing the cheeks with a sharp chisel.

The rails and stretchers spanning the sides of the chair (pieces 6 and 10) enter the legs at a 90° angle and therefore do not need specially angled tenons. Clamp a ¾"-thick spacer block to your table saw fence, keeping the block forward of the blade. Reset the blade to 90° and clamp the fence 1¼" away. This will allow you to cut ½"-long tenons. Rest the stock in your miter gauge, butting one end of the piece against the spacer block. Now cut the square shoulders, making additional passes over the blade to form the tenon cheeks. Repeat this procedure for all four pieces, and cut the edge shoulders in the same way. Carefully smooth the cheeks with a chisel, refining the tenons until they fit snugly into their mortises.

Making the Slats

Cut the five slats for the back rest (pieces 12) from ⁴/₄ material. Rip five strips 1½" wide and lay out the slat profile on the edge of each strip. Cut the ⁷/₁₆"-thick slats on the band saw with the same medium-toothed, ½"-wide blade you used earlier, staying outside of the lines so you can sand down to the finished dimension.

Belt-sand the front of the slats so they're even and smooth. Now use the drum sanding setup on your drill press

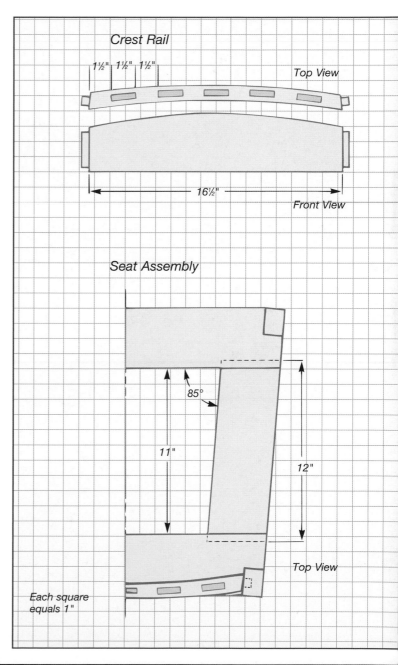

Crest Rail

1½" 1½" 1½"

Top View

16½"

Front View

Seat Assembly

85°

11"

12"

Top View

Each square equals 1"

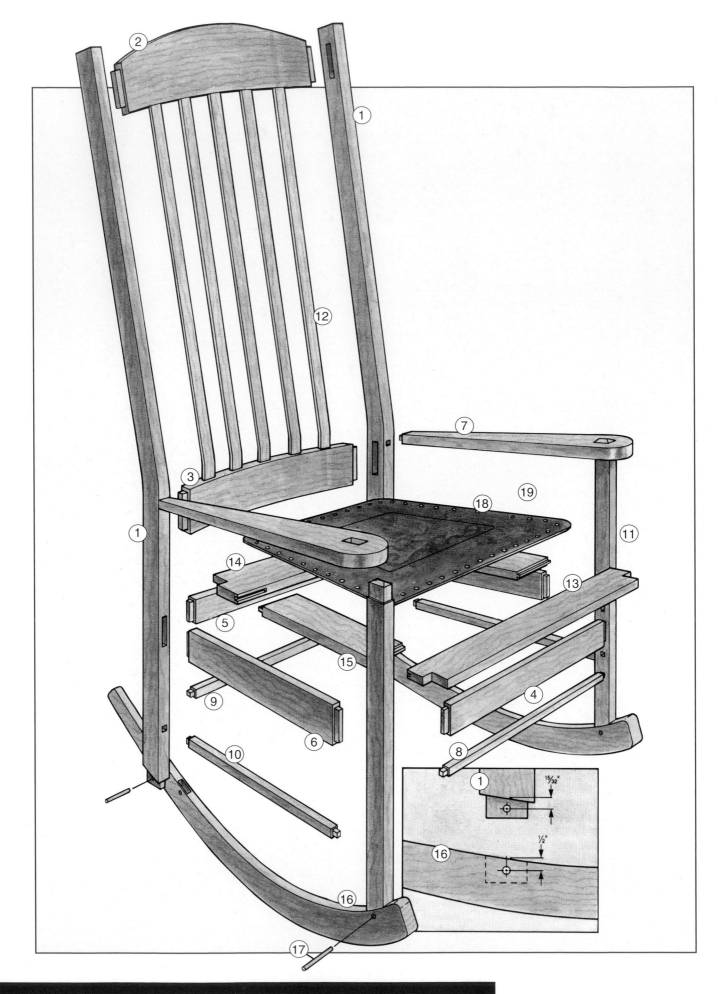

Material List - Rocker

		T x W x L
1	Back Legs (2)	1¼" x 5" x 46"
2	Crest Rail (1)	1½" x 4" x 17½"
3	Lower Rail (1)	1½" x 3" x 17½"
4	Front Support Rail (1)	¾" x 2½" x 20³⁄₁₆"
5	Back Support Rail (1)	¾" x 2½" x 17½"
6	Side Support Rails (2)	¾" x 2 ½" x 16¼"
7	Arms (2)	1" x 3" x 18½"
8	Front Stretcher (1)	¾" x 1" x 20³⁄₁₆"
9	Back Stretcher (1)	¾" x 1" x 17½"
10	Side Stretchers (2)	¾" x 1" x 16¼"
11	Front Legs (2)	1¼" x 1¾" x 21⅜"
12	Slats (5)	¾" x 1½" x 21"
13	Front Seat Rail (1)	¾" x 4" x 21¹¹⁄₁₆"
14	Back Seat Rail (1)	¾" x 4" x 19⁹⁄₁₆"
15	Side Seat Rails (2)	¾" x 4" x 12"
16	Rockers (2)	1¼" x 5" x 30½"
17	Dowel Pins (4)	¼" x 2"
18	Leather Seat (1)	16" Rectangular
19	Upholstery Tacks (1)	Pack of 100; Antique Finish

to sand the back sides of the slats to a uniform thickness of ⅜". Again, make sure to sand against the drum's rotation.

Assembling the Chair

By this time you've made most of the parts of the chair. Those parts that are left—the arms, rockers and the seat—are made after the main structure is assembled.

Gather together all the pieces you've made so far and organize them into three groups. The first group should include all the parts that make up the back of the chair, including the back legs, the crest rail and the lower rail, the slats, the back seat support rail and the back stretcher. The second group should include the parts for the front of the chair, which are the front legs, the front seat support rail and the front stretcher. The final group includes the side seat support rails and the side stretchers.

Dry-assemble all the parts in the back and, once everything fits properly, spread glue in all the mortises of the crest rail and the lower rail and insert the slats into position. Now apply glue in all the mortises of the back legs and on the tenons of the rails and stretcher. Slip the right leg onto the crest rail and lower rail tenons, then add the seat support rail and the stretcher. Pull the left leg onto the assembly and check for squareness by taking each diagonal measurement from the crest rail to the lower rail. When the spans are equal, the unit is square. Clamp the assembly and let the glue dry.

Assembling the front section is much easier since there are a lot fewer parts. Spread glue in the leg mortises and on the tenons of the front seat support rail and the stretcher. Draw the legs onto the stretchers, check for squareness and clamp the assembly for a couple hours.

After the glue on the front and back assemblies dries, put glue in the mortises for the side seat support rails and the stretchers. Insert these pieces into the back leg mortises, then glue the front assembly onto their other ends. Set the chair aside to allow the glue plenty of time to dry.

Building the Seat

The four pieces of the seat (pieces 13, 14 and 15) are 4" wide, so rip enough ¾"-thick material to this width, leaving the pieces overly long for the moment. The two side pieces are joined to the front and back pieces by mortise and tenon joints, however, since the seat is tapered from front to back, the joints form an 85° angle.

Cut each piece to length, remembering that all the crosscuts must be made at an 85° angle. Once cut to length, stop-mortise the front and back pieces for the joints using the dimensions shown on page 155. This can easily be done on the router table with a stop block on the fence. Mount a ⅜" straight bit in the router, raise the bit ½" above the table and adjust the fence so the bit cuts exactly down the center of the ¾"-thick seat pieces. Clamp a stop block 4⅜" beyond the bit and then rout the four mortises.

Next, form the tenons on the seat side rails. Remove the router from the router table and add the edge guide to its base. Install a ½" straight bit and set it to cut ³⁄₁₆" deep. Adjust the edge guide to limit the cut to ½" in width. Following the angled end of each side piece, rout one side of the tenon and then flip the piece over to make the second cut. When the joints fit properly, glue the seat together and use the inside diagonals to check for squareness. Sand the seat flush when you remove the clamps, and notch each corner of the seat to fit around the legs as shown in the Seat Assembly Drawing on page 155. Run a bead of glue along the seat support rails and clamp the seat into position. By gluing the seat to the rails, the overall strength of the chair will increase tremendously.

Forming Arms and Rockers

The arms (pieces 7) are cut from 1"-thick material, which must be planed from thicker stock. Rip two pieces of 1¼"-thick oak to 3" in width and cut them 20" long. Try to find highly figured stock for these pieces, as they'll show off the chair more than any other single component. Mill the stock down to 1" thick.

Lay out the through mortise location on the front end of both arms. The mortises must be cut at a 5° angle to allow the arms to slope properly. To do this, tilt your drill press table 5° and install a ⅜" bit in the chuck. Now bore through the mortise area to remove the waste, being sure to drill around the perimeter of the mortise first so you get the slope properly laid out. Once the bulk of the material is removed, clean up the mortise with a sharp chisel, being careful to preserve the 5° angle.

Rest the right arm on the outside shoulder of the front leg tenon and align

Figure 4: *Position the rocker on the legs, then trace the curve to lay out the tenon shoulders accurately.*

the arm mortise with the tenon. The arm is now positioned as it will be when installed, sloping 5° to the back leg. Put a mark on the arm (see Figure 3) where it intersects the back leg. In addition, draw lines on the leg indicating the top and bottom of the arm. Now lay out a ½"-high by ¾"-wide mortise on the back leg, centering it between the arm intersection marks and across the width of the back legs. At the mark you just made on the arm's edge, lay out the angled tenon, using the angled tenon template shown on page 153. Repeat this process on the left arm.

Drill out the bulk of the waste in the ½"-deep mortises with a ½" bit, then square the walls with a sharp chisel. Cut the angled tenons on the arms using the table saw and long miter gauge fence, just as you earlier cut the other angled tenons. Once the tenons are formed, layout the shape of the arm on the stock and cut this profile on the band saw. Belt-sand the edges smooth. Next, cut the tenon side shoulders and edges with a handsaw and chisel, paring down the shoulders and the cheeks for a perfect fit. Put glue on all the mortises and tenons and slip the arms into place. Use clamps to draw the arms tightly against the back legs.

Now that the basic chair is made you can move on to make the rockers. Cut two rockers (pieces 16) out of 1¼"-thick material following the Rocker Scale Drawing on page 154. Clamp the two rockers together to sand their bottom edges smooth, ensuring the two pieces match exactly. Now pass the rockers over the drum sander to smooth their inside curves. Mark the position where the rockers intersect the legs as shown in the elevation drawings.

Set the chair on its left side and lay the right rocker onto the legs, as shown in Figure 4 above. Align the marks you

---

*Quick*Tip

Moisture Meter Prevents Surprises when Buying Air-dried Lumber

Your local sawmill may be a great source for inexpensive lumber, but moisture can be a problem if the mill doesn't kiln-dry its stock. Most small mills pile up logs and store them out in the weather. When they rip them into boards, they usually store these green boards outside in unprotected stickered stacks. Even if the lumber gets stored out of the elements, be sure to bring a moisture meter with you, and crosscut a board a few inches in from an end to test it. Don't test the exposed ends, which dry faster than areas deeper in the board. Ideally, lumber used for furniture projects should have no more than 12% moisture content.

Figure 5: *Re-create this symbol of superior craftsmanship from the Arts & Crafts era using a 1" chisel, a tenon saw and your hand tool skills.*

just made on the rocker with the points of intersection on the legs (see the drawings). Holding the rocker in place, trace the curve of the rocker onto the legs and outline the position of the legs on the rocker. Flip the chair over and repeat this process for the other rocker.

Lay out the leg tenons below the shoulder lines following the elevation drawing on page 154. Using a dovetail saw, make straight cuts close to the shoulder lines, then pare the shoulders with a chisel to match the curved lines. Cut the side shoulders and edges with the dovetail saw.

On the rockers, lay out the mortises between the lines you traced off the leg positions. When you drill out the waste with a ½" bit, drill ¾" deep at the shallow end of each mortise and drill slightly deeper as you follow the rising curve of the rocker. If you do this you'll end up with nice, flat-bottomed mortises that easily fit the tenons. Clean up the walls with a chisel.

Drill a ¼" hole through the center of the four mortises on the rockers (see exploded view detail on page 156) and then mount the rockers onto the leg tenons. Use an awl to mark the center of these holes onto the tenons, then remove the rockers. Now drill a ¼" hole through each tenon ¹⁄₃₂" above your awl mark.

Put glue on the tenons and in the mortises and drive the rockers onto the legs. Now chamfer the ends on four lengths of ¼" dowel rod and drive these into the pin holes at each joint—the offset holes will draw the joints tightly together so clamps won't be necessary. Cut off the dowels flush.

Cut off the top of the back legs 1" above the crest rail, then saw and chisel the ends into pyramid shapes as shown in Figure 5. Sand the entire chair to 180 grit.

Applying Finish

Arts & Crafts furniture was traditionally finished with a fumed ammonia process. Ammonia causes woods high in tannic acid, like oak, to darken considerably, and the longer the wood is exposed to the fumes the darker it becomes. Controlling this process requires a fair amount of experience and a plastic tent or other enclosure to contain the fumes (see page 15 for more on ammonia fuming). If you'd rather not fume your chair, modern stains and dyes can closely duplicate the colors that result from ammonia fuming. Watco Danish Oil Finish in medium dark walnut matches the tone of the traditional craftsman colors closely. You can easily darken or lighten the color by using other shades of this product. Apply one coat of Watco Oil and let it dry for a couple of days, then follow with two coats of tung oil finish or satin varnish to complete the finishing process.

Figure 6: *Trim the leather to lap onto the side rails by 1" and 2" on the front and back rails. To prevent splitting, drill pilot holes for the nails 1" apart.*

Adding a Leather Seat

The leather seat is held to the chair by upholstery nails, which have large, dome-shaped heads. First trim the leather with a sharp razor blade to overlap the seat opening by 1" on the left and right sides and by 2" on the front and back. After lightly coloring the freshly cut edges with a brown stain, begin securing the leather by driving one nail in the center of each side (see Figure 6, above). Work toward the corners from these points, installing more nails and leaving about ½" between the heads. Hide any discrepancies by varying the spacing.

All that's left to do now is find a quiet corner of your home to place this classic rocker. By making this chair you have fulfilled one of the original precepts of the Arts & Crafts Movement; that is, combining the best of hand and power tool techniques in order to create quality furniture that is pleasant to build, unpretentious and sturdy enough to last for generations.

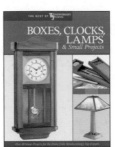

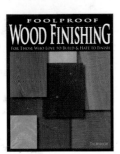

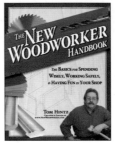